Medical Law in Canada

Medical Law in Canada

Second Edition

Trudo Lemmens
Jennifer Bergman
Kanksha Mahadevia Ghimire
Maryam Shahid

This book was originally published as a monograph in the International Encyclopaedia of Laws/Medical Law.

Founding Editor: Roger Blanpain
General Editor: Frank Hendrickx
Volume Editor: Herman Nys

Wolters Kluwer

Published by:
Kluwer Law International B.V.
PO Box 316
2400 AH Alphen aan den Rijn
The Netherlands
E-mail: international-sales@wolterskluwer.com
Website: lrus.wolterskluwer.com

Sold and distributed by:
Wolters Kluwer Legal & Regulatory U.S.
7201 McKinney Circle
Frederick, MD 21704
United States of America
Email: customer.service@wolterskluwer.com

ISBN 978-94-035-3015-4

e-Book: ISBN 978-94-035-2961-5
web-PDF: ISBN 978-94-035-2962-2

The Authors

This contribution to Kluwer was prepared under general supervision of Trudo Lemmens by Jennifer Bergman, Kanksha Mahadevia Ghimire, Maryam Shahid, and Trudo Lemmens. Maryam Shahid wrote the first draft of the section on Indigenous Health. The three other authors drafted various sections of the monograph and edited all sections of the manuscript. Ashley Qian (verification case law) and Leora Chapman (updating of sources, background research, editing and work on the bibliography and references) provided helpful research assistance. Most of this monograph was written in Toronto. The authors acknowledge that Toronto is the traditional territory of many nations, including the Mississaugas of the Credit, the Anishnabeg, the Chippewa, the Haudenosaunee and the Wendat peoples and is now home to many diverse First Nations, Inuit and Métis peoples. The authors also acknowledge that the territory is covered by Treaty 13 signed with the Mississaugas of the Credit, and the Williams Treaties signed with multiple Mississaugas and Chippewa bands.

Some sections of the earlier monograph prepared by Nola M. Ries, Karen Kellogg, Research Associates with the Alberta Health Law Institute, and Timothy Caulfield, Professor, Faculty of Law and School of Public Health, University of Alberta, who served as the original authors and editor are also included in this monograph.

Trudo Lemmens is Scholl Chair in Health Law and Policy in the Faculty of Law at the University of Toronto, with cross-appointments in the Dalla Lana School of Public Health and the Joint Centre for Bioethics. His research lies at the interface of law, governance, and ethical norms and values in the context of health care, biomedical research, and health product development. His publications include the co-edited volumes *Law and Ethics in Biomedical Research: Regulation, Conflict of Interest, and Liability and Regulating Creation: Law, Ethics and Policy of Assisted Human Reproduction* (both University of Toronto Press), as well as more than one-hundred chapters and articles in national and international law, policy, science, medicine, and bioethics journals. His most recent work focuses on human rights, disability rights, and health. He has taught and been a visiting professor at academic institutions in Argentina, Belgium, Canada, Colombia, New Zealand, the United Kingdom, and the United States.

Jennifer Bergman is a Doctor of Juridical Science (SJD) candidate in the Faculty of Law at the University of Toronto, Cananda. Her doctoral research focuses on the relationship between the law and the unmet mental health service needs of young people with mental health issues who are engaged with the family law (child welfare) and youth criminal justice systems. Jennifer holds an LLM (Health Law, Ethics and

Policy Concentration) from the University of Toronto, Canada as well as an LLM (Alternative Dispute Resolution) from York University, Canada. She is a member of the Bar in Ontario and British Columbia, and she has practiced law in both provinces.

Kanksha Mahadevia Ghimire is a legal practitioner and has worked in multiple countries including Small Island Developing States (SIDS). She has led transactions in premier law firms in India; headed the legal team of a statutory regulator in Vanuatu; and interned at the World Bank's Legal Vice Presidency and the United Nations Office for Disaster Risk Reduction (UNDRR). She is an adjunct faculty at the School of Law, University of the South Pacific, Vanuatu. Kanksha is pursuing her doctoral studies (Doctor of Juridical Science - SJD) in the Faculty of Law at the University of Toronto, Canada. Her research explores mechanisms to improve regulation and governance.

Maryam Shahid graduated from the University of Toronto, Faculty of Law in 2018 with a JD. She articled at a civil litigation boutique in Toronto and, upon being called to the Ontario bar in 2019, she joined public service.

Table of Contents

List of Abbreviations

AC	Canadian Reports Appeal Cases (1828–1913)
ACWS	All Canada Weekly Summaries
Admin. L.R.	Administrative Law Reports
AI	Artificial (or Assisted) Insemination
AIH	Assisted Insemination Homologous
ALL	Acute Lymphoblastic Leukemia
Alta (A)	Alberta
Alta L Rev	Alberta Law Review
Alta L.R.	Alberta Law Reports
AmDec	American Decisions
APR	Atlantic Provinces Reports
AR	Alberta Reports
BCD	British Columbia Decisions
BCLR	British Columbia Law Reports
CA	Court of Appeal (also N.Z. Court of Appeals Reports)
CBS	Canadian Blood Services
CCA	Council of Canadian Academies
CCC	Canadian Criminal Cases
CCH	Commerce Clearinghouse Inc.
CCLT	Canadian Cases on the Law of Torts
CCQ	Civil Code of Quebec
CCSM	Continuing Consolidation of the Statutes of Manitoba
CDSS	Canadian Drugs and Substances Strategy
CIHR	Canadian Institutes of Health Research
CMA	Canadian Medical Association
CRC	Canadian Railway and Transport Cases
CRCS	Canadian Red Cross Society
CT	Connecticut
DI	Donor Insemination
EHR	Electronic Health Record

List of Abbreviations

Gen. Div.	General Division
HC	Haute Cour
Health LJ	Health Law Journal
HL	House of Lords
ICH	International Conference on Harmonisation
ICH-GCP	International Conference on Harmonisation-Guideline for Good Clinical Practice
IVF	In Vitro fertilization
KB	King's Bench
L. Med. Q.	Legal Medical Quarterly
MAiD	Medical Assistance in Dying
MB	Manitoba
McGill LJ	McGill Law Journal
MPR	Maritime Provinces Reports
MRC	Medical Research Council
NB	New Brunswick
NDS	New Drug Submission
NE	North-eastern Reporter
Nfld.	Newfoundland
NH	New Hampshire
NHSC	New Hampshire Supreme Court
NR	National Reporter
NSERC	Natural Sciences and Engineering Research Council of Canada'
NSF	Nova Scotia
NYCA	New York Court of Appeal
NZLR	New Zealand Law Reports
OJ	Ontario Judgments
ON	Ontario
ONCA	Ontario Court of Appeal
ONCJ	Ontario Court of Justice
Ont.	Ontario
Ont. Dist. Ct.	Ontario District Court
Ont. Div. Ct.	Ontario Divisional Court
Ont. Gen. Div.	Ontario Court General Division
Ont. HCJ.	Ontario High Court of Justice
OR	Ontario Reports
OWN	Ontario Weekly Notes
P (2d)	Pacific Reporter Second Series

PC	Privy Council
PEI	Prince Edward Island
PHI	Provincial Health Insurer
PIPEDA	Personal Information Protection and Electronic Documents Act
POG	Pediatric Oncology Group
Prov. Ct.	Provincial Court
Q	Quebec
QB	Queen's Bench
QC	Quebec
QCCS	Superior Court of Quebec
QJ	Quebec Judgments
QL	Quick Law
Que. Sup. Ct.	Quebec Superior Court
R.	Reports
RCNRT	Royal Commission on New Reproductive Technologies
REB	Research Ethics Board
Reg.	Regulations
RFL	Reports of Family Law
RJQ	Receuils de Jurisprudence de Quebec
RSC	Royal Society of Canada
S	Statutes
SA	Statues of Alberta
SC	Supreme Court
SCC	Supreme Court of Canada
Sch.	Schedule
SCJ	Supreme Court Judgments
SCR	Supreme Court Reports
SJ	Saskatchewan Judgments
SSHRC	Social Sciences and Humanities Research Council
Supp.	Supplement
TCPS 2	Tri-Council Policy Statement: Ethical Conduct for Research Involving Humans
TD	Trial Division
TRC	Truth and Reconciliation Commission of Canada
U.F.C.	Unified Family Court
U.S.	United States
USCA. 8th Cir.	United States Court of Appeals 8th Circuit
WCB	Workers Compensation Boards

List of Abbreviations

WLR	Western Law Reporter
WNV	West Nile Virus
WWR	Weekly Western Reports

General Introduction

Chapter 1. The General Background of the Country

§1. Geography and Climate

1. As the second-largest country in the world, Canada covers over 9,970,610 square kilometers of land and freshwater.[1] Bounded to the west, north and east by the respective Pacific, the Arctic and Atlantic oceans, Canada's border to the south with the United States (U.S.) is often referred to as the world's longest undefended border. Most of Canada's geography consists of interior areas made up of lowlands, interior plains, and the massive, uniformly landscaped platform of the Canadian Shield. A rim of highlands, incomplete in the far northwest and along the South, forms the remainder of the country. The Western Cordillera forms the highest and thickest part of the rim, which runs from Alaska in the northwest to the U.S. border in the southwest. Several peaks in the Cordillera reach over 4,500 meters, and the highest peak of M. Logan attains a height of 5,951 meters.

2. Much of the Canadian climate consists of wide variations upon a continental type of climate, marked by long cold winters, short hot summers, and barely adequate rainfall. The Pacific and Atlantic coasts experience more moderate temperatures and greater humidity. Bitterly cold extended winters, short cool summers and little precipitation characterize the Arctic coastal regions.

§2. Cultural Composition

3. In 2019, Canada's population was over 37 million. Cultural and ethnic diversity has increased steadily over the past half-century due to immigration.[2] Canada's

1. B Law, ed., *Corpus Almanac & Canadian Sourcebook,* 28th ed. (Ontario: Gordon Sova, 1993); *The New Encyclopaedia Britannica,* 15th ed. (Chicago: Encyclopaedia Britannica, 1984) vol. 2.
2. Statistics Canada, *Report on the Demographic Situation in Canada* (online: Statistics Canada, Mar. 28, 2019) www150.statcan.gc.ca/n1/pub/91-209-x/91-209-x2018001-eng.htm (Statistics Canada, *Demographic Situation*); Statistics Canada, *Topics, 2016 Census* (online: Statistics Canada) www12.statcan.gc.ca/census-recensement/2016/rt-td/index-eng.cfm (Statistics Canada, *2016 Census*); Statistics Canada, *Immigration and Ethnocultural Diversity in Canada* (online: Statistics Canada) www12.statcan.gc.ca/nhs-enm/2011/as-sa/99-010-x/99-010-x2011001-eng.cfm; Statistics Canada, *Labour Force Survey, April 2019* (online: Statistics Canada, May 10, 2019) www150.statcan.gc.ca/n1/daily-quotidien/190510/dq190510a-eng.htm.

population is now largely the result of immigration. Prior to European contact, the lands now known as Canada were home to many distinct nations. These original settlers and their descendants are often collectively referred to as "Indigenous peoples," and include the First Nations, Inuit, and Métis communities in Canada. These communities thrived prior to contact, but past and present colonial activities have had a devastating effect on the population. As a result, while the Indigenous population (First Nations, Métis, and Inuit) has again been increasing more recently and was estimated in 2016 at 4.9% of the total population, the majority of Canada's population consists of descendants of early colonial settlers and immigrants who arrived since the nineteenth century.[3] Around 32.3% of the population describes their ethnic origin as "Canadian" and a number reported at least one origin as British Isles (32.5%) and French (13.6%). Canada's political structure, legal system, and dominant official languages (English and French) reflect the shifting colonial powers of France and Great Britain from which most of the first colonial settlers and immigrants originated. Over the years, the ethnic diversity has significantly increased. Two-hundred and fifty ethnic origins were reported in the 2016 census and 41.1% of the population reported more than one ethnic origin. Just over 20% of the population is comprised of recent immigrants. The majority of recent immigrants in 2016 were born in Asia (61.8%), followed by African-born newcomers (13.4%). More than one-fifth (22.3%) of Canada's population identified as belonging to a visible minority in 2016, with three out of ten people in this population being born in Canada. South Asians (e.g., East Indians, Pakistanis, Sri Lankans) were Canada's largest visible minority group in 2016, comprising 25.1% of the visible minority population, followed by Chinese people (20.5%) and Black people (15.6%). Degrees of ethnic diversity vary widely across Canada, with most of the visible minority population concentrated in the provinces of Ontario and British Columbia (in the metropolitan areas of Toronto and Vancouver, especially). Part of the Canadian ethos has been a relatively high tolerance for the retention of immigrant culture. Nearly 23% of the population reports a non-official mother tongue—that is, a first language that is neither English nor French.

4. Christianity is the largest religion in Canada, with 67.3% of the population being affiliated with a Christian religion, and the majority of that population belonging to either the Roman Catholic, United, or Anglican Church. As of 2011, 23.9% reported no religious affiliation, a 7.4% increase since 2001. Changing immigration patterns have resulted in increases in the numbers of Canadians professing faith in Islam, Hinduism, Sikhism and Buddhism. The *Canadian Charter of Rights and Freedoms,* part of the Constitution, guarantees "everyone" the fundamental "freedom of conscience and religion."

5. Nearly 80% of Canadians live in urban areas, with 35.5% of the national population clustered in three urban regions: Toronto, Montréal, and Vancouver. In 2016, 60.2% of Canadians were employed—63.8% of men and 56.7% of women. Increased participation in the labor market was subsequently observed, with the unemployment rate dropping from 7.7% in 2016 to 5.7% by April 2019. Over the

3. *See* further for a discussion under indigenous health.

decade 2006–2016, labor force gains continued to be strongest in service-producing industries, principally health care, social assistance and retail trade. Canada's workforce is aging and more people are working beyond the age of 65. Immigrants made up almost one-quarter of the labor force in Canada in 2016.

§3. Political System

6. Canada is an independent parliamentary federation of ten provinces and three territories.[4] Created as the Dominion of Canada by the British North America Act of 1867, Canada did not become a fully independent state, capable of passing its own constitutional amendments, until passage of the *Constitution Act, 1982*.[5] Under the Canadian Constitution, Canada is a country with two official languages, French and English, and maintains a division of legislative jurisdiction between the federal and provincial governments. The law in all provinces but Quebec is common-law based. Quebec has maintained a vibrant civil law system, based on its own modernized Civil Code.[6] Any matters not explicitly enumerated as provincial remain under federal jurisdiction. Under the *Constitution Act,* provincial jurisdiction includes the authority to establish, maintain and manage hospitals, and to have jurisdiction over civil rights within the province. The Federal Health Department is only explicitly responsible for such national concerns as the health of the aboriginal population, the establishment of marine hospitals, and health standards for immigrants. The health-care system is very decentralized in Canada as each province maintains its own health-care education and professional certification programs. However, Federal Parliament's spending authority has allowed it to play a central role in establishing interlocking medical care insurance programs throughout Canada, and coordinating the establishment of national standards.

7. Canada has, like most other liberal democracies, three distinct branches of government, both at the federal and provincial levels: the executive branch (the government), the judiciary, and the legislative branch. At the federal level the legislative branch consists of an appointed upper house (the Senate) and an elected lower house (the House of Commons). Both the House and the Senate may introduce legislation, but proposals for the use of public funds or the imposition of taxes may only be drafted by the House. Legislative bills must gain assent from both the House and the Senate before they can receive royal assent and become law. The executive branch is formally led by the Queen as Canada's Head of State. The Queen is represented in Canada by the Governor-General, whose role is purely formal by convention. The Prime Minister is the head of the government, which is further

4. J Wood, ed., *Canada Year Book 1992*, 125th ed. (Ottawa: Statistics Canada, 1992); *The New Encyclopaedia Britannica*, 15th ed. (Chicago: Encyclopaedia Britannica, 1994) vol. 2.
5. *Constitution Act, 1982*, being Sch. B to the *Canada Act 1982* (UK), 1982, c 11.
6. *Civil Code of Quebec*, CQLR c CCQ-1991.

composed of the Cabinet. As in the United Kingdom, the Prime Minister is normally the leader of the largest party represented in Parliament, and as a result of Canada's first-past-the-post electoral system, often heads a government backed by an absolute majority in Parliament.

8. The third government function is entrusted to an independent judiciary, which is given the power to interpret laws. The judiciary may strike down laws which are unconstitutional, either because they fall outside of the enacting federal or provincial government's jurisdiction, or because they infringe upon the individual democratic protections which are guaranteed in the *Canadian Charter of Rights and Freedoms*. However, the guarantees listed in the Charter are explicitly subject to "reasonable limits prescribed by law as can be demonstrably justified in a free and democratic society" (section 1). Specific Charter rights, such as the section 7 right to "Life Liberty and Security of the Person," also recognize proportional limitations of the rights. These different proportionality tests play an important and distinct role in constitutional litigation, including in areas that are relevant to health. The federal Parliament or a provincial legislative assembly may also expressly declare that an act shall operate notwithstanding the Charter sections which protect rights and freedoms. This "notwithstanding" clause has been very rarely used, and when so primarily for political reasons by the Province of Quebec.

9. The provincial and territorial governments operate with many of the same political institutions and constitutional conventions that function at the federal level. Each province has a Lieutenant Governor, who operates as the Queen's representative and is appointed by the Governor-General. Provincial legislatures, however, are unicameral, consisting of the Lieutenant Governor and an elected legislative assembly. Important categories under the provinces' constitutional jurisdiction include property and civil rights within the province, civil law, municipal government, hospitals, direct taxation within the province for provincial purposes, and other matters of local or private concern. Matters related to health therefore fall largely under provincial and territorial jurisdiction. Canada's three territories—Northwest Territories, Nunavut and Yukon—have their own legislative assemblies as well as a commissioner who serves as the federal government representative.

10. Since local government falls under provincial jurisdiction, each province has developed its own system of municipal government, with territorial divisions into municipalities known variously as counties, cities, towns, villages, etc. There are over 3,700 registered municipalities in Canada, each with delegated powers and responsibilities according to its province's designation. Municipalities are generally governed by directly elected officials.

11. Canada has a multi-party political system. Four parties were represented in the House of Commons after the 2019 general federal election: Liberal, Conservative, Block Québéquois and New Democratic. Members of the Green Party were also elected to the House of Commons, but not in sufficient numbers to be a "recognized party" for parliamentary proceedings. There was also one Member of Parliament elected as an independent.[7] The Conservative and Liberal parties are essentially centrist, the New Democratic Party is leftist (but in comparison with the political positions of most European leftist parties still quite centrist), and the Bloc Quebecois, while in terms of social policies more leftist, focused primarily on leading the province of Quebec toward succession as an independent state. From 1993 to 2011, a period of strong nationalist support in Quebec, it was the second or third-largest party. While its influence subsequently diminished, the party has once again regained official party status, winning thirty-two seats in the 2019 election and becoming the third-largest party in the House of Commons.

12. The number of seats available in the House is based upon representation by population. There is no proportionate representation, and the party that has won a majority of seats is called upon to form the government, with its leader normally becoming the Prime Minister (in theory a coalition government could also be formed). The party with the second-largest number of seats becomes the official opposition. Where, as in the 2019 election, no party receives a majority of seats in the House of Commons, the party with the most seats may form a minority government, but will need the support of other parties to pass legislation and remain in power. The same electoral system exists in the provinces. As a result of the "first-past-the-post" system (the person with the most votes in an electoral district represents the entire district), Canadian federal and provincial elections can result in significant shifts in policy-making, including in the area of health, by parliamentary majorities that at times represent only between 35%–40% of the popular vote. At the same time, the system makes it very difficult for smaller parties with sometimes niche agendas (e.g., environment or health) to have significant representation in federal and provincial parliaments. This system has a moderating impact on the major parties, which need broad political support and therefore may avoid taking on niche issues that may deter some more centrist voters from supporting them.

13. Senate membership is based upon regional representation. Senators are not elected: they are appointed by the Governor-General as advised by the Prime Minister and are usually affiliated with a political party, even though the Liberal Party has recently moved away from including non-elected senators in their parliamentary caucus. There have been long-standing calls for a reform of the non-elected Senate, which can block or significantly delay legislation adopted by the House of Commons. It has done so, for example, in the context of abortion and also threatened to do so in the context of the recent legislation on Medical Assistance in Dying (MAiD).

7. Parliament of Canada, "Party Standings in the House of Commons," online: House of Commons Canada www.ourcommons.ca/Parliamentarians/en/partystandings.

14. While the 2015 federal election saw an increase in voter turnout as compared to the six previous elections, only 68% of enfranchised Canadians voted in 2015. The figures dipped again in the last federal election, with voter turnout at just under 66% in 2019.[8]

§4. Population and Vital Statistics

15. Canada's population in 2019 was 37,314,442.[9] The ratio of males to females is about 97:100. By 2018, the median age had reached 40.8 years, an increase of over ten years since 1984. As of 2016, persons aged 65 years and older comprised 16.9% of the population, exceeding the number of children aged 14 years and younger (16.6%) in the Canadian population for the first time. In contrast to the general aging of Canada's population, only 7.3% of Indigenous people are aged 65 and over; about one-third are under 15 years of age.

16. In 2016, life expectancy was 79.9 years for men and 84 years for women. The life expectancy of men and women in Canada did not increase from 2016 to 2017. This is the first time in over four decades that an annual increase was not observed and is largely attributable to the opioid crisis, discussed further. The infant mortality rate was 4.5 deaths per 1,000 live births in 2016. The "total fertility rate" (the average number of children born per woman) has fallen from 1.62 in 2012 to 1.54 in 2016. Cancer and heart disease were the leading causes of death in Canada in 2016; together, they accounted for 48.6% of deaths. Treatment developments for cancer and other causes of death have led to improvements in life expectancy in recent years. However, these improvements have been offset by losses in life expectancy from other causes, particularly the drug overdose crisis. Between 2015 and 2017 death rates due to drug overdose increased 1.6 times for women and 2.1 times for men in Canada.

17. A significant black eye for Canada's overall equitable social welfare and health-care system is the significant shorter life expectancy and the serious health challenges among Indigenous people. The reason for the health disparities is complex and is discussed further in more detail. It is largely attributed to lower living standards and the colonial legacy, which includes the forced education of Indigenous children in residential schools and forced removal of Indigenous communities from their ancestral lands.

---

8. Elections Canada, "Voter Turnout at Federal Elections and Referendums," online: *Elections Canada* www.elections.ca/content.aspx?section=ele&dir=turn&document=index&lang=e; Elections Canada, "Election Results," online: *Elections Canada* https://enr.elections.ca/National.aspx?lang=e.
9. Statistics Canada, *Demographic Situation*, *supra* note 2; Statistics Canada, *2016 Census*, *supra* note 2; Statistics Canada, *Changes in Life Expectancy by Selected Causes of Death, 2017* (online: Statistics Canada, May 30, 2019) www150.statcan.gc.ca/n1/daily-quotidien/190530/dq190530d-eng.htm; Statistics Canada, *Deaths, Causes of Death and Life Expectancy, 2016* (online: Statistics Canada, Jun. 28, 2018). www150.statcan.gc.ca/n1/daily-quotidien/180628/dq180628b-eng.htm.

§5. Social and Cultural Values Affecting Canadian Health Law and Policy

18. The depth of historical conflicts, the neighboring influence exerted by the enormously powerful U.S., the diversity of Canada's ethnic population, and the sheer size of the land itself are all factors which threaten to make the task of extracting social generalizations about Canada a specious exercise. At the same time, these are the very factors which provide a clue as to what possible generalizations could be drawn.

19. Canada has always given greater recognition than the U.S. to its historical European roots in Britain and France. The country has traditionally maintained a European recognition of government as the agency which bears responsibility for the redistribution of wealth, and the welfare of the poor, the disabled, the elderly and children. A central belief in the importance of offering equality of access has shaped the universality of Canada's social programs, from pensions to health care to sales tax rebates. A Canadian university education, which is generally regarded more as a privilege than a right, is still publicly subsidized much more than a U.S. college education. However, most Canadian post-secondary institutions are increasing tuition fees, particularly in professional programs such as medicine, law, dentistry and business. This has raised concern about access to university education for children of low- and middle-income earners.

20. At the same time, with majorities at federal and most provincial levels fluctuating between center left and center right governments, many Canadians also appear reluctant to be willing to pay much more taxes to further develop social support and health-care systems, or larger infrastructure works. Yet, the concept of government funding for basic medical care seems firmly entrenched and is not even being questioned by the more fiscal conservative governments. But some aspects of health care continue to be underfunded, such as dental care and pharmaceutical treatments (which are not covered under the publicly funded Canadian health-care system), as well as various home care and long-term care services.

21. Canada has been inundated with many core American beliefs, in particular, the necessity of free market competition, the desirability of individual wealth and responsibility, and the needless wastefulness of government administration. Many American commercial and cultural beliefs are embraced in Canada, but U.S. influence is moderated by a distrust of large foreign corporate entities. This may spring in part from the fact that so much of Canada's economic structure is in fact dependent upon foreign ownership and financing. As a nation of great natural resources and low population density, Canadians have traditionally looked to government as the institution responsible for safeguarding a "unique" Canadian identity and cultural values. An interesting variant upon this feeling has occurred as Canada's immigrant population has grown; government is frequently asked to bear responsibility for helping individual ethnic communities maintain their identities.

22. A detailed comparison of some of the differences between the social and cultural values in the predominantly francophone province of Quebec and the rest of Canada—a relation often described with reference to a famous 1945 novel by Hugh MacLennan as one of "two solitudes"[10]—exceeds the scope of this monograph. But it is fair to state that the predominantly francophone province of Quebec has a more clearly defined unique cultural identity. This identity is shaped in large part by its efforts to maintain a strong predominantly francophone culture in a North-American context. The social and cultural norms in Quebec can be seen as a fusion between more traditional continental European, primarily French, and North-American values. In part because of its strong emphasis on the preservation of its own cultural identity, it also has an ambiguous, and at times more tense relationship with the vision of multiculturalism that is promoted as a key component of Canadian identity in the rest of the country. Quebec has, for example, imposed legal restrictions on religious headwear by public officials, embracing the French notion of secularism, while this is seen as an unacceptable interference with cultural and religious diversity elsewhere in Canada. Quebec's overall approach to social policy tends to be more closely aligned with some of the more left-leaning social democracies in Europe although fiscal conservative parties have also at times been elected to govern the province. Worth noting further is that the presence of significant French-speaking communities outside Quebec, and the recognition of French as an official federal language as well as a fully official (New Brunswick (NB)) or protected language in other provinces (e.g., Ontario), also forms an important part of Canada's identity. According to the 2016 Census, French is the mother tongue for 20.6% (or 7.2 million) of Canadians.

23. Canadians have a certain penchant toward patience and civil obedience. However, advocacy and litigation to enforce health-care-related rights have become more common in Canada. Class-action litigation in the context of pharmaceuticals and medical devices, or in other health-related areas (e.g., against the government for West-Nile virus infections), is now more common. Canada's tort litigation remains, however, more restrained than in the U.S., in part because it does not allow the sometimes astronomically high jury-awards for medical negligence cases.

24. In the Canadian context, litigation to enforce health-care rights usually takes place with recognition of the government's role in funding social policies, including health care, and in ensuring equal access to health care. The absence of a specific constitutional "right to health" notwithstanding, constitutional rights related to the right to life, liberty and security of the person, the right to equality, and the right to be free from cruel and unusual treatment have been invoked in the courts to enforce health-related rights. A 2018 federal court case also invoked the Charter's right of Freedom of Speech (section 2) in a decision that imposed on Health Canada, Canada's drug regulator, a duty to disclose clinical trials data related to pharmaceutical products.[11]

10. Hugh MacLennan, *Two Solitudes* (Toronto: Macmillan of Canada, 1945).
11. *Doshi v. Canada (Attorney General)*, 2018 FC 710; *see* Matthew Herder, Peter Doshi & Trudo Lemmens, *Precedent Pushing Practice: Canadian Court Orders Release of Unpublished Clinical Trials*

25. But some health-care related decisions by the Canadian Supreme Court and other courts based on Charter or related rights have an increasingly individual rights-focused flavor, which may undermine public interest-oriented policies. This has been the case, as is discussed further, with the *Chaoulli v. Quebec (Attorney General)* decision, which resulted in a declaration of invalidity of Quebec's restrictions on offering private health insurance contracts for some medically necessary services.[12] This restriction was aimed at protecting the publicly funded health-care system. Although the decision was ultimately based on the Quebec Charter of Fundamental Rights and Freedoms, the decision has opened the door to new Charter-based challenges against the Canadian publicly funded health-care system, as discussed further. More recent decisions by the Supreme Court and even more so by a Quebec trial court, which invalidated respectively Canada's absolute prohibition on Medical Assistance in Dying and a new law's restriction of Medical Assistance in Dying to the end-of-life context, can also be seen as favoring individual rights, and arguably undermining broad legislative schemes aimed at upholding social health-care-related values and norms, and protecting vulnerable people against premature death.[13]

26. The distinct cultural identity and values of the different Indigenous people have historically been ignored and even oppressed in Canada. This explains also the tensions that have arisen in the application of health law to Indigenous people. We devote in this monograph a special section to "Indigenous health" in which this is developed in more detail.

Data (Jul. 19, 2018), online (blog): *BMJ Blogs* https://blogs.bmj.com/bmj/2018/07/19/precedent-pushing-practice-canadian-court-orders-release-of-unpublished-clinical-trial-data/.

12. *Chaoulli v. Quebec (Attorney General)*, 2005 SCC 35 [*Chaoulli*]. Worth noting is the critique on the case in *Cambie Surgeries Corporation v. British Columbia (Attorney General)*, 2020 BCSC 1310 [*Cambie*], see infra at Chapter 2, §1, General Review of the Health-Care System.
13. *See* infra.

Chapter 2. General Description of the Health-Care System

§1. General Review of the Health-Care System

27. "Medicare," a comprehensive universal system of health services, has been offered in every Canadian province since 1971.[14] Under Medicare, government administers a publicly funded universal health insurance program which seeks to preserve freedom of choice for consumers and caregivers. Given the country's constitutional division of powers, the provincial governments are responsible for Medicare administration, but the need for federal funding allows Parliament to enact criteria which provincial health insurance plans must meet in order to qualify for full federal contributions. The 1984 Canada Health Act statutorily recognized five principles of Canadian health care: universality, portability, non-profit administration, no extra billing, and equal accessibility. Federal funding is also legislatively linked to population size, and economic indicators such as gross national product and inflation. Canadians are generally covered by Medicare even if they are outside of their province of residence, though the extent of coverage available may vary.

28. Health care in Canada is actually delivered by a mix of government and non-profit agencies and institutions, and private for-profit agencies. Hospitals form the core of the country's health-care network, with most of the larger hospitals offering both acute and long-term care. As of 2018, there were almost 1,500 hospitals in Canada.[15] In 2017, the number of acute care hospital beds was 2.0 per 1,000.[16] Rehabilitation and home care services are provided by public and voluntary agencies, in and out-patient hospital facilities, and Workers' Compensation Board Centres; also increasingly by private agencies in some provinces. Non-government administered health plans do exist in Canada; for instance, millions of Canadians choose to subscribe to private dental insurance plans. Financing of these services is generally public or voluntary, and some programs are covered by Medicare.

29. In 2017, there were 234 physicians for every 100,000 persons living in Canada, an increase of 6.6% since 2013.[17] Only allopathic physicians are fully licensed to practice medicine in Canada, and there are no Canadian medical schools of osteopathic medicine. Licencing requirements for physicians vary, with different regulatory bodies governing the practice of medicine in their respective provinces and territories.

---

14. J Wood, ed., *Canada Year Book 1992*, 125th ed. (Ottawa: Statistics Canada, 1992); M Rachlis & C Kushner, *Strong Medicine* (Toronto: Harper-Collins, 1994).
15. Government of Canada, *Summary: Canadian Industry Statistics* (online: Government of Canada, Feb. 14, 2018) strategis.ic.gc.ca/app/scr/app/cis/summary-sommaire/622.
16. Organization for Economic Co-operation and Development, "Hospital Beds" (2019), online: *OECD* data.oecd.org/healtheqt/hospital-beds.htm.
17. Canadian Institute for Health Information, "Summary Report, February 2019: Physicians in Canada, 2017" (February 2019) at 13-14, online (pdf): *Canadian Institute for Health Information* https://secure.cihi.ca/free_products/Physicians_in_Canada_2017.pdf (CIHI, "Physicians 2017").

30. Canada's total health-care expenditure for 2018 was forecast to reach CAD 253.5 billion, approximately 11.3% of the country's gross domestic product. Hospital expenditures account for the bulk of spending, at 28.3% of total health-care costs. Spending on drugs was expected to grow by 3.2% in 2018, to account for 15.7% of total health costs. Physician services were also forecast to increase by 2.2% over the last year, accounting for 15.1% of total health-care spending. Additional categories reported in the national health accounts include other health-care institutions and professionals and capital expenditures. The per capita health expenditure in 2018 was expected to be CAD 6,839.[18]

31. In 2017–2018, the average length of stay in an acute care hospital in Canada was 6.8 days.[19] The length of patient stays has decreased in recent years due to early discharge programs and greater reliance on home care services. Likewise, the focus on psychiatric hospitals has decreased as there is a trend toward community-based treatment, although the availability of community-based treatment services continues to be limited in many regions.

32. Canadian health care is currently undergoing a number of central changes, prompted in large part by the desire on the part of some provinces to integrate greater private market competition in the delivery of health care. Even as the U.S. attempted to undertake a massive national reorganization of their health-care system, and looked to Canada for inspiration, Canada has been forced to re-evaluate the costs of publicly maintaining universal health care. The solution will clearly require intense cooperation between the two levels of Canadian government, and, despite clear criticism, may result in a level of private medical care which has not hitherto been seen in Canadian health care. Arguably paving the way for increased privatization is a 2005 highly criticized[20] decision[21] of the Supreme Court of Canada (SCC), the highest court in the country, in which prohibitions against private health-care insurance were struck down by a 5–4 majority as unjustified infringements of Quebec's *Charter of Human Rights and Freedoms.* There was no majority of the Court to find the impugned Quebec legislation also in violation of

18. Canadian Institute for Health Information, "National Health Expenditure Trends, 1975 to 2018" (2018) at 1, 15, online (pdf): *Canadian Institute for Health Information* https://secure.cihi.ca/free_products/NHEX-trends-narrative-report-2018-en-web.pdf (CIHI, "Health Expenditure Trends").
19. Canadian Institute for Health Information, "CIHI Snapshot April 2019: Inpatient Hospitalization, Surgery, Newborn, Alternate Level of Care and Childbirth Statistics, 2017-2018" (2019) at 2, online (pdf): *Canadian Institute for Health Information* https://secure.cihi.ca/free_products/dad-hmdb-childbirth-quick-stats-2017-2018-snapshot-en-web.pdf.
20. *See* in general Colleen M Flood, Kent Roach & Lorne Sossin, eds., *Access to Care, Access to Justice: The Legal Debate over Private Health Insurance in Canada* (Toronto: University of Toronto Press, 2005).
21. *Chaoulli, supra* note 12.

the *Canadian Charter of Rights and Freedoms*. In the absence of a finding of violation of the Canadian *Charter*, the case was not binding in other provinces as a precedent. The decision only resulted in small changes to the Quebec provincial health-care system, in particular it resulted in legislative changes that enabled private health insurers to offer targeted insurance contracts for elective hip, knee, and cataract surgeries.

33. But similar challenges have since been brought in other Canadian provinces. The most prominent challenge is the 2020 case of *Cambie Surgeries Corporation v. British Columbia (Attorney General)*, a constitutional challenge to various provisions of British Columbia's *Medicare Protection Act*, R.S.B.C. 1996, c 286, which ban parallel private insurance for publicly insured services and prohibit physicians in the public system from extra billing patients for private-pay medically necessary health services. In challenging the impugned provisions, the plaintiffs in *Cambie* argued that it was "unconstitutional to prevent patients from accessing private medically necessary healthcare, including private surgeries, when they are unable to access timely care in the public system." Following a lengthy and contentious trial, the British Columbia Supreme Court dismissed the plaintiffs' claim, finding that the impugned provisions did not violate either section 7 (rights to life, liberty and security of the person) or section 15 (equality rights) of the *Charter*. In reaching this conclusion, the Court found that the "purpose of the impugned provisions is to preserve and ensure the sustainability of a universal public healthcare system that ensures access to necessary medical care is based on need and not on an individual's ability to pay" and that their effect was "one of suppressing and discouraging the emergence of a parallel duplicative private healthcare system." The Court further found that the introduction of duplicative private healthcare would create a two-tier system which would allow "access to preferential treatment … based on the ability to pay," result in increased wait times in the public system, and exacerbate existing inequities in access to timely care.[22] Given what was at stake in the case, there is a good chance this case will be appealed by the plaintiffs and eventually wind its way up to the SCC.

§2. Regulation of the Health-Care System

34. Most health-care matters are regulated by the provinces, according to their constitutional jurisdiction under the *British North America (BNA) Act* of 1867.[23] The provinces directly legislate in a variety of areas and have also delegated certification and regulatory functions to numerous agents, such as professional organizations and public agencies created by statute. Canadian health-care regulation is

22. *Cambie, supra* note 12 at paras. 4, 14–19, 1969–2043, 2077–2082, 2308–2465, 2562–2669; for a discussion of *Chaoulli, supra* note 12, *see also* paras. 1394–1429, 1495–1529. *See also* Colleen M Flood & Bryan Thomas, "A Successful Charter Challenge to Medicare? Policy Options for Canadian Provincial Governments" (2018) 13:3–4 Health Economics, Policy, and Law 433; consider also *Allen v. Alberta*, 2015 ABCA 277, leave to appeal to SCC refused, 2016 CarswellAlta 203.
23. *Chaoulli, supra* note 12.

highly decentralized, as each province is responsible for the administration of public health insurance within the province and maintains its own system of professional and institutional certification. The provincial licensing authorities of any given profession may elect to use a national licensing exam. Physician examinations are set by the Medical Council of Canada, for example. However, such a national requirement could not be imposed federally. Similarly, licensing reciprocity may not be difficult to obtain, but it is not automatic. Direct federal jurisdiction is generally restricted to particular segments of the Canadian population, as listed in the BNA Act, and to federal matters such as the interprovincial transportation of hazardous wastes.

35. Provincial governments have the constitutional jurisdiction to regulate virtually every aspect of any type of health service. The actual degree to which physician services, dental care, hospitals, ambulance service and public health is regulated varies according to political, social and economic changes within and between the provinces. Legislatures have the jurisdiction to set general health-care policy, allocate resources, determine the services which are covered by public health insurance, and establish professional and institutional standards. All the provinces have elected to exercise direct involvement in most areas of health care, particularly in the area of costs and setting minimum standards.

36. However, the provincial governments are rarely directly involved in daily health-care management, though there are exceptions, such as psychiatric hospitals. Actual management and service delivery are frequently delegated to various public, volunteer, professional, or private bodies. Health-care provider organizations exist for health-care workers, for some types of institutions such as hospitals, and in service areas such as mental health. These organizations often occur at national, regional and provincial levels, with the provincial associations wielding the greatest legislative authority since health care is a provincial matter.

37. Bodies with delegated regulatory authority may impact on health care directly or indirectly. For example, employment-related disability is regulated through the Workers Compensation Boards (WCB). These are non-profit, health-related agencies which are funded by employers but are also generally held accountable to a provincial government minister for their activities and decisions. They exist to compensate workers and provide long-term support for work-related injuries or diseases, including those which employees may have caused or contributed to themselves. In return, employees have a restricted right to bring legal action for negligence at the workplace. With the exception of a few municipalities that contribute directly to hospital costs, municipalities generally have little to do with primary health care. However, municipal levels of government have important public health functions and municipal regulatory jurisdictions often include areas such as zoning and land use, the handling and disposal of toxic wastes, and the creation of halfway houses and group homes, which indirectly impact on health planning.

38. Although health care is primarily an area of provincial jurisdiction, the federal government is responsible for administering a number of health-related statutes and regulations that address food and drugs, environmental safety, medical devices, consumer safety, and tobacco products. The federal government responds to national public health threats, such as human infectious disease outbreaks, through the Public Health Agency of Canada, in cooperation with other relevant federal, provincial and local authorities. Criminal law is under federal jurisdiction and may affect health-care regulation in matters such as the legalization of abortion, euthanasia and medicinal marijuana use (as well as legalization of marijuana more generally). The federal government also ensures health services are available to First Nation and Inuit communities, although many aboriginal communities are working with the federal government to transfer greater authority over health care to those communities.

39. The federal government also wields considerable influence by virtue of federal control over the most effective revenue-producing taxation methods. Federal statutes, such as the *Canada Health Act* (1984),[24] established certain conditions for the provincial provision of health care. These conditions must be met if the provinces are to receive the full grant monies to which they are entitled under federal law. Public administration is one of the conditions of federal financing, so public insurance tends to cover all basic hospital and physician services.

§3. Financing of the Health-Care System

40. Medicare, Canada's universal health insurance program, is financed by both the public and private sectors.[25] Public sector funding, which includes payments by governments at the federal, provincial/territorial and municipal levels and by Workers' Compensation Boards and other social security schemes, accounts for about 69% of Canada's total health expenditures. The additional 31% is funded by the private sector, that is, individuals and private insurance firms. While the balance between public and private funding has remained stable in recent years, the source of funding varies significantly by category: the bulk of physician (98.4%) and hospital (90%) costs are funded by the public sector and over 60% of prescription and non-prescription drug costs are financed by the private sector.

41. As Medicare is administered by individual provinces, the exact financial proportions and administration of health care vary across the country. Most of the provinces fund health insurance through general revenues alone. Until recently, the only two provinces to have health insurance premiums were British Columbia and Ontario. Both had income-based premiums. In British Columbia, the maximum premium was around CAD 37.50 per month for one person and CAD 75.00 per month for family coverage. Premiums were reduced for those earning less than CAD

24. *Canada Health Act*, SC 1984, c 6.
25. CIHI, "Health Expenditure Trends," *supra* note 18 at 10–12, 19; Ontario, "Health Premium" (Feb. 21, 2018), online: *Ontario* www.ontario.ca/page/health-premium; British Columbia, "Monthly Premium Rates" (2018), online: *British Columbia* www2.gov.bc.ca/gov/content/health/health-drug-coverage/msp/bc-residents/premiums/rates.

42,000 per year, and no premiums were paid by those earning under CAD 26,000. The Medical Services Plan premiums in British Columbia were eliminated by the provincial government as of January 1, 2020. The Ontario health premium is deducted from employee and pension payments or, if not automatically deducted, paid when income taxes are filed, and individuals who earn less than CAD 20,000 in taxable income are exempt. Since 2016, the federal government has completed health-care funding deals with the provincial and territorial governments. Under these agreements, the federal government made key commitments to the rate of annual increases in funding through the Canada Health Transfer program and to allocate a specific envelope of funding for mental health and addictions services and home and community care over ten years.

§4. HEALTH-CARE INSURANCE

42. While Medicare covers most basic hospital and physician services, the actual extent of service and provider coverage does vary to some extent between provinces. For instance, some provinces may provide some funding for drugs, glasses, prosthetics, home care, ambulance service, dentistry, optometry and chiropractics. Even some services offered in hospitals and by doctors may not be covered such as optional immunizations and cosmetic surgery. It should be no surprise that private health plans are most prevalent in those service areas for which Medicare provides little or no coverage. Most provincial insurance plans do provide an extended range of service coverage for certain groups such as seniors and veterans.

43. Medicare is generally portable between provinces, though some provinces reduce the monetary extent of coverage available for treatment given outside of the resident province. The amounts which may be recovered from provincial health insurance, for medical treatment either in other provinces or outside of the country, are usually limited to the amounts which would have been allowed for equivalent medical service within the home province.

44. Approximately 73% of payments to physicians are paid for on a fee-for-service basis, representing a considerable decline from approximately 90% in the 1990s.[26] The remaining costs are paid for through arrangements such as uniform per capita fees, straight salary, sessional payment, contract services, and salary incentives for medical practice in remote rural and northern areas. Direct patient payment, both full and partial, is clearly discouraged under the federal *Canada Health Act*. However, it is not uncommon to find extra billing for services which are not fully covered under a province's health insurance plan, such as long-term institutional care and ambulance service.

45. Finally, there are a variety of health-related services and products which are not covered under Medicare, and for which the general population frequently does

26. CIHI, "Physicians 2017," *supra* note 17 at 31, 32.

not obtain private insurance. Such medical items as vision products, pharmaceuticals and home care products are usually paid for out of pocket.

46. The federal government administers compassionate caregiving benefits and leave program that makes short-term employment insurance benefits available in certain circumstances to employees who must be absent from work to care for someone who is critically ill or injured or who needs end-of-life care and who is "like" family.[27]

§5. Pharmacare

47. Canada is the only country in the world that has a comprehensive universal public health-care system that does not include universal coverage for pharmaceuticals. The lack of universal drug coverage has left Canadians to rely on a patchwork of public and private drug insurance plans for coverage and/or to pay out of pocket for needed prescription medications. It has also meant that many Canadians have had to cut spending on other necessities (e.g., food) to pay for their medications or have had to forgo filling needed prescriptions entirely, for purely financial reasons.[28]

48. While no national program currently exists, the Province of Quebec has had a comprehensive drug coverage system in place since 1997. The Quebec system combines public and private coverage and requires that all residents have prescription drug insurance, either through a private plan or, if unavailable, through the Public Prescription Drug Insurance Plan. Private plans are accessed through employment or professional groups, through a spouse or through a parent (for children and students) and must provide at least the minimum drug coverage available under the public plan. Quebec residents aged 65 and over who qualify for a private plan can choose to get coverage under that plan, under the public plan, or under a combination of both plans.[29]

49. There have long been calls to extend Canada's Medicare system to include a universal drug coverage system which would provide Canadians with consistent coverage across the country and allow them to access prescription drugs based on the need rather than the ability to pay.[30] In February 2018, the federal government

---

27. Government of Canada, *Caregiving Benefits and Leave: What Caregiving Benefits Offer* (online: Government of Canada, Jan. 2, 2019) www.canada.ca/en/services/benefits/ei/caregiving.html.
28. Government of Canada, *A Prescription for Canada: Achieving Pharmacare for All, Final Report of the Advisory Council on the Implementation of National Pharmacare, June 2019* (Ottawa: Health Canada, June 2019) at 7, 9.
29. Régie de l'assurance maladie Québec, *Know the Eligibility Conditions for the Public Plan* (online: Régie de l'assurance maladie Québec) www.ramq.gouv.qc.ca/en/citizens/prescription-drug-insurance/Pages/eligibility.aspx; *Act Respecting Prescription Drug Insurance*, CQLR c A-29.01.
30. Government of Canada, *A Prescription for Canada: Achieving Pharmacare for All, Final Report of the Advisory Council on the Implementation of National Pharmacare, June 2019* (Ottawa: Health Canada, June 2019) at 1, 14.

created an Advisory Council on the Implementation of National Pharmacare. The Council released their final report in June 2019, recommending that the Canadian government implements "universal, single-payer, public pharmacare."[31] To implement this system, the Council recommended the enactment of new federal legislation "embodying the five fundamental principles in the *Canada Health Act*" (universal, comprehensive, accessible, portable, and public).[32] The Council also recommended the creation of a Canadian drug agency to establish a list of drugs to be covered, provide guidance on the use of drugs, and monitor drug safety and effectiveness once on the market.[33]

50. Like Canada's Medicare system, national pharmacare would require cooperation between the federal and provincial and territorial governments.[34] A major issue to be negotiated between the federal and provincial and territorial governments will be the nature and amount of the federal investment in national pharmacare. The Council recommended that the federal government establishes a new fiscal transfer program, which would be separate from the Canada Health Transfer, and would provide long-term, predictable, fair funding to each of the provinces and territories in a manner agreeable to them.[35]

51. The introduction of a national pharmacare system is expected to carry significant costs; however, the Council suggested that it could ultimately save the country money for two reasons. First, prescription medication prices currently differ from province to province and are often established through secret negotiations between provinces and pharmaceutical companies. Creating a pan-Canadian system would promote efficient decision-making and increase the government's negotiation power. Second, making drugs available to all who need them would prevent the avoidable "health crisis" which can occur where a patient cannot afford needed medications.[36] The Council also suggested that the program could be expected to provide considerable savings to individual Canadians and to businesses, by reducing out of pocket spending on prescription drugs and eliminating the need for private drug coverage plans.[37]

52. While they have voiced a commitment to introducing a national pharmacare program, and while steps have been taken in this regard,[38] the federal government is yet to enact legislation to implement universal drug coverage in Canada. A Bill to

31. *Ibid.*, at 8, 10.
32. *Ibid.*, at 11.
33. *Ibid.*, at 11–12.
34. *Ibid.*, at 13, 12.
35. *Ibid.*, at 13–14, 22.
36. *Ibid.*, at 2, 14, 15–16.
37. *Ibid.*, at 14–15.
38. *See* for example, Health Canada, *Government of Canada Announces Changes to Lower Drug Prices and Lay the Foundation for National Pharmacare* (online: Health Canada, Aug. 9, 2019) www.canada.ca/en/health-canada/news/2019/08/government-of-canada-announces-changes-to-lower-drug-prices-and-lay-the-foundation-for-national-pharmacare.html; Health Canada, *Statement*

implement national pharmacare[39] was tabled in the House of Commons by the New Democratic Party in 2020; however, with only a fraction of the number of Members of Parliament needed for a majority vote, the Bill is unlikely to be passed without the support of the governing Liberal Party.

§6. The Opioid Crisis

I. Opioid Addiction and the Health-Care System

53. One of the most significant challenges the Canadian health-care system has been facing in the past decades is the impact of opioid addiction on the health and well-being of Canadians. Opioids are among the most powerful pain medications.[40] They are also considered highly addictive. Commonly prescribed opioids include codeine, hydromorphone, oxycodone, morphine, fentanyl, methadone and tramadol.[41] Opioids can be legally prescribed by a health-care professional to treat short-term acute or long-term chronic pain.[42] But they are also widely distributed illegally and available as "street drugs."[43]

54. In recent years there has been a staggering increase in fatal and non-fatal opioid-related overdoses in Canada.[44] Opioid-related overdoses and deaths have become a serious public health crisis across the country.[45] The numbers speak for

---

from the Government of Canada on the Final Report from the Advisory Council on the Implementation of National Pharmacare (online: Health Canada, Jun. 12, 2019) www.canada.ca/en/health-canada/news/2019/06/statement-from-the-government-of-canada-on-the-final-report-from-the-advisory-council-on-the-implementation-of-national-pharmacare.html; Employment and Social Development Canada, *Budget 2019: Moving Forward on Implementing National Pharmacare* (online: Government of Canada, Mar. 25, 2019) www.canada.ca/en/employment-social-development/news/2019/03/budget-2019-moving-forward-on-implementing-national-pharmacare0.html.

39. Bill C-213, *An Act to Enact the Canada Pharmacare Act*, 1st Sess, 43rd Parl, 2019–2020 (first reading Feb. 24, 2020).
40. Government of Canada, *Opioids: What Are They?*, ISBN 978-0-660-28932-8, online (pdf): www.canada.ca/content/dam/hc-sc/documents/services/publications/healthy-living/opioids-what-are-they.pdf (Government of Canada, *Opioids: What Are They?*).
41. Tara Gomes et al., "Comparing the Contribution of Prescribed Opioids to Opioid-Related Hospitalizations Across Canada: A Multi-Jurisdictional Cross-Sectional Study" (2018) 191 Drug & Alcohol Dependence 86 at 88; Canadian Institute for Health Information, *Pan-Canadian Trends in the Prescribing of Opioids and Benzodiazepines, 2012 to 2017*, ISBN 978-1-77109-719-2 (Ottawa: Canadian Institute for Health Information, 2018) (CIHI, *Trends*) at 8.
42. Government of Canada, *Opioids: What Are They?*, *supra* note 40.
43. *Ibid.*
44. Health Canada, *Government of Canada: Actions on Opioids, 2016 and 2017*, Catalogue No H14-236/2017E-PDF (Ottawa: Health Canada, November 2017) (Government of Canada, *Actions on Opioids*) at 1; CIHI, *Trends*, *supra* note 41 at 5; Special Advisory Committee on the Epidemic of Opioid Overdoses, *National Report: Apparent Opioid-Related Deaths in Canada* (Ottawa: Public Health Agency of Canada, April 2019), online: *Government of Canada* infobase.phac-aspc.gc.ca/datalab/national-surveillance-opioid-mortality.html (Special Advisory Committee, *National Report*).
45. Government of Canada, *Actions on Opioids*, *supra* note 44 at 1; Mohammad Karamouzian et al., "Correlates of Seeking Emergency Medical Help in the Event of an Overdose in British Columbia, Canada: Findings from the Take Home Naloxone Program" (2019) 71 International Journal of Drug Policy 157 at 157.

themselves. According to Canada's Public Health Infobase, between January 2016 and December 2019, the death of more than 15,000 people was related to opioids. The same period saw close to 20,000 hospitalizations for opioid-related poisoning and 21,000 suspected opioid overdoses.[46] The opioid crisis has impacted every province and territory, with some regions being more heavily impacted than others.[47] British Columbia has experienced particularly high rates of fatal and non-fatal opioid-related overdoses, prompting the province to declare the opioid crisis as a public health emergency in April 2016.[48]

55. One of the major factors contributing to the current public health crisis is the high rate of opioid prescribing. Historically increased rates of opioid addiction and overdose largely coincided with increases in opioid prescribing, fueled by marketing efforts by pharmaceutical companies and the resulting perception that opioids were safe for long-term use for chronic pain management.[49] While these prescription and promotion practices are associated with the original rise in opioid addiction and resulting deaths, there has been a shift toward an illicit distribution and consumption of opioids.[50]

56. The more recent steep increase in drug-related harms, including high numbers of opioid-related deaths, is now largely attributed to the contamination of street drugs with strong opioids, particularly fentanyl.[51] Fentanyl is a strong synthetic opioid which may be legally prescribed to treat severe pain.[52] It is much more potent than heroin or morphine, and consumption of even a very small amount can lead to death.[53] A significant number of fatal opioid-related overdoses are accidental.[54] In many instances, individuals unknowingly consume drugs contaminated with fentanyl or other toxic substances and then experience an overdose.[55]

---

46. Government of Canada, *Opioid-Related Harms in Canada* (online: Government of Canada, June 2020) health-infobase.canada.ca/substance-related-harms/opioids/.
47. Special Advisory Committee, *National Report*, *supra* note 44.
48. Government of Canada, *Actions on Opioids*, *supra* note 44 at 1; Karamouzian et al., *supra* note 45 at 158; Gomes et al., *supra* note 41 at 86.
49. Tony Antoniou et al., "'Like Being Put on an Ice Floe and Shoved Away': A Qualitative Study of the Impacts of Opioid-Related Policy Changes on People Who Take Opioids" (2019) 66 International Journal of Drug Policy 15 at 15; Gomes et al., *supra* note 41 at 86.
50. Gomes et al., *supra* note 41 at 86–87; Antoniou et al., *supra* note 49 at 16.
51. Government of Canada, *Canada's Opioid Crisis*, ISBN 978-0-660-28942-7 (Government of Canada, *Opioid Crisis*); Health Canada, *Joint Statement of Action to Address the Opioid Crisis: A Collective Response, Annual Report, 2016-2017* (Ottawa: Canadian Centre on Substance Use and Addiction, 2017) at 4; Gomes et al., *supra* note 41 at 86; Government of Canada, *Actions on Opioids*, *supra* note 44 at 2.
52. Government of Canada, *Opioids: What Are They?*, *supra* note 40; Government of Canada, *Actions on Opioids*, *supra* note 44 at 2.
53. Government of Canada, *Opioids: What Are They?*, *supra* note 40.
54. Special Advisory Committee, *National Report*, *supra* note 44; Government of Canada, *Actions on Opioids*, *supra* note 44 at 2.
55. Government of Canada, *Actions on Opioids*, *supra* note 44 at 2; Special Advisory Committee, *National Report*, *supra* note 44.

II. The Response: Efforts to Curtail the Opioid Crisis

A. *Regulating Prescriptions and Pharmaceutical Manufacturers*

57. In response to the opioid crisis, Federal and provincial and territorial governments have enacted legislation to regulate the prescribing of opioids. For example, in Ontario certain long-acting and high-strength opioids have been removed (delisted) from the province's drug benefit program, and a "Narcotic Monitoring System" implemented to monitor the prescribing of opioids.[56] Ontario also introduced a program to try to curb the misuse or diversion of prescribed fentanyl patches from the illicit drug market.[57] Specifically, through "Patch-for-Patch" programs, patients with prescribed fentanyl patches must return their used patches before additional prescribed patches are dispensed.[58] Guidelines regarding the use of non-opioid pain management, tapering of opioid prescriptions, and restrictions of maximum opioid dosages have also been enacted.[59] For example, the 2017 Canadian Guideline for Opioids for Chronic Non-cancer Pain provides a series of recommendations for clinical practice surrounding chronic non-cancer pain management and the prescribing of opioids.[60]

58. Recently enacted changes to the *Food and Drug Regulations* allow the Federal Minister of Health to require pharmaceutical companies manufacturing opioids to have a "risk management plan" to monitor and mitigate the risks associated with the use of these products once they are on the market.[61] The amendments also require a "patient information handout" and a "warning sticker" to be provided along with prescription opioids when they are sold.[62] The Federal Government has also taken steps to restrict the marketing and advertising of opioids in Canada. Specifically, the Minister of Health is looking at imposing additional terms and conditions on pharmaceutical companies that would restrict advertising materials to statements that have been authorized by Health Canada.[63] These steps are being taken in an effort to address the over-prescribing of opioids and the influence that

---

56. Antoniou et al., *supra* note 49 at 15; Diana Martins et al., "Impact of Delisting High-Strength Opioid Formulations from a Public Drug Benefit Formulary on Opioid Utilization in Ontario, Canada" (2019) 28 Pharmacoepidemiology & Drug Safety 726 at 727.
57. Mina Tadrous et al., "Evaluation of the Fentanyl Patch-for-Patch Program in Ontario, Canada" (2019) 66 International Journal of Drug Policy 82 at 82–83.
58. *Ibid.,* at 83.
59. Martins et al., *supra* note 56 at 727; Antoniou et al., *supra* note 49 at 15.
60. Jason Busse, ed., *The 2017 Canadian Guideline for Opioids for Chronic Non-cancer Pain* (Ontario: National Pain Center, 2017).
61. Government of Canada, *Actions on Opioids*, *supra* note 44 at 9; *Food and Drug Regulations*, CRC, c 870, s C.01.014.21.
62. *Food and Drug Regulations*, *supra* note 61, s C.01.005.1(1); Government of Canada, *Actions on Opioids*, *supra* note 44 at 9.
63. Government of Canada, *Restricting the Marketing and Advertising of Opioids* (online: Government of Canada, Mar. 11, 2019) www.canada.ca/en/health-canada/services/substance-use/problematic-prescription-drug-use/opioids/responding-canada-opioid-crisis/advertising-opioid-medications.html (Government of Canada, *Restricting Marketing and Advertising*); *Food and Drug Regulations*, *supra* note 61, s C.01.014.21.

pharmaceutical companies' marketing and advertising efforts can have on health-care professionals' prescribing practices.[64]

59. Efforts have also been made to encourage transparency about the financial relationships between pharmaceutical companies and doctors and other health-care professionals. For example, in 2017, the Ontario Liberal Government introduced the *Health Sector Payment Transparency Act, 2017*, to require public disclosure of "financial relationships" that exist within the province's health-care system.[65] However, the legislation has not yet come into force and, with the election of the Conservative Government in Ontario in 2018, the implementation of the act and related regulations remains in question.[66]

60. While regulatory efforts may have had some effect on curtailing the prescribing of opioids, these policies may also have had unintended consequences. For example, they may have increased stigma, contributed to a reticence on the part of health-care providers to work with individuals with substance use disorders, or undermined the relationship between patients who use opioids and their primary health-care providers.[67] Restrictions on the prescribing of opioids may also explain the steep rise in illicit opioid consumption, which may be more dangerous and carry a heightened risk of overdose.[68]

B. Harm Reduction Strategies

61. Harm reduction strategies are broadly aimed at promoting the health and safety of people who use drugs and reducing the "negative effects" of substance use on individuals and communities.[69] Harm reduction was first endorsed by the Federal Government as a policy objective in the late 1980s.[70] In the latter part of the 1990s, the Federal Government included harm reduction as one of four approaches in their drug strategy, along with enforcement, prevention, and treatment.[71] While the Federal Government continued to endorse harm reduction approaches until 2006, critics argued that harm reduction strategies lacked funding (as compared to spending for enforcement, prevention, and treatment) and were embraced more in theory than in practice.[72] Federal support for harm reduction ceased in 2006, with

64. Government of Canada, *Restricting Marketing and Advertising*, *supra* note 63.
65. *Health Sector Payment Transparency Act, 2017*, SO 2017, c 25, Sch. 4, s. 1.
66. Kelly Grant, "Ford PCs Leave Drug-Company Transparency Law in Limbo," *The Globe and Mail* (Nov. 5, 2018), online www.theglobeandmail.com/canada/article-ford-pcs-leave-drug-company-transparency-law-in-limbo/.
67. *See* Antoniou et al., *supra* note 49 at 16–17, 19.
68. Gomes et al., *supra* note 41 at 89; Government of Canada, *Actions on Opioids*, *supra* note 44 at 2; Antoniou et al., *supra* note 49 at 19.
69. Elaine Hyshka et al., "Principles, Practice, and Policy Vacuums: Policy Actor Views on Provincial/Territorial Harm Reduction Policy in Canada" (2019) 71 International Journal of Drug Policy 142 at 143; Government of Canada, *Actions on Opioids*, *supra* note 44 at 4.
70. Hyshka et al., *supra* note 69 at 143.
71. *Ibid.*
72. *Ibid.*

the Conservative Government of the day opposing harm reduction throughout the next decade.[73] Although the Federal Government's opposition to harm reduction did not prevent the provinces or territories from investing in harm reduction, expansion of services remained "modest."[74]

62. In 2016, efforts to address the harms related to opioid addictions and death gained new energy. In November 2016, the Federal Ministry of Health, various provincial and territorial Ministries of Health, and numerous other stakeholders came together to discuss the ways to address and reduce opioid-related harms in Canada, resulting in a Joint Statement of Action to Address the Opioid Crisis containing commitments to action by the various parties.[75] In December 2016, with the Liberal Party in office, the Federal Government's National Anti-Drug Strategy was replaced with the Canadian Drugs and Substances Strategy (CDSS).[76] With the introduction of the CDSS, harm reduction was once again endorsed by the Federal Government, along with prevention, treatment and enforcement as the four pillars needed to respond to problematic drug and substance use.[77] The provinces and territories, alone and in conjunction with the Federal Government and other stakeholders, have also introduced and expanded harm reduction efforts in recent years.[78]

63. Supervised consumption sites are one of the programs introduced to reduce opioid-related harms. In order to operate a supervised consumption site, an exemption from the prohibition on possessing controlled substances must be obtained pursuant to section 56.1 of Canada's *Controlled Drugs and Substances Act*. Through legislative changes adopted in May 2017, the Federal Government simplified the requirements to apply for this exemption.[79] Supervised consumption sites allow individuals to use drugs in the presence of trained personnel and may also facilitate access to other health and social services.[80] Until late 2016, Vancouver was the only city with supervised consumption services and injectable opioid agonist treatment.[81] Health Canada has now approved around forty supervised consumptions sites in Alberta, British Columbia, Ontario, Quebec, and Saskatchewan.[82]

---

73. *Ibid.*
74. *Ibid.*
75. Government of Canada, *Actions on Opioids*, *supra* note 44 at 3, 5; Health Canada, *Joint Statement of Action to Address the Opioid Crisis: A Collective Response, Annual Report, 2016-2017* (Ottawa: Canadian Centre on Substance Use and Addiction, 2017) at 4.
76. Government of Canada, *Actions on Opioids*, *supra* note 44 at 3.
77. *Ibid.*, at 3, 4.
78. *Ibid.*, at 2–3, 5; Health Canada, *supra* note 75 at 4.
79. Government of Canada, *Actions on Opioids*, *supra* note 44 at 7; *Controlled Drugs and Substances Act*, SC 1996, c 19, s. 56.1(2).
80. Government of Canada, *Actions on Opioids*, *supra* note 44 at 7.
81. Hyshka et al., *supra* note 69 at 143; Government of Canada, *Actions on Opioids*, *supra* note 44 at 7.
82. Government of Canada, *Supervised Consumption Sites: Status of Applications* (online: Government of Canada, Apr. 8, 2020) www.canada.ca/en/health-canada/services/substance-use/supervised-consumption-sites/status-application.html#app; Government of Canada, *Actions on Opioids*, *supra* note 44 at 7.

64. The effects of an opioid overdose (e.g., unconsciousness, breathing issues) can be temporarily reversed and death prevented by administering the drug naloxone.[83] In March 2016, Health Canada removed naloxone from the prescription drug list, making it easier for individuals and organizations to access naloxone kits.[84] Take-home naloxone kits can now be obtained, usually free of charge, from pharmacies or other health authorities in most regions in Canada.[85] For example, the British Columbia take-home naloxone program provides educational and training resources and naloxone kits to various registered sites, including emergency departments, pharmacies, correctional facilities, and settings in Indigenous communities.[86] These sites distribute the naloxone kits to individuals who may be at risk of overdose or who may witness an overdose, free of charge.[87]

65. Legislation has also been enacted to encourage people to call for medical or law enforcement help when they experience or witness a drug overdose.[88] The Federal *Good Samaritan Drug Overdose Act* extends certain legal protections to people who seek emergency assistance by exempting them from charges for possession of illegal substances and charges for violating certain conditions or orders relating to an offense of possession.[89] People experiencing or witnessing a drug overdose may be reluctant to call 9-1-1 for various reasons, including fears about police involvement, child custody, or incurring criminal charges for drug possession.[90] The intention of the legislation is to reduce fears surrounding involving authorities in drug overdose situations and to encourage the delivery of life-saving medical interventions.[91] However, to be effective, the new legislation must be known to people who may experience or witness an overdose.[92] Furthermore, as the legislation only addresses charges for possession and violations of certain related conditions or court orders, people fearful of other reprisals (e.g., more serious drug charges, losing custody, eviction, police harassment) may still be reticent to contact the authorities in the event of a drug overdose.[93]

83. Government of Canada, *Actions on Opioids*, *supra* note 44 at 8; Karamouzian et al., *supra* note 45 at 157.
84. Government of Canada, *Actions on Opioids*, *supra* note 44 at 8.
85. *Ibid.*, at 3.
86. Karamouzian et al., *supra* note 45 at 158.
87. *Ibid.*
88. Government of Canada, *About the Good Samaritan Drug Overdose Act* (online: Government of Canada, Apr. 23, 2019) www.canada.ca/en/health-canada/services/substance-use/problematic-prescription-drug-use/opioids/about-good-samaritan-drug-overdose-act.html (Government of Canada, *GSDOA*); *Good Samaritan Drug Overdose Act*, SC 2017, c 4, Summary.
89. *Good Samaritan Drug Overdose Act*, *supra* note 88, s. 4.1.
90. Karamouzian et al., *supra* note 45 at 158.
91. Government of Canada, *GSDOA*, *supra* note 88.
92. Karamouzian et al., *supra* note 45 at 161.
93. *Ibid.*, at 2, 5; Government of Canada, GSDOA, *supra* note 88.

III. Legal Proceedings

66. Class action lawsuits have been pursued in various jurisdictions in Canada against Purdue Pharma (and related entities) relating to the "manufacture, marketing, sale, distribution, labelling, prescription and use of OxyContin® and OxyNEO® in Canada."[94] In 2007, lawsuits were commenced in Ontario, Nova Scotia and Quebec, and in 2012 in Saskatchewan.[95] Seven additional class actions also started in various jurisdictions between 2007 and 2012.[96] The proceedings contained similar claims alleging a breach of the defendants' duty to warn the addictive properties of the drugs which they "manufactured, marketed and/or sold or otherwise placed in the stream of commerce in Canada."[97] Pursuant to conditional certification orders granted in the Ontario, Nova Scotia, Quebec and Saskatchewan proceedings, the class descriptions in these proceedings, taken together, encompassed "all persons who, between January 1, 1996 and February 28, 2017 inclusive, ingested OxyContin and/or OxyNEO prescribed for them in Canada."[98]

67. In spring 2016, a series of mediation sessions were held, and the parties to Ontario, Nova Scotia, Quebec and Saskatchewan proceedings ultimately reached an "Agreement in Principle" in April of that year.[99] The following year, in March 2017, the parties entered into a Settlement Agreement, which increased the agreed-upon payment from CAD 19 million to CAD 20 million, reflecting a CAD 1 million increase in the monies earmarked for Provincial Health Insurers (PHI), to settle their claims for medical services provided, and to be provided to class members relating to their use of OxyContin and/or OxyNEO.[100] Specifically, the Settlement Agreement provided that the class members and the PHIs would release their claims against the defendants for CAD 20 million dollars, with CAD 2 million being paid to the PHIs and the remaining CAD 18 million to "satisfy the costs of administering the Settlement Agreement, the legal costs of Class Counsel [$4.5 million] and the approved claims of all class members."[101]

68. The Settlement Agreement was approved by the Courts in Ontario, Nova Scotia and Quebec, but would only remain effective if it was also approved in the Saskatchewan proceedings.[102] However, in March 2018, Justice Barrington-Foote of the Saskatchewan Court of Queen's Bench declined to approve the settlement. He observed that under the Settlement Agreement the estimated "average compensation for an approved claimant would be between $11,000 and $13,500, including legal fees," and that this amount would be further reduced by taking into account

94. *Perdikaris v. Purdue Pharma*, 2017 SKQB 287, 14 CPC (8th) 402 (*Perdikaris 1*) at paras. 1, 5.
95. *Ibid.*, at para. 5.
96. *Ibid.*
97. *Perdikaris 1, supra* note 94 at paras. 3, 5.
98. *Ibid.*, at para. 22.
99. *Ibid.*, at paras. 7–15.
100. *Ibid.*, at paras. 16, 25.
101. *Ibid.*, at paras. 23–26.
102. *Ibid.*, at paras. 29–32; *Perdikaris v. Purdue Pharma*, 2018 SKQB 86, 17 CPC (8th) 119 (*Perdikaris 2*) at para. 5.

the CAD 2 million payable to PHIs and non-refundable expenses and other costs related to notice and administration of the agreement.[103] He further observed that there was "no evidence that the amount payable to Saskatchewan pursuant to the Settlement Agreement—which Ball J. estimated to be $57,350—would constitute payment in full of the cost of the health services provided or to be provided in Saskatchewan."[104] Justice Barrington-Foote was ultimately "not satisfied that the assumptions identified by class counsel as to range of damages, average recovery, total recovery and the number of potential claimants were sound" and was also troubled by the "limited evidence and analysis as to the likelihood of success."[105]

69. Other legal proceedings have also recently been instituted against Purdue Pharma and a number of other opioid producers. In August 2018, the Government of British Columbia became the first province to commence legal proceedings against a number of opioid producers and distributers, including Purdue Pharma, to seek compensation for the health-care costs incurred by the province in relation to the opioid crisis.[106] The lawsuit alleges that the companies contributed to the current opioid crisis by downplaying the risks and addictive nature of opioids in marketing the drugs to health-care professionals.[107] The government has structured the lawsuit as a class action, so other provinces and territories can join the proceedings, and has introduced legislation, the *Opioid Damages and Health Care Costs Recovery Act*, to expedite the proceedings.[108] A number of other provinces have since joined the class-action lawsuit and enacted their own legislation in relation to the proceedings.[109]

IV. The Ongoing Crisis

70. The opioid crisis is a complex public health issue, with opioid-related harms stemming from both (over)prescribed and illicit opioids.[110] While policies aimed at curbing the prescribing of opioids may be contributing to a reduction in opioid prescriptions and efforts at harm reduction may be helping to avert overdose deaths,

103. *Perdikaris 2, supra* note 102 at paras. 12, 62.
104. *Ibid.*, at para. 51; *See also Perdikaris 1, supra* note 94 at paras. 77–78.
105. *Perdikaris 2, supra* note 102 at paras. 62–68.
106. Megan Thomas, "B.C. Aims to Accelerate Lawsuit Against Opioid Makers with New Legislation," *CBC News* (Oct. 2, 2018), online www.cbc.ca/news/canada/british-columbia/b-c-aims-to-accelerate-lawsuit-against-opioid-makers-with-new-legislation-1.4846388; Nate Raymond & Mike Spector, "OxyContin Maker Purdue Reaches $270-million Settlement in Oklahoma Opioid Case, Source Says," *The Globe and Mail* (Mar. 26, 2019), online www.theglobeandmail.com/world/article-oxycontin-maker-purdue-agrees-to-settle-oklahoma-opioid-case-source-2/.
107. Thomas, *supra* note 106.
108. *Ibid.*; *Opioid Damages and Health Care Costs Recovery Act*, SBC 2018, c 35.
109. The Canadian Press, "Ontario Passes Bill to Join Opioid Class-Action Lawsuit Launched by B.C.," *CBC News* (Dec. 12, 2019), online www.cbc.ca/news/canada/toronto/ontario-opioid-class-action-suit-1.5394066; *See also* for example, *Opioid Damages and Health Care Costs Recovery Act*, SA 2019, c O-8.5; *Opioid Damages and Health Care Costs Recovery Act, 2019*, SO 2019, c 17, Sch. 2.
110. Gomes et al., *supra* note 41 at 86–87; Government of Canada, *Opioid Crisis*, *supra* note 51; Government of Canada, *Actions on Opioids*, *supra* note 44 at 2.

the rates of fatal and non-fatal overdoses continue to rise, and the harms related to opioid addiction and death remain a significant public health crisis in Canada.[111] The opioid crisis in Canada presents a complex public health issue, one which requires a multi-faceted response which addresses the over-prescription of opioids, the illicit production of opioids, access to treatment services, and the underlying health and social factors that are fueling this crisis.[112]

111. Consider Tadrous et al., *supra* note 57 at 85; Government of Canada, *Actions on Opioids*, *supra* note 44 at 1; Special Advisory Committee, *National Report*, *supra* note 44.

112. Consider Gomes et al., *supra* note 41 at 86–87, 89, 90; Tadrous et al., *supra* note 57 at 85; Antoniou et al., *supra* note 49 at 20.

Chapter 3. Medical Law

§1. Definition and Function

71. While medical negligence and forensic litigation have long been recognized as areas in which the professions of law and medicine intersect, medical law as a discrete area of law has only come to prominence in the last few decades. Canadian recognition of the field has been encouraged by issues raised in American litigation and developments in medical entrepreneurship and science. For example, corporate and general business law is relevant to the business enterprises and tax planning of medical professionals, patent law is stretched by scientific innovations in genetics, and constitutional law is relevant for various health-related debates, such as abortion, MAiD and assisted human reproduction. Thus, while the traditional study and practice of medical negligence law continue, other branches of health law are expanding, both as fields of academic study and of practice.

§2. Sources of Medical Law

72. English Canada's legal system is common law based, which means that precedent, established through previous cases, forms the foundation for deciding cases currently before the courts. Yet, within all common law jurisdictions, statutory law plays an increasingly important role. While medical negligence and the physician-patient relationship continues to be dominated by the common law in Canada, statutory law plays an increasingly important role, particularly in the regulation of new areas of health law. Statutes and regulations commonly operate in the licensing and discipline of health-care professionals, in the establishment of health-care institutions, in the funding and administration of the health system and universal insurance, and in the care and treatment of people with mental health issues. Legislation has also encroached upon negligence issues; for example, many provinces have enacted "Good Samaritan" laws to protect health-care personnel against negligence when they provide emergency care, by explicitly confirming that they are liable only for gross negligence in those circumstances.

73. The province of Quebec has a civil law system, governed by codified rules and their interpretation by jurisprudence and doctrine. Book One, Title Two, of the *Civil Code of Quebec* (CCQ) (Certain Personality Rights) establishes rights relevant to medical liability—rights regarding medical care, psychiatric evaluation, integrity of the person and confinement in establishments.[113]

74. The common law and the civil law comprise distinct legal traditions, and Quebec is the only province in Canada which follows a civil law system. However, as the SCC deals with both common law and civil law cases, and as other courts also at times refer to cases from both the common law provinces and Quebec, there

113. The Quebec Code of Ethics of Physicians sets out duties and obligations specific to physicians. RRQ, c M-9, r 17.

is some convergence and cross-fertilization between these two legal systems in Canada. While both systems are relevant to understanding medical law in Canada, in this monograph we focus primarily on the Canadian common law, with limited discussion of the Quebec civil law.

75. Canada publishes a small number of specialized health law journals, and health law articles appear regularly in general medical and legal publications. Health law treatises published over the last decade have focused on topics ranging from the traditional study of medical negligence to the latest bioethical concerns.

Part I. The Medical Profession

Chapter 1. Access to the Medical Profession

§1. Training of Physicians

76. A Canadian medical education typically requires a minimum of two years of study, leading toward a bachelor's degree, followed by four years of professional medical education. However, a large majority of medical students have completed a four-year bachelor's degree before entering into the "undergraduate" program leading toward the Medical Doctor (M.D.) degree in allopathic medicine. The M.D. degree is followed by a period of residency, which consists of practical postgraduate training in an approved hospital or clinic. While each province sets its own requirements for the practice of medicine, no Canadian province requires less than one residency year. "Internship" is generally used to refer to the first year of practical training after graduation. A general residency may be "straight" or rotating or mixed. The College of Family Physicians of Canada offers a family medicine training program which requires a minimum of two years of residency. For specialties such as pediatrics, ophthalmology, and internal medicine, four to five years of postgraduate training is generally required. Any further medical education after specialization generally takes the form of independent or supervised study in the latest developments of a particular medical field.

77. Undergraduate and postgraduate medical education is provided by seventeen university faculties in Canada; there are no accredited schools of osteopathic medicine. Continuing professional education is generally provided by professional organizations, medical faculties or private health-care companies. Since 1979, Canada has had its own medical faculty accreditation body—the Committee on Accreditation of Canadian Medical schools. Canadian medical schools are currently accredited by both the Canadian Committee, as well as the U.S. Liaison Committee on Medical Education. In 2013, a Memorandum of Understanding was signed which conferred more independence on the Canadian Committee in decision-making, setting standards, and modifying the accreditation process.[114]

114. Committee on Accreditation of Canadian Medical Schools, "About CACMS," online: *CACMS/CAFMC* cacms-cafmc.ca/about-cacms.

78. From a low of 1,577 in 1997, national first-year enrolment in Canadian medical schools has risen significantly in recent years—to 2,916 as of 2017.[115] Medical school tuition ranges between a low of around CAD 4,000, on average, per year for Quebec residents attending Quebec medical schools, to approximately CAD 28,000 a year in other parts of Canada.[116] In the early 1990s, there was a general perception that Canada had a surfeit of medical students and a number of faculties introduced explicit enrolment quotas. Two decades later, concerns centered on perceived physician shortages. However, in the last decade, the number of physicians in Canada has been increasing, and from 2013 to 2017 increases in the number of physicians outpaced population growth, leading to more physicians per 100,000 people in 2017 than ever before.[117] The ratio of family medicine physicians and specialists were relatively equal, with family medicine practitioners comprising 119 of the 224 physicians per 100,000 population, and specialists comprising 115.[118] However, some parts of Canada, particularly rural and remote regions, continue to have trouble recruiting and retaining general practitioners; people living in rural communities constitute around 19% of the population in Canada, but only about 8% of physicians practice in rural areas.[119]

§2. HEALTH HUMAN RESOURCE PLANNING

79. There is no national program for physician distribution in Canada. The provinces license and control their own physician populations, so that interprovincial practice is subject only to the requirement of meeting a given province's licensing requirements. Within each province, physicians are free to establish their practice wherever they choose. In fact, their right to do so has been judicially interpreted as a part of the individual's constitutional right to liberty under the *Canadian Charter of Rights and Freedoms.*[120] Furthermore, various provincial attempts to structure financial remuneration under Medicare so as to discourage physicians from establishing practices in over-serviced urban areas have been the subject of successful legal challenges.[121] Equality and mobility rights under the *Charter* make it difficult

115. The Association of Faculties of Medicine of Canada, *Canadian Medical Education Statistics 2018*, vol. 40 (Ottawa: AFMC, 2019) at 138.
116. *Ibid.,* at 15.
117. CIHI, "Physicians 2017," *supra* note 17 at 11, 12.
118. *Ibid.*, at 13.
119. Canadian Medical Association, "Quick Facts on Canada's Physicians" (2019), online: *CMA* www.cma.ca/quick-facts-canadas-physicians.
120. *Wilson v. British Columbia* (1989), 2 WWR 1 (BCCA), leave to appeal to SCC refused (1989), 3 WWR LXXI (holding that provinces could not force physicians to practise in certain geographic areas, or restrict them to *locum tenens* work, by threatening to withhold the issuance of a Medicare billing number).
121. *Waldman v. British Columbia (Medical Services Commission)* (1997), 150 DLR (4th) 405 (BCSC), in which B.C.'s *Medicare Protection Act,* and its restriction on new billing numbers to remuneration at 50% of the province's normal fee schedule, was found to be a violation of physicians' *Charter* rights to both interprovincial mobility and the equal benefit of the law. The restrictions were not saved by s. 1 of the *Charter* as there was no evidence of a rational connection between the enacted measures and the government's objective of controlling the quality and cost of medical services within the province; aff'd (1999), 177 DLR (4th) 321.

for any one province to effectively initiate physician supply measures, since restricting fee payments in an over-serviced area will invariably have the greatest effect on those physicians who wish to move inter- or intra-provincially, or risk incurring the political opposition of established physicians.[122] Legal and political constraints on the provinces' ability to regulate physician supply may encourage provincial and federal cooperation in devising a national policy for physician distribution. The enactment of strictly additive financial incentives for practicing medicine in rural and remote Northern areas of Canada has never been, and are unlikely to be, subject to legal challenge.

80. Physician workforce issues were addressed in the *Barer Stoddart Report toward Integrated Medical Resource Policies for Canada,* written for the Federal/Provincial/Territorial Conference of Deputy Health Ministers held in June 1991.[123] The report found that Canada lacked consensus on a policy objective for managing the physician resource sector and suggested that physicians should be managed in order to efficiently meet the health needs of the population. In the evaluation of physician resources, purely technical means of data collection and statistical methodology were deemed to be insufficient for finding the "optimal" number of physicians. The report also found that the health-care system should use incentives and be structured so as to increase the responsiveness of physicians to the universal goals and needs of public health care. While conceding that national unanimity on specific health-care policies could not be achieved, the Report supported developing a national policy framework which would encourage provinces and territories to coordinate policies and cooperate with one another. Since the federal government lacks a solid constitutional basis for legislating and enforcing regulations on Canada's physician workforce, any national policy could only rest on provincial goodwill and cooperation.

81. In 2009, an agreement on national standards for licensure eligibility was reached by the thirteen provincial and territorial medical regulatory authorities. The *Model Standards for Medical Registration in Canada*, which continue to evolve, provide for a Canadian standard for registration and full licensure of physicians and supports the mobility of physicians across jurisdictions.[124] Other national reports on the Canadian health-care system have identified current concerns regarding physician workforce and other health human resource issues. For example, in spring 2017, the federal Standing Senate Committee on National Finance released its first

---

122. *See* Linette McNamara, "Case Comment: Waldman v. British Columbia (Medical Services Commission)" (1997) 6:2 Health L Rev 24 for more in-depth discussion of the issues involved in enacting physician supply measures.
123. Morris Barer & Gregory Stoddart, "Barer Stoddart Report Toward Integrated Medical Resource Policies for Canada" (1991) Centre for Health Economics and Policy Analysis Working Paper Nos. 91-7, 91-8.
124. Federation of Medical Regulatory Authorities of Canada, "Model Standards for Medical Registration in Canada" (February 2018), online: *Federation of Medical Regulatory Authorities of Canada* fmrac.ca/wp-content/uploads/2018/04/Model-Standards-for-Medical-Registration-in-Canada-updated-February-2018.pdf.

interim report titled, "Getting Ready: For a New Generation of Active Seniors."[125] This report recognized that in the coming decades people aged 65 and over will "put greater pressure on the country's health care system and public finances" and recommended that the Federal government, in collaboration with provincial, territorial, and Indigenous partners, develop a "national seniors strategy," to: control increases in spending while ensuring appropriate and accessible care; implement measures to allow seniors to receive support services at home; introduce measures to increase labor force participation by underrepresented groups to match labor demand and supply and mitigate the negative impact of an aging population on the labor market and economy; and contemplate including demographic considerations in the calculation of federal transfer payments to ensure all regions have the resources needed to address the demands that arise from their aging populations. In reaching these recommendations, the Committee considered the limitations of the current health-care system in Canada, regional disparities in accessibility of needed health-care services, and the need to reorganize the way the system operates in order to respond to these realities and address the challenges posed by an aging population.

82. Canada's immigration policy also influences the physician workforce. In 2017, 26.5% of Canada's physicians were graduates of foreign medical schools.[126] Applicants for Canadian permanent residence with experience as a physician or resident-in-training who want to immigrate to Canada as a skilled worker are not required to provide evidence of licensing as a pre-condition of admission to Canada. Once admitted to Canada, however, applicants intending to practice as physicians in Canada must complete the Medical Council of Canada Qualifying Examinations as well as a series of licensing requirements established by the province in which they intend to practice.

§3. Licensing of Physicians

83. The Royal College of Physicians and Surgeons of Canada is the national body which certifies all specialties in clinical, laboratory and surgical medicine, excepting family medicine which has its own national college. Almost one-hundred areas of specialty, subspecialty and special programs and areas of focused competence are recognized in Canada. However, the obtainment of a certificate of qualification by the Royal College does not automatically give a graduate license to practice medicine. The provinces have the jurisdiction to both require registration as a condition for the practice of medicine, and set qualifications for obtaining registration.[127] Hospital management boards have the power to fix regulations for obtaining hospital privileges in public hospitals.

125. Standing Senate Committee on National Finance on Canada's Aging Population, *Getting Ready: For a New Generation of Active Seniors* (June 2017) (Chair: Percy Mockler).

126. CIHI, "Physicians 2017," *supra* note 17 at 20.

127. *Hutfield v. College of Physicians & Surgeons (Alberta)* (1989), 96 AR 85 (CA); leave to appeal to SCC refused (1989), 101 AR 320. *See also*, Part III, Ch. 3, s. 2.

84. All of the provincial licensing authorities generally have four main requirements:

(1) A degree from a recognized school of medicine.
(2) Postgraduate medical training.
(3) Successful sitting of the examinations set by the Medical Council of Canada.
(4) Evidence of "good character."

Any further conditions, such as a citizenship requirement, would likely be found to be unconstitutional. In *Andrews v. Law Society of British Columbia,*[128] a provincial law society's requirement of Canadian citizenship for entry into the legal profession was struck down as an unreasonable limit on the right to equality contained in the *Canadian Charter of Rights and Freedoms.* Under the requirement of "good character," some provincial licensing authorities reserve the right to refuse registration to any person who has been convicted of an indictable offense.

128. *Andrews v. Law Society of British Columbia* [1989] 1 SCR 143 [1989] 2 WWR 289.

Chapter 2. Illegal Practice of Medicine

§1. Legal Definition of the Offense

I. Statutory Definition

85. Every province is responsible for legislatively defining the parameters of medical practice within the province.[129] The practice of medicine is difficult to precisely define, and obviously there are going to be areas of overlap in activities which are routinely undertaken by other health professions. Most of the provinces have enacted a "Medical Act" or a "Medical Practitioner" or "Medical Professions" Act, which defines "medical practice" very broadly.

86. Generally, the "practice of medicine" encompasses any individual who holds himself or herself out, by advertisement or otherwise, as someone able and willing to diagnose, prevent or treat any human disease or injury. Particular enumerated activities include the examination or giving of advice on any person's mental or physical condition; the prescription or administration of any drug or remedial substance; the application of any appliance or device as a cure or prevention for human disease or defect; and acting as agent, assistant or associate or a person who practices medicine. Anyone who engages in these or other defined activities, and is not registered as a physician in that province, is engaged in the unlawful practice of medicine. Other licensed health professionals are then statutorily exempted from prosecution for engaging in activities which are statutorily defined in their own governing acts.

87. It is increasingly common for Canadian provinces to have "umbrella" legislation, commonly called a *Health Professions Act,* that provides an overarching regulatory framework for all regulated health professions. Such legislation replaces a number of profession-specific statutes. Under health professionals legislation, many regulated health professional groups, such as physicians, nurses, dentists and pharmacists, are authorized to establish a self-governing regulatory college. The health professions statutes typically define controlled or restricted acts (e.g., communicating medical diagnosis; setting bone fractures and joint dislocations; and prescribing, dispensing and selling statutorily defined drugs) that may only lawfully be performed by specific regulated health professional groups.

88. The dearth of available physicians in remote areas of Northern Canada has prompted a number of provinces to legislatively recognize "hybrid professions," capable of performing certain medical functions which would normally be classified as the illegal practise of medicine. This occurs most frequently in the context of nursing, whereby registered nurses with particular training and experience are

129. CED (West), vol. 21, title 88 (Medicine); CED (Ont), vol. 14, title 72 (Hospitals and Health Care); Canadian Abridgement, vol. R18, *Health Law* and supplement (1992–1994); Gilbert Sharpe, *The Law & Medicine in Canada,* 2nd ed. (Toronto: Butterworths, 1987) at 238–240.

given the authority to engage in diagnostic, treatment and drug handling acts without the direct supervision of an attending physician; such tasks are outside the usual scope of authority of nurses.[130] Interestingly, the recent Canadian legislation related to Medical-Aid-in-Dying permits also nurse practitioners to perform life-ending measures.[131]

89. All of the provincial schemes make some exceptions to prosecution for the unlawful practice of medicine. These exceptions include situations in which medical aid is given for emergency first aid, treatment is given according to religious tenets and without hope of profit or gain, or assistance is given to the members of one's own household.

II. Judicial Interpretation

90. Canadian courts do not seem to have developed a single way of interpreting provincial legislation regulating medical practice. On the one hand, it has been decided that the unlawful practice provisions of a medical professions act should be strictly and narrowly interpreted since the act's main purpose was said to be protection of the monopoly of practice, and not protection of the public against "quacks" or unregistered practitioners.[132] On the other hand, the court is clearly willing to penetrate beyond an individual's title or claimed activities, and question whether an accused person is substantively engaging in actions which constitute the practice of medicine.[133]

§2. Regulating Alternative and Complementary Approaches to Health Care

91. Individual provinces have the legal authority to decide whether to recognize alternative and complementary health-care practitioners as regulated health professions. Chiropractors, massage therapists, midwives, naturopaths, and practitioners of traditional Chinese medicine and acupuncture are examples of professional groups that have attained legal recognition in many provinces. Public funding for

---

130. For example, *see* s. 5.1 of Ontario's *Nursing Act, 1991*, SO 1991, c 32.
131. *An Act to Amend the Criminal Code and to Make Related Amendments to Other Acts (Medical Assistance in Dying)*, SC 2016, c 3; *See also infra* at Chapter 3: Specific Activities, §7.
132. *R v. Wong* [1979] 6 WWR 163 (Alta. Prov. Ct.), in which an acupuncturist was not in violation of Alberta's *Medical Profession Act* since acupuncture was not recognized as a branch of medical practice; *R v. Windrum* (1994), 126 Sask. R. 15, 25 WCB (2d) 497 (Sask. QB), in which a conviction for contravening Saskatchewan's *The Medical Profession Act, 1981*, was upheld against an unlicensed individual found to have diagnosed and treated another individual for gain.
133. *R v. Sandhar* (1987), 78 AR 70 (QB), affirmed (1988), 86 AR 241 (CA), in which the accused claimed to be practising homeopathy, and was convicted of diagnosing human illness and prescribing drugs in violation of *Alberta's Medical Professions Act*. Consider also *R v. Baig* [1992] BCJ No. 2567, 21 BCAC 59 (BCCA), in which convictions against an individual who was not registered to practice medicine were upheld in relation to violating BC's *Medical Practitioner's Act* by having held himself out as qualified to treat and diagnose a variety of human ailments.

services provided by such professions is a separate policy decision, however, and many complementary and alternative therapies are excluded from provincial health insurance programs. Private health insurance coverage offered by employers, for example, may fund a limited number of visits to a complementary/alternative practitioner.

Chapter 3. Control over the Practice of Medicine

§1. Disciplinary Organizations and Professional Codes

I. Government Licensing Agencies

92. The responsibility for medical licensure, supervision, and professional discipline falls under provincial jurisdiction. The province ultimately controls the right to practice of physicians, nurses, nurse practitioners, chiropractors, osteopaths, naturopaths, midwives, and other paramedical personnel such as respiratory therapists.[134] This section will specifically address the licensure of physicians.

93. Each province has delegated the authority for control over licensure to a self-governing body. The licensing authority's name varies from province to province. Some examples are: College of Physicians and Surgeons, Medical Council, or Medical Board. These licensing authorities are quasi-public institutions created for the protection of the professional capacity of members and as a safeguard to the health and welfare of the public.[135] The two main functions of licensing authorities are to maintain a register of the names of all those who have applied and met the requirements for licensing and to regulate those so registered by ensuring that the register contains only those whose conduct and competence meets the standards.[136]

94. The authorities set and administer the standards for professional licensure and the Code of Professional Conduct. Moreover, licensing authorities establish mechanisms for dealing with complaints against doctors and questions of professional discipline, and they monitor and maintain the standards of medical practice. The licensing authorities are enabled by legislation to censure, reprimand, suspend, qualify, limit or revoke the license to practice, collect costs of operations and fine delinquents.[137] Each licensing authority consists of a council made up of elected medical members of the authority.[138]

95. To qualify for registration, the physician will be required to furnish proof of qualification and training, or if previously registered elsewhere, a "certificate of good standing" from that licensing body, which states that practice has been competent and ethical, and no charges of misconduct are pending or under review.

96. A licensing authority has the responsibility to:[139]

---

134. HE Emson, *The Doctor and the Law: A Practical Guide for the Canadian Physician,* 2nd ed. (Toronto: Butterworths, 1989) at 16–17.
135. Sharpe, *supra* note 129 at 227.
136. *Palmer School & Infirmary of Chiropractic v. Edmonton (City)* [1921] 2 WWR 6 (Alta. SC); *Brand v. College of Physicians & Surgeons (Saskatchewan)* (1990), 83 Sask. R. 218 (CA), reversed in part on other grounds 86 Sask. R. 18 (CA); *Wakeford v. College of Physicians & Surgeons (British Columbia)* (1993), 84 BCLR (2d) 171, 105 DLR (4th) 543 (BCCA).
137. Emson, *supra* note 134 at 18.
138. *Health Professions Act,* RSA 2000, c H-7, ss. 5–6.
139. Sharpe, *supra* note 129 at 228.

(1) determine the validity of diplomas presented to it;
(2) assure itself that the person presenting it is, in fact, the person named in the diploma;
(3) equate the qualification and competence of graduates from medical schools in various countries;
(4) determine supplementary requirements for the graduates of designated schools to bring them up to the established standard.

97. There are several types of registration possible. An applicant may be registered:[140]

(1) on the General Register with an unqualified license;
(2) on a Temporary Register, with an unqualified license for a specified period of time;
(3) on a Special Register, with a license restricted as to scope of practice or restricted to a defined area, such as an academic institution, hospital, the public service or an underserviced area; or
(4) on an Educational Register, with a license restricted to a hospital or institution where post-doctoral study is undertaken or where a clinical clerkship is being served.

II. Procedural Requirements

98. Provincial legislation enables licensing councils to hear disciplinary matters. They act as a quasi-judicial body; depending on the jurisdiction, appeals from their licensing decisions may be heard before a court or before an appointed Board.[141]

99. The licensing authorities have a duty to act fairly. The lack of respect for rules of natural justice and procedural fairness give rise to grounds for appeal. If an application for licensure is refused, therefore, the authorities must provide reasonable access to evidence against the applicant.[142] Reasonable access to evidence also must be furnished to those who are appealing a decision of the Discipline Committee.

100. In reviewing an application for registration, the licensing authorities may look behind certificates of qualification to determine the suitability of an applicant.

140. *Ibid.*, at 229.
141. *Ibid.*; Emson, *supra* note 134 at 18.
142. *Bakht v. College of Physicians & Surgeons (British Columbia)* (1980), 20 BCLR 43 (SC), affirmed 30 BCLR 89 (CA), leave to appeal to SCC refused 41 NR 268n; *Farhat v. College of Physicians and Surgeons of Alberta*, 2014 ABQB 731, 603 AR 35. For an overview of the principles of natural justice, *see* David Phillip Jones & Anne S de Villars, "Natural Justice and the Duty to Be Fair: Historical Development and General Principles" in *Principles of Administrative Law*, 6th ed. (Scarborough: Carswell, 2014) at 217.

III. Substantive Grounds for Discipline in the Medical Profession

A. *General*

101. In 2018, the Board of Directors of the Canadian Medical Association (CMA) approved an updated Code of Ethics and Professionalism that provides ethical guidance in core areas of medical practice, including diagnosis, treatment and prevention of disease and patient care, advocacy, education and research.[143] The Code instructs that "Physicians should be aware of the legal and regulatory requirements that govern medical practice in their jurisdictions." The Code recognizes three major areas of ethical principles:

(1) Virtues to be exemplified by the ethical physician, namely compassion, honesty, humility, integrity, and prudence.
(2) Fundamental commitments of the medical profession, of which the first is the need to "[c]onsider first the well-being of the patient," and also include commitments to respect for persons, justice, professional integrity and competence, professional excellence, self-care and peer support, and inquiry and reflection.
(3) Professional responsibilities, including:
   - Responsibilities to the patient and the practice of medicine, which are further broken into particular areas involving the initiation and dissolution of the patient/physician relationship, the need for communication and informed decision-making and consent, the right to confidentiality, and the management and minimizing of conflicts of interest.
   - Responsibilities to society, including admonitions to "[s]upport the profession's responsibility to promote equitable access to health care resources" and "promote resource stewardship."
   - Responsibilities to colleagues.
   - Responsibilities to oneself.

102. Although individual disciplinary actions involve more specific transgressions than are set out in the Code of Ethics, physicians are expected to respect its general tenor, and disciplinary actions arise from not doing so.

103. More specifically, every registered practitioner is subject to regulation and discipline by the licensing authority in the province or territory where registered. If found guilty of professional misconduct, a physician's license may be suspended or revoked. Professional misconduct resulting in suspension or withdrawal of a license is elaborated on in a variety of ways in provincial and territorial statutes.

143. Canadian Medical Association, *CMA Code of Ethics and Professionalism*, online (pdf): *Canadian Medical Association* https://policybase.cma.ca/documents/policypdf/PD19-03.pdf.

104. An example of one approach is provided by Ontario's *Regulated Health Professions (Code)*[144] which states that a panel must find that a member has committed an act of professional misconduct if:

(1) the member has been found guilty of an offense that is relevant to the member's suitability to practice;
(2) the governing body of another health profession in Ontario, or the governing body of a health profession in a jurisdiction other than Ontario, has found that the member committed an act of professional misconduct that would, in the opinion of the panel, be an act of professional misconduct under this section or as defined in the regulations;
(3) the member has failed to co-operate with the Quality Assurance Committee or any assessor appointed by that committee;
(4) the member has sexually abused a patient; or
(5) the member has committed an act of professional misconduct defined in the regulations.

105. The *Regulated Health Professions Act*[145] in Manitoba provides an example of disciplinary measures that may be taken in cases where an inquiry panel has found that an investigated member has engaged in professional misconduct or is unfit to practice. The panel may make an order doing one or more of the following:

(a) reprimanding the member;
(b) suspending the member from practicing the profession for a stated period;
(c) suspending or restricting the member's practice until he or she has satisfactorily completed a specified course of studies or supervised practical experience;
(d) suspending the member until such time that an ailment, emotional disturbance or addiction no longer impairs his or her ability to practice the regulated health profession;
(e) accepting the member's undertaking to limit his or her practice;
(f) imposing conditions on the investigated member's right to practice a regulated health profession, for example, by requiring the member to limit his or her practice, practice under supervision, and/or permit periodic inspections or audits of his or her practice;
(g) requiring the member to take counseling or receive treatment;
(h) directing the member to repay money that was paid to him or her where payment was unjustified for any reason; or
(i) barring the member from practice (cancellation of registration).

144. *Regulated Health Professionals* Act, SO 1991, c 18, Sch. 2, s. 51.
145. *Regulated Health Professions Act,* SM 2009, c 15, s. 126(1).

B. *Burden of Proof of Professional Misconduct*

106. The burden of proof of professional misconduct is a civil standard of proof on a balance of probabilities, the onus of which rests on the disciplinary committee.[146] As a result of this civil standard of evidence, physicians who are accused, for example, of sexual assault may still be disciplined even if they are not found guilty in criminal court.

C. *Discipline for Non-registration as a Medical Practitioner*

107. Health professions statutes prohibit the practice of a regulated health profession without being registered/licensed with the relevant regulatory/licensing authority. It is a statutory offense to practice or profess to practice a regulated health profession without a valid registration/license.[147]

D. *Discipline for Incompetency*

108. To prove incompetency, a disciplinary panel must prove that the member's professional care of a patient displayed a lack of knowledge, skill or judgment of a nature or to an extent that demonstrates that the member is unfit to continue to practice or that the member's practice should be restricted.[148]

E. *Discipline for Incapacity*

109. Licensing authorities are empowered to suspend, revoke or restrict the license of members who are found to be incapacitated. According to the Alberta *Health Professions Act,*[149] a health professional is incapacitated if "suffering from a physical, mental or emotional condition or disorder or an addiction to alcohol or drugs as defined in the *Pharmacy and Drug Act* or other chemicals that impairs the ability to provide professional services in a safe and competent manner."

110. In such cases when the licensing authority believes that a member may be incapacitated, a complaints committee will be established to investigate and report on its findings to an executive committee. If the complaints committee gives the executive committee a referral to investigate further, the executive committee must give the member notice of its intention to appoint a board of inquiry.

---

146. *Green v. College of Physicians & Surgeons (Saskatchewan)* (1984), 31 Sask. R. 119 (Med. App. Trib.), affirmed 51 Sask. R. 241 (CA); *Taylor v. College of Physicians and Surgeons of Ontario*, 2018 ONSC 4562, 298 ACWS (3d) 649.
147. *See* for example, Manitoba's *The Regulated Health Professions Act,* SM 2009, c 15, s. 54.
148. *See* for example, the Ontario *Regulated Health Professions Act,* SO 1991, c 18, Sch. 2, s. 52(1).
149. RSA 2000, c H-7, s. 1(1)(s).

F. Discipline for Sexual Misconduct with Patient

111. The sexual misconduct of a physician provides grounds for licensing authorities to take disciplinary action. The penalties range from revoking the member's certificate of registration, to suspending of registration, to placing conditions on the member's certificate of registration.

G. Appeals

112. Medical practitioners who have been found guilty of professional misconduct or incompetence may appeal the decision to a court. The provisions relating to the time within which notice must be given, and the court to which appeal may be taken, vary from province to province and are outlined in the relevant statutes. Where a right of appeal exists, the doctor may not be required to take this route if the decision is being challenged on jurisdictional ground or where a "reasonable apprehension of bias" on the part of the decision maker is alleged.[150]

IV. Judicial Review of Grounds for Disciplinary Action

113. In addition to the right to appeal decisions of a Discipline Committee, there also exists the potential for judicial review of decisions. The right to judicial review exists in cases where the principles of "natural justice" or "fairness" have been violated. In many jurisdictions in Canada the relevant legislation sets out the minimum standard of procedural fairness in administrative decision-making. However, where the legislation is silent on the procedural question, the common law principles apply.[151]

114. As is the case for licensing decisions above, basic administrative law principles regarding decision-making apply to disciplinary decisions. The decision-making body must have the appropriate jurisdiction to make the decision in question. The physician must be adequately notified of the hearing and must have the opportunity to respond.[152] The physician is entitled to be heard by unbiased decision makers[153] and to be represented by legal counsel. All evidence should be disclosed and the physician must be able to cross-examine with respect to this evidence. If any of these principles of fair decision-making have not been respected, the right to judicial review arises.

---

150. Sharpe, *supra* note 129 at 243.
151. For an overview of the principles of natural justice, *see* David Phillip Jones & Anne S de Villars, *supra* note 142 at 217.
152. *Murthy v. College of Physicians & Surgeons (Sask.),* 52 Sask. R. 314, affirmed 56 Sask. R. 307 (CA); *Swart v. College of Physicians and Surgeons of Prince Edward Island*, 2014 PECA 20, 361 Nfld. & PEIR 5 [*Swart*].
153. *Re Yat Tung Tse and Ontario College of Physicians & Surgeons* (1979), 3 L. Med. Q. 44 (Ont. Div. Ct.) [*Re Yat Tung Tse*]; *College of Physicians & Surgeons Alberta v. Ali*, 2017 ABCA 442, 67 Alta. LR (6th) 16 [*Ali*].

A. Judicial Review of Disciplinary Action

115. The following is a statement of the fundamental principles which apply in cases of judicial review of disciplinary action:[154]

- The preconditions to jurisdiction must be met.
- Discretion as to whether a hearing is to be held should be exercised properly.
- Any disciplinary proceedings must commence within a reasonable length of time after the events giving rise to them.
- Notice of any hearing must be provided.[155]
- The parties are entitled to an unbiased decision maker.[156]
- All evidence upon which the tribunal will base its decision should be disclosed.
- Cross-examination in relation to important contested facts should be permitted.
- Physicians are entitled to be represented by lawyers at a disciplinary hearing.

V. Challenges to the Professions Regulatory System: Ontario Developments as an Example

116. Particularly in the last decade, a number of controversies related to different health professions have exposed key shortcomings of the regulatory regime in Ontario, Canada's largest province.[157] These controversies reveal failures by some of the health professions to set and enforce proper educational and practice standards in specific areas and to conduct timely investigations into potential misconduct by professionals. For example, investigations following the death of a woman undergoing a liposuction procedure revealed problematic cosmetic surgery practices by general practitioners and the absence of clear criteria for qualification as cosmetic surgeon.[158] In response, the regulatory college, in collaboration with the government, took a number of steps, including changing the scope of practice, improving public information, and introducing monitoring of the practice.[159]

---

154. The discussion which follows is derived largely from Sharpe, *supra* note 129 at 243–248.
155. *Murthy v. College of Physicians & Surgeons (Saskatchewan)*, 52 Sask. R. 314, affirmed 56 Sask. R. 307 (CA); *Swart, supra* note 152.
156. *Re Yat Tung Tse, supra* note 153; *Ali, supra* note 153.
157. Trudo Lemmens & Kanksha Mahadevia Ghimire, "Regulation of Health Professions in Ontario: Self-Regulation with Statutory-Based Public Accountability" (2019) 19:3 Revista de Direito Sanitário / Journal of Health Law 124 at 151–154.
158. *See* Colleen M Flood, Bryan Thomas & Leigh Harrison Wilson, "Cosmetic Surgery Regulation and Regulation Enforcement in Ontario" (2010) 36 Queen's Law Journal 31.
159. The College of Physicians and Surgeons of Ontario, "Action Taken by the College to Improve Patient Safety with Respect to Cosmetic Procedures," online (pdf): *The College of Physicians and Surgeons of Ontario* https://www.cpso.on.ca/admin/CPSO/media/Documents/physician/polices-and-guidance/statements-positions/cosmetic-procedures-initiative.pdf; The College of Physicians and Surgeons of Ontario, "Out-of-Hospital Premises Inspection Program (OHPIP): Program Standards" (2013), online (pdf): *The College of Physicians and Surgeons of Ontario* www.cpso.on.ca /uploadedFiles/policies/guidelines/office/ohp_standards.pdf.

117. A Public Inquiry into another high-profile controversy, involving the former chief child pathologist of Ontario, Dr. Charles Smith,[160] highlighted the gaps in self-regulation arising on account of lack of formal and explicit quality standards governing pathology. It also revealed the professional regulatory system's failure to challenge at times the practice of incompetent professionals with significant authority within their area of practice. The case further highlighted the potentially devastating consequences of poor quality control, in this case, with tragic consequences for individuals who were wrongfully convicted based on flawed pathology expert reports.[161]

118. Lack of timely regulatory intervention and problems with communication of professional misconduct have also been revealed within the context of the nursing profession, in the wake of the murder conviction of a nurse practitioner, Elizabeth Wettlaufer, who killed over a ten-year time span eight of her patients and attempted to murder many others.[162] The murder trial revealed that she had been fired for medication errors and behavioral problems, yet future employers were not warned about her behavior, which was not further investigated by the profession.[163] A public inquiry by a commissioner explored the role and shortcomings in the functioning of the Ontario College of Nurses and the Ministry of Health and Long Term Care.[164]

---

160. Ontario, *Inquiry into Pediatric Forensic Pathology in Ontario*—Report (Toronto: Ministry of the Attorney General, 2008).
161. For a good discussion, *see* KA Collins & RW Bynard, *Forensic Pathology of Infancy and Childhood* (New York: Springer, 2014); DH Ubelaker, ed., *The Global Practice of Forensic Science* (West Sussex, UK: Wiley-Blackwell, 2015) at 37.
162. Peter Goffin, "Gap Existed Between Watchdog and Wettlaufer Care Home: Inquiry Commissioner," *CTV News* (Jul. 25, 2018), online https://www.ctvnews.ca/canada/gap-existed-between-watchdog-and-wettlaufer-care-home-inquiry-commissioner-1.4028006; Nora Loreto, "Vulnerable Patients Were Easy Prey for Ontario Serial Killer," *National Observer* (Jul. 4, 2018), online www.nationalobserver.com/2018/07/04/opinion/vulnerable-patients-were-easy-prey-ontario-serial-killer.
163. Kate Dubinski, "Nursing Home Didn't 'Paint Full Picture' of Wettlaufer, Inquiry Hears," *CBC News* (Jul. 25, 2018), online www.cbc.ca/news/canada/london/long-term-care-inquiry-elizabeth-wettlaufer-college-of-nurses-of-ontario-1.4760740; Liam Casey, "Serial Killer Guilty of Professional Misconduct by Nursing College," *Canada's National Observer* (Jul. 25, 2017), online www.nationalobserver.com/2017/07/25/news/serial-killer-guilty-professional-misconduct-nursing-college.
164. Ontario, *Public Inquiry into the Safety and Security of Residents in the Long-Term Care Homes System* (Toronto: The Honourable Eileen E. Gillese, Commissioner, Jul. 31, 2019); Goffin, *supra* note 162; Trish Audette-Longo, "Advocates Warn Against Treating Nursing Home Murders as an Isolated Case," *Canada's National Observer* (Jun. 26, 2017), online www.nationalobserver.com/2017/06/26/news/advocates-warn-against-treating-nursing-home-murders-isolated-case.

§2. PROFESSIONAL LIABILITY

I. Civil Liability

A. General

119. Civil liability for professional malpractice comes within the realm of tort law, and generally will lie either in battery or in negligence, depending on the circumstances.[165] Therefore, establishing a claim of medical malpractice liability requires proof of the same elements as are required to establish tortious liability in other contexts. However, it will be seen that there are some defenses available to a medical practitioner that are specific to the medical malpractice context.

B. Battery

120. Battery is an intentional tort, in that liability turns on whether the defendant had obtained consent for the invasion of the person's bodily integrity, which forms the basis of the plaintiff's action. Consent is a complete defense against claims of battery.[166] In Canada, with limited exceptions, every individual's body has been long considered inviolate, and any medical intervention in which a physician touches the body of a patient requires the patient's consent. An action for battery may lie if the physician has proceeded without first having obtained valid consent for the particular treatment or procedure performed.[167] Valid consent comprises certain requisite elements, the absence of any of which will vitiate consent as a defense to a battery action. For consent to be valid, it must be:

(a) given voluntarily and without undue influence, coercion or misrepresentation;
(b) given by a patient with the capacity to consent;
(c) referable to the particular proposed treatment or procedure;

---

165. *See* generally G Robertson & Justice E Picard, *Legal Liability of Doctors and Hospitals in Canada*, 5th ed. (Toronto: Thomson Reuters Canada Limited, 2017) at 158–161; I Kennedy & A Grubb, *Medical Law: Text with Materials*, 2nd ed. (London: Buttersworth, 1994) at 137–160; AJ Meagher, PJ Marr & RA Meagher, *Doctors and Hospitals: Legal Duties* (Toronto: Butterworths, 1991) at 83–86; JC Irvine, PH Osborne & MJ Shariff, *Canadian Medical Law: An Introduction for Physicians, Nurses and Other Health Care Professionals*, 4th ed. (Toronto: Carswell, 2013) at 58; Emson, *supra* note 134 at 121–122; Lorne Rozovsky, *Canadian Law of Consent to Treatment*, 3rd ed. (Toronto: LexisNexis Butterworths, 2003) at 115–121. *See also* GB Robertson, "Ontario's New Informed Consent Law: Codification or Radical Change?" (1994) 2 Health LJ 88 at 90–94; Trudo Lemmens, "Informed Consent" in Bartha Knoppers & Yann Joly, eds., *Routledge Handbook of Medical Law and Ethics* (Routledge, 2014) at 38–44.

166. *See* C Sappideen & P Vines, eds., *Fleming's the Law of Torts*, 10th ed. (Sydney: The Law Book Company Ltd., 2011) at 31–32; *Reibl v. Hughes* [1980] 2 SCR 880 [*Reibl*]. *See also Bollman v. Soenen*, 2014 ONCA 36, 236 ACWS (3d) 1032 [*Bollman (2014)*].

167. *Nancy B.* (1993), 86 DLR (4th) 385 (Que. Sup. Ct.); *Malette v. Shulman* (1987), 43 CCLT 62 (Ont. HC), affirmed (1990), 2 CCLT (2d) 1 (Ont. CA); *Fleming v. Reid* (1991), 4 OR (3d) 74 (Ont. CA) [*Fleming*]. For an early statement of this postulate, *see Schloendorff v. Society of New York Hospital* (1914), 105 NE 92 (NYCA).

(d) given by an informed patient.[168]

121. To respond to a claim of battery, it will suffice for the defendant physician to show that these four elements have generally been satisfied; the adequacy of the disclosure is an issue which is addressed in the law of negligence. Battery can only be invoked in the absence of consent or in cases of fraud or misrepresentation, for example, misrepresentation as to the nature of the medical intervention. Where the physician violates the plaintiff's right to self-determination without justification, punitive or exemplary damages may be awarded.[169]

122. Absence of consent can only be justified in exceptional situations, such as an emergency situation. This will be the case, for example, when a patient is unable to consent because of unconsciousness, the treatment is necessary to preserve life and is not a mere convenience, there are no reasonable alternatives available to the proposed treatment, and there are no indications the patient would not consent to the treatment if he or she were able.[170]

C. Burden of Proof

123. Once it is established that the touching occurred, a prima facie case of battery is made out; the action does not require proof of causation. At that point the burden shifts to the defendant, who can supply a complete defense to the battery

168. *See* Lousie Bèlanger-Hardy, "Informed Choice in Medical Care" in Joanna N Erdman, Vanessa Gruben & Erin Nelson, eds., *Canadian Health Law and Policy,* 5th ed. (Toronto: LexisNexis, 2017) at 329–348. *See also Health Care Consent Act, 1996*, SO 1996, c 2, Sch. A, ss. 4, 11. *See* Robertson & Picard, *supra* note 165 at 74; A Meagher, Marr & R Meagher, *supra* note 165 at 95; Rozovsky, *supra* note 165; Sharpe, *supra* note 129 at 30–34; Kennedy & Grubb, *supra* note 165 at 180–215; M Somerville, *Law Reform Commission of Canada, Consent to Medical Care, Protection of Life Series, A Study Paper* (Ottawa: Department of Justice Canada, 1980) at 46–58; *Gerula v. Flores* (1995), 126 DLR (4th) 506 (Ont. CA); *Re T* [1992] 4 All ER 649 (Eng CA); *Ney v. Canada* (1993), 79 BCLR (2d) 47 [*Ney*] at 53 (BCSC); *Re W* [1992] All ER 627 (Eng CA); *Johnston v. Wellesley Hospital* (1970), 17 DLR (3d) 139 at 144–145 (Ont. HC); *Manitoba (Director of Child & Family Services) v. C.(A.)*, 2009 SCC 30 [*C.(A.)*]; *Norberg v. Wynrib* [1992] 2 SCR 226; *Re D and Council of College of Physicians & Surgeons of BC* (1970), 11 DLR (3d) 570 (BCSC); *Schweizer v. Central Hospital* (1974), 6 OR (2d) 606 (HC) [*Schweizer*]; *Parmley v. Parmley* [1945] 4 DLR 81 (SCC); *Hopp v. Lepp* (1980), 112 DLR (3d) 67 (SCC) [*Hopp*]. *See also Carter v. Canada (Attorney General)*, 2015 SCC 5 [*Carter*] at paras. 67, 106.

169. *Hankai v. York County Hospital* (1981), 9 ACWS (2d) 354 (Ont. CA); *Norberg v. Wynrib* [1992] 2 SCR 318, supplementing [1992] 2 SCR 226, reversing 44 BCLR (2d) 47, which affirmed 27 BCLR (2d) 240; *B.(A.) v. F.(E.)*, 2004 NBQB 259, 278 NBR (2d) 310, affirmed 2005 NBCA 2.

170. *Marshall v. Curry* [1933] 3 DLR 260 (NSSC); *Murray v. McMurchy* [1949] 2 DLR 442 (BCSC) [*Murray*]. *See also Mulloy v. Hop Sang* [1935] 1 WWR 714 (Alta. CA); *Allan v. New Mount Sinai Hosp* (1980), 109 DLR (3d) 634 (Ont. HCJ), reversed on other grounds (1981), 125 DLR (3d) 276 (CA); *Malette v. Shulman* (1987), 43 CCLT 62 (Ont. HCJ), affirmed (1990), 2 CCLT (2d) 1 (Ont. CA). Generally, *see* Robertson & Picard, *supra* note 165 at 68–73; A Meagher, Marr & R Meagher, *supra* note 165 at 124–125; Rozovsky, *supra* note 165 at 13; Bèlanger-Hardy, *supra* note 168 at 331.

action by proving consent to the treatment.[171] Although not conclusive, written consent forms are useful evidence in this respect and are often used to obtain and document consent for additional procedures unforeseen at the time consent for the intended procedure is given.[172]

D. Negligence

124. Unlike battery, negligence is not an intentional tort, so it does not depend on the presence or absence of consent. Rather, it is founded on the breach of a duty of care of a recognized standard. To establish liability in a negligence action, the plaintiff must prove the existence of four elements:

(1) a duty of care owed by the defendant to the plaintiff;
(2) the defendant's breach of that duty, or failure to meet the standard of care to which he or she is subject;
(3) loss or injury to the plaintiff as a result of the breach of the duty of care; and
(4) the defendant's breach of the duty of care as the proximate cause of the plaintiff's loss or injury.[173]

1. Duty of Care

125. The early English view of the medical profession was that it was a common calling, in which the physician was seen to owe the patient a duty of care upon engaging in the practice of medicine with that patient. The nature of this duty was delictual, and the content of the duty was the exercise of proper skill and care.[174] Today, the duty of care is seen to be inherent in the physician-patient relationship and is generally expressed as the duty to use reasonable care, skill and judgment in the practice of the profession.[175] Prior to the creation of a physician-patient relationship, the physician has no legal duty to treat an individual. Once the relationship is formed, however, the duty of care arises and continues for the duration of the relationship.[176]

---

171. *Reibl, supra* note 166; *Norberg v. Wynrib* [1992] 2 SCR 226.
172. *Doiron v. Orr* (1978), 86 DLR (3d) 719 (Ont. HC); *Schweizer, supra* note 168; *O'Bonsawin v. Paradis* (1993), 15 CCLT (2d) 188 (Ont. Gen. Div.); *Brushett v. Cowan* (1990), 3 CCLT (2d) 195 (Nfld. CA); *Pridham v. Nash* (1986), 33 DLR (4th) 304 (Ont. HC); *Tomeh v. Cheah*, 2013 ONSC 6074, 235 ACWS (3d) 827. Generally, *see* Robertson & Picard, *supra* note 165 at 59–60.
173. *See* Bèlanger-Hardy, *supra* note 168 at 307–316; Robertson & Picard, *supra* note 165 at 268–368; Kennedy & Grubb, *supra* note 165 at 143–160; Irvine, Osborne & Shariff, *supra* note 165 at 90–132; Emson, *supra* note 134 at 87–106; *Chan (Litigation Guardian of) v. Tang*, 2012 ONSC 2050 [2012] OJ No. 1436 [*Chan*].
174. *Everard v. Hopkins* (1615), 2 Bulstrode 332, 80 ER 1164 (Eng. KB). *See* Robertson & Picard, *supra* note 165 at 1.
175. Robertson & Picard, *supra* note 165 at 2. *See also* Gerald Robertson et al., "Legal Norms Relevant to the Practice of Human Genetics: A Background Paper" (1995) 3 Health LJ 187 at 188.
176. *Pellerin v. Stevenson* (1945), 18 MPR 345 (NBCA). *See* Robertson & Picard, *supra* note 165 at 269; A Meagher, Marr & R Meagher, *supra* note 165 at 14–15. Note that where a prescription is

126. In a number of cases, a third party, such as a biological father, has brought action to recover economic losses incurred because of reliance on a physician's negligent advice or treatment. While Canadian courts may recognize that a third party's reliance can be both reasonable and foreseeable, they have generally resisted attempts to extend the physician's duty of care beyond those with whom a "special relationship" has been formed, giving rise to a duty of care. At the very least, the plaintiff third party must establish that the physician knew of his or her existence, and the fact of reliance on the physician's advice.[177] Some jurisdictions have clearly indicated their reluctance to extend the physician's duty of care, by striking claims of liability "for the negligent act of a physician to a third party who received neither treatment nor advice, and where the claim is not derivative to a claim by the patient herself."[178]

127. The duty of care comprises certain specific functions, including attendance on the patient, consultation and referral if necessary, diagnosis, disclosure of information relating to treatment, provision of care and instruction as to future treatment.[179] A general practitioner has a duty to consult with or refer the patient to a specialist when he or she is unable to diagnose the cause of the patient's symptoms, when the patient is not responding to treatment, when the physician must protect against his or her own inexperience or when the physician is unable to continue treatment of the patient.[180]

128. The duty of care also responds to advances in medical and genetic technologies. Physicians who fail to refer pregnant patients for, or negligently perform,

---

given, the relationship is deemed to continue as long as the patient is taking the prescribed medication: *Cook v. Abbott* (1980), 112 DLR (3d) 234 at 241 (NSTD), affirmed (1980), 113 DLR (3d) 88 (NSCA); *See also Stone v. Hipp* [2008] OJ No. 1002, 165 ACWS (3d) 825.

177. *Kovacvich v. Henshaw* (1995), 25 CCLT (2d) 295 (BCSC), in which the defendant physician had been sued successfully in negligence by the biological mother, who had recovered damages for pain and suffering and loss of income during the pregnancy; the biological father now brought an independent action for recovery of the maintenance costs which he had been ordered to pay under B.C.'s *Child Paternity and Support Act. See also Yarmie v. Armstrong*, 2014 MBQB 40, 237 ACWS (3d) 876, where parents brought derivative claims on the basis of negative impacts from medical treatment received by their daughter.

178. *Freeman v. Sutter* [1996] 4 WWR 748 at 751 (Man. CA); also *Kines Estate v. Lychuk Estate* [1996] 10 WWR 426 (Man. QB), affirmed (1997), 15 CPC (4th) 378 (QB), affirmed (1997), 123 Man R (2d) 151 (CA), in which the family of a psychiatric patient's fatally wounded victim brought action for the alleged negligence of four of the patient's physicians. *See also* Robertson & Picard, *supra* note 165 at 279–284.

179. Robertson & Picard, *supra* note 165 at 269; Kennedy & Grubb, *supra* note 165 at 143; A Meagher, Marr & R Meagher, *supra* note 165 at 17. *See Fraser v. Vancouver Gen Hospital* [1952] 2 SCR 36; *Layden v. Cope* (1984), 28 CCLT 140 (Alta. QB); *Dillon v. Leroux* [1994] 6 WWR 280 (BCCA); *Kooijman v. Bradshaw*, 2016 BCSC 2316, 273 ACWS (3d) 652 [*Kooijman*].

180. *Vancouver Gen Hosp v. Fraser* [1952] SCR 36; *MacDonald v. York County Hosp.* (1973), 41 DLR (3d) 321 (Ont. CA), affirmed [1976] 2 SCR 825; *Turriff v. King* (1913), 3 WWR 862 (Sask. SC); *Osburn v. Mohindra* (1980), 29 NBR (2d) 340 (QB); *Bell v. R* (1973), 44 DLR (3d) 549 (Fed. TD) [*Bell*]; *Fraser v. Vancouver General Hospital* [1952] 2 SCR 36; *Wilson v. Stark* (1967), 61 WWR 705 (Sask. QB); *Kooijman, supra* note 179.

genetic counseling and testing may be found liable for both general damages for wrongful birth, and the costs of future care, at least where a child is born in ill health with increased care costs.[181]

2. Standard of Care and Breach of Duty of Care

a. General

129. The standard of care required of a physician has been traditionally stated to be that degree of care and skill which could reasonably be expected of a normal, prudent practitioner of the same experience and standing.[182] In undertaking to treat a patient, a physician does not provide a guarantee of success; perfection is not required of a physician. He or she simply undertakes to use a reasonable degree of skill and learning and exercise reasonable care, on the objective standard of the average fellow professional in like circumstances.[183] However, the law makes no distinction between experienced and inexperienced physicians. Interns and residents are judged not on the standard of the other interns and residents but on the same standard as licensed physicians. The degree of skill undertaken by interns must be no less than the ordinary skill of a junior doctor in appreciation of the indications of the injury, as well as in appreciation of his or her own limitations.[184]

b. Specialists

130. The law does differentiate between the standard of care required of a general practitioner and that required of a specialist. A higher degree of skill is expected of a specialist than is expected of a general practitioner performing treatment in the

181. *H(R) v. Hunter* (1996), 32 CCLT (2d) 44 (Ont. Gen. Div.); *Jones (Guardian ad litem of) v. Rostvig*, 2003 BCSC 1222, 124 ACWS (3d) 585. *See also* BM Knoppers, "Physician Liability and Prenatal Diagnosis," CCLT 18 (1981): 169; BM Dickens, "Legal Approaches to Genetic Diagnosis and Counselling" (1980) 1:25 Health L in Can; BM Knoppers, "Modern Birth Technology and Human Rights" (1985) 33:1 Am J Comp Law 1; Lori B Andrews, "Torts and the Double Helix: Malpractice Liability for Failure to Warn of Genetic Risk" (1992) 29:1 Houston L Rev 149; Maeghan Toews & Timothy Caulfield, "Physician Liability and Non-invasive Prenatal Testing" (2014) 36:10 J Obstetrics & Gynaecology Can 907; Mark Pioro et al., "Wrongful Birth Litigation and Prenatal Screening" (2008) 179:10 CMAJ 1027.

182. *Crits v. Sylvester* (1956), 1 DLR (2d) 502 at 508 (Ont. CA), affirmed [1956] SCR 991. *See also Wilson v. Swanson* (1956), 5 DLR (2d) 113 (SCC); *Gent v. Wilson* (1956), 2 DLR (2d) 160 at 165 (Ont. CA); *Wine v. Kernohan* (1978), 2 L. Med. Q. 129 at 134 (Ont. HC); *Torrison v. Colwill* (1987), 42 CCLT 51 (BCSC), affirmed (1988), 47 CCLT 198 (BCCA). *See also Chasney v. Anderson* [1950] 4 DLR 223 (SCC); *Aynsley v. Toronto Gen Hosp* (1971) [1972] SCR 435; *Cherry (Guardian ad litem of) v. Borsman* (1990), 75 DLR (4th) 668, reversed in part on other grounds (1992), 70 BCLR (2d) 273 (CA); *Kooijman, supra* note 179. Generally, *see* Robertson & Picard, *supra* note 165 at 286–288; A Meagher, Marr & R Meagher, *supra* note 165 at 206–208.

183. *Crits v. Sylvester*, 1 DLR (2d) 502 (Ont. CA); *Cardin v. Montreal (City)* (1961), 29 DLR (2d) 492 at 494 (SCC); *Roe v. Minister of Health* [1954] 2 QB 66 (Eng. CA); *Challand v. Bell* (1959), 27 WWR 182 (Alta. SC); *Kooijman, supra* note 179. *See* Irvine, Osborne & Shariff, *supra* note 165 at 102–103.

184. *Fraser v. Vancouver Gen Hospital* [1952] 2 SCR 36 at 46; *Wills v. Saunders* (1989), 93 AR 282 (QB). *See also Ares v. Venner* [1970] SCR 608; *McKeachie v. Alvarez* (1970), 17 DLR (3d) 87 at 101 (BCSC); *Kooijman, supra* note 179. *See also* Robertson & Picard, *supra* note 165 at 295.

same field.[185] While the standard of care required of a general practitioner is that of a reasonable medical person,[186] a specialist must meet the standard of an average specialist in the same field of expertise.[187]

131. This higher standard may encompass not only the duty to make an accurate diagnosis and relay a precise diagnosis to a patient's treating physician but also the duty to exercise their expert judgment and interpret a diagnosis so as to warn of the potential of child abuse.[188]

3. Defenses Applicable to the Standard of Care

a. Locality

132. An earlier principle in Canadian law which has operated as a defense to a claim of a failure to meet the standard of care is the rule of similar locality. To compensate for vast differences between the facilities, equipment and resources available to the rural physician and those available to an urban physician, the courts developed the principle that the standard of skill expected of a physician would be measured against practitioners in similar communities in similar circumstances.[189] Today, however, because of improved communications, transportation and access to resources, continuing education and standardized testing, the locality rule is applied in only a limited sense, as merely one circumstance to be considered in determining whether the standard of care is met, and not an absolute limit.[190] Several Canadian judgments have recently suggested the locality rule ought to be abandoned.[191] Nonetheless, public policy interests in minimizing deterrence to the establishment

---

185. *McCaffery v. Hague* [1949] 2 WWR 539 (Man. KB); *Quintal v. Datta* [1988] 6 WWR 481 (Sask. CA). *See also* Robertson & Picard, *supra* note 165 at 289–294; A Meagher, Marr & R Meagher, *supra* note 165 at 217.
186. *Crits v. Sylvester* (1956), 1 DLR (2d) 502 (Ont. CA), affirmed [1956] SCR 991 [*Crits*]; *Cryderman v. Ringrose* [1977] 3 WWR 109, affirmed [1978] 3 WWR 481 (Alta. CA); *McCormick v. Marcotte* [1972] SCR 18; *Worth v. Royal Jubilee Hosp* (1980), 4 L. Med. Q. 59 [1980] BCJ No. 1336 (BCCA); *McKenzie v. Lee* (1991), 113 AR 284 (QB).
187. *Rietze v. Bruser (No 2)* (1978) [1979] 1 WWR 31 at 45 (Man. QB); *Leadbetter v. Brand* (1980), 37 NSR (2d) 581 at 590 (TD); *McBride v. Langton* (1982), 22 Alta. LR (2d) 174 at 184 (Alta. QB). *See also Crits, supra* note 186; *Konkolus v. Royal Alexandra Bd of Gov* (1982), 21 Alta L.R. (2d) 359 (QB); *Kooijman, supra* note 179.
188. *Brown (Next Friend of) v. University of Alberta Hospital* (1997), 145 DLR (4th) 63 (Alta. QB).
189. *McCormick v. Marcotte* [1972] SCR 18; *Wilson v. Swanson* [1956] SCR 804; *Tiesmaki v. Wilson* [1975] 6 WWR 639 at 650 (Alta. CA); *McBride v. Langton* (1982), 22 Alta. L.R. (2d) 174 (QB). Generally, *see* Robertson & Picard, *supra* note 165 at 314–318; A Meagher, Marr & R Meagher, *supra* note 165 at 209–211.
190. *Haughian v. Paine* (1986), 46 Sask. R. 186 at 190–191 (QB), reversed in part (1987), 55 Sask. R. 99 (CA), leave to appeal to SCC refused [1987] 6 WWR LIX (n.). *See also* Robertson & Picard, *supra* note 165 at 316–317; Timothy A Caulfield, "Health Care Reform: Can Tort Law Meet the Challenge?" (1994) 32:4 Alta Law Rev 685 at 703–705. *Sunnucks (Litigation Guardian of) v. Tobique Valley Hospital* (1999), 216 NBR (2d) 201 (QB); *Pinch (Litigation Guardian of) v. Morwood*, 2016 BCSC 75, 262 ACWS (3d) 664 [*Pinch*].
191. *Crawford (Litigation Guardian of) v. Penney* (2003), 14 CCLT (3d) 60 at paras. 250–254 (Ont. SCJ); *Holan Estate v. Stanton Regional Health Board*, 2002 NWTSC 26, 11 CCLT (3d) 34 at para. 85.

of badly needed general practitioners in rural areas of Canada have been cited in one court as justification for holding the rural medical general practitioner to a less stringent standard of care than the specialist, or even the urban general practitioner.[192]

b. Approved Practice

133. An allegation of breach of the standard of care may be defended on the basis that the physician followed approved practice in performing the treatment or conducting the test. The physician using this defense takes the position that procedures followed were in accordance with those generally accepted and employed by other physicians at the time, and consequently he or she should not be found negligent.[193] In addition, a physician generally will be absolved from liability where he or she has acted in accordance with a respected body of professional opinion, even though that opinion is shared only by a minority of members of the profession.[194] Because the approved practice defense is based on accepted procedures prevailing at the time of the event in question, the content of the defense will evolve over time, as older procedures grow obsolete and lose approval and new ones gain acceptance.[195] If a physician chooses to use an older tool or technique or an innovative but yet uncommonly used procedure, he or she is at greater risk of being found negligent.[196]

134. In the context of this defense the medical profession itself plays a large role in determining the appropriate standard of care, in that evidence relating to approved practice is usually given by experts from the profession.[197] The extent to which a court will defer to such evidence, however, is not absolute. It is open to a court to reject evidence of approved practice, or to find that medical custom which

192. *Elofson v. Davis* (1997), 144 DLR (4th) 143 (Alta. QB).

193. *See* generally Robertson & Picard, *supra* note 165 at 451–463; Kennedy & Grubb, *supra* note 165 at 405–420; *Vancouver General Hospital v. McDaniel* [1934] 4 DLR 593 at 597 (PC). *See also Neufeld v. McQuitty* (1979), 18 AR 271 (TD); *Goodwin v. Brady* (1991), 7 CCLT (2d) 319 (BCSC), affirmed [1994] 89 BCLR (2d) 27 (CA); *Pinch, supra* note 190.

194. *Maynard v. West Midlands Regional Health Authority* [1984] 1 WLR 635 (UKHL); *Achneepineskum (Litigation Guardian of) v. Laine*, 2013 ONSC 1261, 226 ACWS (3d) 585, affirmed 2014 ONCA 644; *see also* Kennedy & Grubb, *supra* note 165 at 405–408.

195. *McCormick v. Marcotte* (1971) [1972] SCR 18; *Hajgato v. London Health Assn* (1982), 36 OR (2d) 669 (HC), affirmed (1983), 44 OR (2d) 264 (CA); *Pittman Estate v. Bain* (1994), 112 DLR (4th) 257 (Ont. Gen. Div.); *McQuay v. Eastwood* (1886), 12 OR 402 (CA); *Cataford v. Moreau* (1978), 114 DLR (3d) 585 (Que. SC). *See* Robertson & Picard, *supra* note 165 at 451–453.

196. *Eady v. Tenderenda* (1974) [1975] 2 SCR 599; *Zimmer v. Ringrose* (1978), 89 DLR (3d) 646 (Alta. TD), affirmed (1981), 124 DLR (3d) 215 (Alta. CA); leave to appeal to SCC dismissed [1981] SCCA No. 200. *See also* Robertson & Picard, *supra* note 165 at 457–459.

197. *See* Robertson & Picard, *supra* note 165 at 451–457; Kennedy & Grubb, *supra* note 165 at 405–420; *Villemure v. Turcot* [1973] SCR 716; *Chasney v. Anderson* [1949] 4 DLR 71, affirmed (1950), 4 DLR 223 (SCC). However, *see Eldridge v. British Columbia (Attorney General)* (1997), 151 DLR (4th) 577 (SCC), in which the Supreme Court of Canada found the province's discretionary refusal to fund sign language interpreters for medical services to the deaf to be a discriminatory violation of the equality rights guaranteed under the *Charter of Rights and Freedoms*. While the case does not deal directly with a physician's standard of care, it clearly indicates that there are limits to how far legal standards will go to accommodate cost containment goals.

was formerly approved no longer should be so. Those cases in which a court may intervene and refuse to rely solely on expert opinion about approved practices are primarily those in which the procedures in question deal not with technical matters or matters requiring expertise, but instead are subject to the common sense of the layperson.[198] The SCC stated that standard practice itself should be found to be negligent only in situations where the practice is fraught with obvious risks such that anyone is capable of finding it negligent, without the necessity of diagnostic or clinical expertise. In practice it is rare that the courts will substitute their own view and reject established practice evidence.[199] However, it has been argued that such clear deference to physician decision-making should only be shown in those areas where a practice has been influenced by "purely" medical or scientific expertise, and not extended to considerations of fiscal constraint and social policy.[200]

c. Error of Judgment

135. A defense which will often operate to relieve a physician of liability for breach of the standard of care is that a mistake or act resulting in injury was an error of judgment and not negligence. This is frequently the point on which a medical malpractice liability action will turn. The Canadian courts have long distinguished an error of judgment from an act of unskillfulness, carelessness or a lack of knowledge. A physician is not an insurer of an outcome; instead, the honest and intelligent exercise of judgment satisfies the professional obligation.[201] Where the physician's mistake involves the exercise of clinical judgment the court will determine whether the error is one that no reasonable physician would have made in similar circumstances.[202] However, while one error, such as an initial diagnosis, may be an error of judgment, an accumulation of errors may constitute negligence.[203]

198. *Pittman Estate v. Bain* (1994), 112 DLR (4th) 257 at 314 (Ont. Gen. Div.); *Hajgato v. London Health Assn* (1982), 36 OR (2d) 669 at 692–693 (HC), affirmed (1983), 44 OR (3d) 264 (CA); *Chasney v. Anderson* (1949), 4 DLR 71 at 74 (Man. CA), affirmed [1950] 4 DLR 223 (SCC).

199. *ter Neuzen v. Korn* (1995), 127 DLR (4th) 577 (SCC) [*ter Neuzen*]; *Samms v. Moolla,* 2019 ONCA 220 [*Samms*]; G Robertson et al., "Legal Norms Relevant to the Practice of Human Genetics: A Background Paper" (1995) 3 Health LJ 187 at 189.

200. Timothy A Caulfield, "Case Comment: Ter Neuzen v. Korn and the Standard of Care: A Call for Caution" (1996) 34:4 Alta L Rev 986.

201. *Wilson v. Swanson* (1956), 5 DLR (2d) 113 at 120 (SCC); *Samms, supra* note 199. *See* generally Robertson & Picard, *supra* note 165 at 463–467; A Meagher, Marr & R Meagher, *supra* note 165 at 186–190; Sharpe, *supra* note 129 at 17–18; G Robertson et al., "Legal Norms Relevant to the Practice of Human Genetics: A Background Paper" (1995) 3 Health LJ 187 at 188.

202. *Lapointe v. Hopital Le Gardeur* (1992), 90 DLR (4th) 27 (SCC); *Challand v. Bell* (1959), 81 DLR (2d) 150 (Alta. TD); *Ostash v. Sonnenberg* (1968), 63 WWR 257 (Alta. CA). *See also Pinch, supra* note 190.

203. *Edmison v. Boyd* (1985), 62 AR 118 (QB), affirmed (1987), 51 Alta. L.R. (2d) 43 (CA), leave to appeal to SCC refused, 20412 (Jun. 23, 1987).

d. Cost Containment and the Availability of Resources

136. The Canadian law recognizes that facilities are resources and limiting factors for the practice of medicine, and the standard of care has been adjusted downward where these are inadequate.[204] However, when there is a choice of facilities, the physician must act in accordance with the best medical interests of the patient.[205] In the context of these principles, an emerging issue in the Canadian law relating to the standard of care is the applicability of a defense relating to cost containment or adherence to a broader resource allocation policy. The courts have recognized that they may accept a lower standard of care than is desirable because of resource allocation limitations, including the availability of trained and experienced personnel.[206] However, the courts have also stated that where there is a choice between a physician's responsibility to an individual patient and the responsibility to the medical insurance system overall, the former must take precedence in many cases.[207]

4. Resulting Injury

137. The third requisite element of a negligence action is the proof of material loss or injury.[208] Therefore, where a patient has received substandard care but has suffered no loss, the proper course of action would be a complaint to the governing professional association[209] or, if there is an issue as to whether consent was obtained, a battery action, for which injury is not a requisite element. For example, where a physician removed part of a patient's uvula during a tonsillectomy, damages were not recoverable in negligence as the patient suffered no disability or injury.[210]

138. In recent decades, a number of plaintiffs have brought action against their physicians for an incorrect birth control prescription, a lack of warning regarding

204. *Bateman v. Doirn* (1991), 8 CCLT (2d) 284 at 291–293 (NBQB), affirmed (1993), 18 CCLT (2d) 1 (NBCA), leave to appeal to SCC refused, 20 CCLT (2d) 320 (May 5, 1994); *Rodych v. Krasey* [1971] 4 WWR 358 (Man. QB); *Feller v. Roffman* (1978), BCD 34698–74 (BCSC); *Bell, supra* note 180 at 550.
205. *Kangas v. Parker* [1976] 5 WWR 25 (Sask. QB), affirmed [1978] 5 WWR 667 (CA). *See also Prevost v. Ali*, 2011 SKCA 50, 371 Sask R 166.
206. *Bateman v. Doirn* (1991), 8 CCLT (2d) 284 at 291 (NBQB), affirmed (1993), 18 CCLT (2d) 1 (CA), leave to appeal to SCC refused (1994), 20 CCLT (2d) 320.
207. *Law Estate v. Simice* (1994), 21 CCLT (2d) 228 at 240 (BCSC), affirmed (1995), 27 CCLT (2d) 127 (CA), where the issue was whether an expensive CT scan should have been ordered earlier in the circumstances of the patient's symptoms. *See also* John C Irvine, "Case Comment: Law Estate v. Simice," CCLT 21 (2d) (1994): 259; *McLean v. Carr Estate* (1994), 363 APR 271 at 288 (Nfld. TD).
208. *See* Robertson & Picard, *supra* note 165 at 325–328; Sappideen & Vines, *supra* note 166 at 122; *See also* Kennedy & Grubb, *supra* note 165 at 151–153.
209. *See* §1 *supra.*
210. *McNamara v. Smith* [1934] 2 DLR 417 (Ont. CA). *See also Mang v. Moscovitz* (1982), 37 AR 221 (Alta. QB); *Davidson v. Connaught Laboratories* (1980), 14 CCLT 251 (Ont. HC); *Ferguson v. Hamilton Civic Hosp* (1983), 23 CCLT 254 (Ont. HC).

the inherent risk of failure in sterilization operations, or the unsuccessful performance of an abortion. Where all the other elements of negligence have been proven, and the result of the physician's failure has been the birth of a disabled child, the courts have found liability and awarded damages.[211] Where, however, the negligence has resulted in the birth of a healthy child, albeit unplanned, the courts have had to consider characterizing the "blessed event" as a resulting injury. These "wrongful birth" or "wrongful life" cases have typically awarded damages for the mother's pain and suffering and for economic loss incurred because of the pregnancy,[212] but have only recently considered awarding damages for the ordinary costs of raising a healthy child.[213] However, the possibility of recovering child-rearing costs may be subject to a complex inquiry into a woman or a couple's reasons for avoiding pregnancy in the first place. In other words, since the claim's "essential character and purpose is to redress injury to an economic interest,"[214] pure tort principles may not be applied strictly when a couple's reasons for avoiding pregnancy were non-economic (i.e., they simply wanted to avoid another pregnancy, not the costs of another child). One court has found that the mere fact that the economic costs of raising a child were foreseeable was not enough to lead to compensation where the parents' ability to fulfill their responsibilities to their newborn in a relationship of mutual support and dependency had not been compromised in any way by the defendant's negligent act.[215]

5. Causation

139. Where it is proved that the physician failed to meet the required standard of care and the patient has suffered an injury, a finding of negligence requires further that there be a causal link between the breach of duty and the injury. The physician's conduct must be both a factual cause and the proximate cause of the plaintiff's injury; that is, the injury would not have occurred but for the physician's

---

211. *Cherry v. Borseman* (1991), 75 DLR (4th) 668 (BCSC), varied (1992), 94 DLR (4th) 487 (CA), leave to appeal to SCC refused (1993), 99 DLR (4th) vii (note); *H.(R.) v. Hunter* (1996), 32 CCLT (2d) 44 (Ont. Gen. Div.); *Arndt v. Smith* (1997), 148 DLR (4th) 48 (SCC) [*Arndt*]. *See also* Robertson & Picard, *supra* note 165 at 334–335; Erin Nelson & Gerald Robertson, "Liability for Wrongful Birth and Wrongful Life" (2001) 2 ISUMA: Can J of Policy Research 102.
212. Even where a woman attains a successful abortion after a "wrongful pregnancy," she may still be awarded damages for pain and suffering and actual expenses incurred: *Zimmer v. Ringrose* (1978), 89 DLR (3d) 646 (Alta. SC), affirmed (1981), 124 DLR (3d) 215 (CA), leave to appeal to SCC refused (1981) [1981] SCCA No. 200.
213. *Suite v. Cooke* [1995] RJQ 2765 (Que. CA); *Kealey v. Berezowski* (1996), 136 DLR (4th) 708 (Ont. Gen. Div.) [*Kealey*]; *Bevilacqua v. Altenkirk*, 2004 BCSC 945, 35 BCLR (4th) 281. Various earlier Canadian cases had dismissed such claims as "ridiculous" or "grotesque": *Cryderman v. Ringrose* [1978] 3 WWR 481 (Alta. CA); *Doiron v. Orr* (1978), 86 DLR (3d) 719 (Ont. HC); *Keats v. Pearce* (1984), 48 Nfld. & PEIR 102 (Nfld. SC); *see also* GB Robertson, "Civil Liability Arising from Wrongful Birth Following an Unsuccessful Sterilization Operation" (1978) 4 Am J L & Med 131.
214. *Kealey, supra* note 213, at 732.
215. *Ibid.*

negligence.[216] The reasonable foreseeability test is used in determining whether a particular act or omission was a proximate cause of injury. A physician will not bear liability for an unforeseeable accident occurring during the normal course of treatment.[217] A court will consider whether a reasonable person would have anticipated that the injury or loss could be a natural result of the particular conduct.[218] In some cases, pursuant to the doctrine of *res ipsa loquitur,* a court can draw a common sense or intuitive inference of causation from the established facts of the mere occurrence of the injury.[219] To rebut the inference, the defendant must offer an explanation that is as consistent with no negligence as with negligence.[220]

140. In practice, it is a complicated and uncertain task to determine whether a physician's negligent conduct caused a patient's injury. The court must be presented with factual and expert evidence which will satisfy it of a causal connection between the patient's loss and the particular conduct complained of, and further that without that negligent conduct, the patient would not have suffered the loss.[221] The burden on the patient in establishing causation is seen to have been reduced somewhat by a SCC decision which confirmed that causation is to be measured on the balance of probabilities and not on the standard of scientific certainty.[222] However, even the balance of probability test may be difficult to meet. Even where the patient introduces believable evidence which could indicate that the physician's conduct was a proximate cause of the injury, a court will not draw an inference of causation if the defendant introduces incontrovertible evidence to the contrary.[223]

6. Other Defenses to Medical Negligence Actions

a. Contributory Negligence of Patient

141. While a physician clearly owes duties to the patient, the patient also has duties toward the physician and toward himself or herself. These duties must be exercised with the standard of care of the reasonable and prudent patient.[224] Contributory negligence in respect of a loss may be found if the patient is in breach of these duties and that breach is a proximate cause of the loss. Such a finding will not

216. *See* Robertson & Picard, *supra* note 165 at 339–368; Kennedy & Grubb, *supra* note 165 at 151–153, 426–452; *Ediger (Guardian ad litem of) v. Johnston*, 2013 SCC 18 [2013] 2 SCR 98 [*Ediger*].
217. *Cardin v. Montreal* [1961] SCR 655.
218. *University Hospital Board v. Lepine* [1966] SCR 561*; Monckton v. Lepine* [1966] SCR 561.
219. *Kapur v. Marshall* (1978), 85 DLR (3d) 566 (Ont. HC); *Rietze v. Bruser* (1978) [1979] 1 WWR 31 (Man. QB).
220. *Finlay v. Auld* (1973) [1975] 1 SCR 338 [*Finlay*].
221. *Wilson v. Stark* (1967), 61 WWR 705 (Sask. QB); *Fraser v. Vancouver Gen Hosp* [1952] 2 SCR 36; *Finlay, supra* note 220.
222. *Snell v. Farrell* (1990) 2 SCR 311. *See also Ediger, supra* note 216; *Benhaim v. St-Germain*, 2016 SCC 48 [2016] 2 SCR 352.
223. *Cranwill v. James et al.* (1994), 164 AR 241 (QB), affirmed (1997), 193 AR 204 (CA), leave to appeal to SCC refused (1997), 212 AR 235 (note); *See also Benhaim, supra* note 222.
224. *See* Robertson & Picard, *supra* note 165 at 467–468.

disentitle the patient to compensation for the loss suffered but will reduce the damages by an amount commensurate with the patient's contributory negligence.[225] In determining whether to make a finding of contributory negligence, a court will consider whether the reasonableness of the physician's decision to shift responsibility to the patient is negligent or not. It may be reasonable for the physician to do so where, for example, the patient has been instructed to take prescribed drugs,[226] refrain from eating or drinking prior to surgery,[227] or to return for further treatment or to use crutches after a bone biopsy.[228]

b. Expiration of Limitation Period

142. It is an absolute defense to any action, including one for medical negligence, that the limitation period to which the action is subject has expired.[229] The practical basis for limitation periods is known as the stale evidence rationale: recollections of relevant facts fade with time, location of witnesses becomes difficult or impossible, records get lost or destroyed. Further, potential defendants are seen to be entitled after the passage of a certain period of time to be free of a lingering apprehension of a negligence action.[230] While limitations of action legislation in some Canadian jurisdictions used to provide a shorter limitation period for medical malpractice actions than other causes of action, this is no longer the case.[231]

143. The phrase "termination of professional services," as the triggering event for a limitation period, has been subject to strict interpretation itself. A partnership of defendant physicians was unable to rely upon the protection of a two-year limitation period for medical malpractice because none of them had established an actual physician/patient relationship with the plaintiff so as to provide professional services, but only engaged in general supervision of the employee technician who had performed the negligent act.[232]

225. *See* AM Linden et al., *Canadian Tort Law*, 11th ed. (Toronto: LexisNexis, 2018); Sappideen & Vines, *supra* note 166 at 322–323. *See also Savoie v. Bouchard* (1982), 23 CCLT 83 (NBQB), affiliated (1983), 26 CCLT 173 (NBCA); *Chan, supra* note 173.
226. *Crossman v. Stewart* (1977), 82 DLR (3d) 677 (BCSC). *See also Chan, supra* note 173.
227. *Barsy v. Manitoba* (1966), 57 WWR 169 (Man. QB).
228. *Ostrowski v. Lotto* [1973] SCR 220; *Brushett v. Cowan* (1990), 69 DLR (4th) 743 (Nfld. CA); *Anderson (Litigation Guardian of) v. Nowaczynski* [1999] OJ No. 4485 (QL) (SCJ); *Patmore v. Weatherston* [1999] BCJ No. 650 (QL) (SC).
229. *Whiston v. Deane* (1979), 95 DLR (3d) 184 (BCSC).
230. *See* Robertson & Picard, *supra* note 165 at 477–478.
231. For example, *Limitations Act,* RSA 2000, c L-12, and *Limitations Act, 2002*, SO 2002, c 24.
232. *Narynski v. Dow Corning Canada* (1997), 147 DLR (4th) 208 (Man. CA). Consider also *Brown v. Baum*, 2016 ONCA 325, 397 DLR (4th) 161.

§3. Indigenous Peoples' Health

I. Background: The Sociological Realities of Indigenous Health

144. The term "Indigenous peoples of Canada" is a collective noun for Canada's original inhabitants and their descendants.[233] Pursuant to section 35(2) of the *Canadian Charter of Rights and Freedoms*, it includes the First Nations, Inuit, and Métis peoples of Canada.[234] The 2016 Census of Population reported that Indigenous people in Canada account for 4.9% of the population, totaling approximately 1,673,785.[235] This was a "breathtaking 42.5 per cent increase since 2006, a growth rate more than four times that of their non-Indigenous counterparts."[236] The next population census scheduled for 2021 will indicate whether this growth rate has slowed, if at all.[237]

145. The steep increase in Canada's Indigenous population reinforces the pressing need to address its health crisis. Over the past two decades, numerous sources have reported on the jarring health disparities between Indigenous and non-Indigenous Canadians.[238] For example, Tuberculosis incidence rates are almost 300 times higher among the Inuit than for non-Indigenous Canadians.[239] Active tuberculosis incidence rates are thirty-two times higher for First Nations people living on reserve than for Canadian-born non-Indigenous people.[240] Suicide rates among Inuit are six to eleven times higher than the Canadian average.[241] Indeed, the Indigenous population as a whole has a higher incidence of mental health issues.[242] In May 2018, the Government of Canada reported that "[t]he prevalence of arthritis, asthma,

233. National Collaborating Centre for Aboriginal Health, "An Overview of Aboriginal Health in Canada" (2013), online (pdf): *National Collaborating Centre for Aboriginal Health* https://www.ccnsa-nccah.ca/docs/context/FS-OverviewAbororiginalHealth-EN.pdf.
234. *Canadian Charter of Rights and Freedoms*, s. 35(2), Part I of the *Constitution Act, 1982*, being Sch. B to the *Canada Act 1982* (UK), 1982, c 11. The *Charter* uses the term "Aboriginal peoples."
235. Statistics Canada, *Aboriginal Peoples in Canada: Key Results from the 2016 Census* (online: Statistics Canada, October 2017) www150.statcan.gc.ca/n1/daily-quotidien/171025/dq171025a-eng.htm.
236. Kristy Kirkup, "Canada's Indigenous Population Growing 4 Times Faster than Rest of Country," *Global News* (October 2017), online: globalnews.ca/news/3823772/canadas-growing-indigenous-population/.
237. Statistics Canada, *2021 Census of Population Program Consultation* (online: Statistics Canada, January 2019) www12.statcan.gc.ca/census-recensement/2021/consultation/index-eng.cfm.
238. *See*, for example, Naomi Adelson, "The Embodiment of Inequity: Health Disparities in Aboriginal Canada" (2005) 96 Can J of Public Health S45–S61; JB Waldram et al., *Aboriginal Health in Canada: Historical, Cultural, and Epidemiological Perspectives*, 2nd ed. (Toronto: University of Toronto Press, 2006); Alika Lafontaine, "Opinion: Close the Gap Between Indigenous Health Outcomes and the Rest of Canada," *CBC News* (Mar. 19, 2018), online www.cbc.ca/news/Indigenous/opinion-Indigenous-health-alika-lafontaine-1.4547798.
239. J Vachon, V Gallant & W Siu, "Tuberculosis in Canada" (2016) 44:3/4 Can Commun Dis Rep 75.
240. Public Health Agency of Canada, "Key Health Inequalities in Canada: A National Portrait—Executive Summary" (online: Government of Canada, May 28, 2018) www.canada.ca/en/public-health/services/publications/science-research-data/key-health-inequalities-canada-national-portrait-executive-summary.html.
241. Saman Khan, "Aboriginal Mental Health: The Statistical Reality" (2008) 5:1 Visions J 6.
242. Khan, *supra* note 241.

diabetes, and obesity were higher among First Nations adults living off reserve, First Nations adults living on reserve and in northern communities, and Métis adults than among non-Indigenous adults."[243] These are only a few examples.

146. The reasons for these disparities are numerous. The factors that affect a population's health, referred to as the "social determinants of health," include physiological, psychological, historical, sociological, cultural, economic, and environmental factors. The health of Indigenous population in Canada is a "product of a complex web" of these social determinants.[244] Waldram et al. aptly summarize the crisis and its complexity as follows: "In Canada, one of the most telling examples of how [the social determinants of health] interact can be found in the health of the country's Aboriginal people. Long considered to be the most disadvantaged group in an otherwise affluent society, Aboriginal people today paradoxically experience the kinds of health problems most closely associated with poverty, problems linked to their historical position within the Canadian system."[245]

147. Adding to this complexity are the differences in the "socio-economic circumstances and lived world experiences of First Nations, Inuit, and Métis peoples, between status and non-status, on reserve and off-reserve as well as urban and rural Aboriginal populations."[246] Moreover, although census data and other sociological research certainly show a persistent gap between the health of Indigenous and non-Indigenous Canadians, there are also significant data limitations in this area of research. The National Collaborating Centre for Aboriginal Health explains: "[I]n Canada there exists a serious deficit in the availability of accurate, complete, and up-to-date statistical information about the health of certain sub-populations of First Nations, Inuit, and Métis peoples. Many Aboriginal health data initiatives, for example, have not collected data on non-registered First Nations people, or on Métis or Inuit people living in urban areas" [citations omitted].[247]

148. It is also important to acknowledge that "quantitative and largely deficit-based indicators do not adequately incorporate Indigenous concepts of health and wellness."[248] They are even "harmful if used incorrectly, as they risk continuing to label Indigenous peoples with negative stereotypes."[249] In *Moving Aboriginal Health Forward*, Yvonne Boyer notes that definitions for the term "health" can be inconsistent across Indigenous and Western medicine.[250]

149. Notwithstanding these data and conceptual limitations, one thing that is clear is that the health-care system in Canada has thus far failed the Indigenous

243. Public Health Agency of Canada, *supra* note 240.
244. Waldram et al., *supra* note 238 at 6.
245. *Ibid.*
246. National Collaborating Centre for Aboriginal Health, *supra* note 233.
247. *Ibid.*
248. Public Health Agency of Canada, *supra* note 240.
249. *Ibid.*
250. Y Boyer, *Moving Aboriginal Health Forward: Discarding Canada's Legal Barriers* (Saskatoon: Purich Publishing Limited, 2014) at 126–127.

population that it is meant to serve equally. The difficult realities must be kept in mind when considering the legal landscape discussed below. The law is an important determinant of health and several of the barriers faced by Indigenous population in accessing adequate health care are legal in nature.[251]

II. Legal Framework

150. The effects of law on the health of Indigenous people are numerous. Canadian laws can criminalize actions that Indigenous people perceive as positive and normal.[252] The law also plays a significant role in shaping the social determinants of Indigenous health. It is important to acknowledge that the health of Indigenous Canadians was, in many ways, measurably better prior to European contact.[253] It has since deteriorated both because colonizers brought disease and pathogens from Europe to Canada[254] and because the non-Indigenous population "destroyed the pre-existing [Indigenous] lifestyles and medicine practices that had maintained good health over countless generations."[255] The legal structure of health care in Canada as it pertains to Indigenous Canadians demonstrates the interconnectedness of law and health.

151. Canada's Constitution is largely silent on health, and so it has been up to courts to decide how governmental powers should best be divided to meet the population's health-care needs.[256] Unfortunately, this has resulted in a dangerous and problematic tug of war between the two levels of government.[257] Each has a significant amount of control over Indigenous health care through various heads of power.

152. For example, without naming health specifically, the federal government's criminal law power[258] and its power over "Indians and Lands Reserved for Indians"[259] significantly affect Indigenous health. Inuit are included as "Indian" for the purpose of section 91(24) of the *Constitution Act, 1867.*[260]

251. *Ibid.*, at 92.
252. *Ibid.*
253. Waldram et al., *supra* note 238 at 24–72; Boyer, *supra* note 250 at 15–28.
254. Waldram et al., *supra* note 238 at 24–72.
255. Boyer, *supra* note 250 at 93.
256. *Ibid.*
257. *Ibid.*, at 93–94.
258. *Constitution Act, 1867*, 30 & 31 Victoria, c 3 (UK), s. 91(27).
259. *Constitution Act, 1867*, 30 & 31 Victoria, c 3 (UK), s. 91(24).
260. *Reference as to whether "Indians" includes in s. 91 (24) of the B.N.A. Act includes Eskimo in habitants of the Province of Quebec* [1939] SCR 104.

153. Provinces, on the other hand, are responsible for health-care delivery for Métis and non-status Indians. Provincial heads of power that affect Indigenous health care include health institutions,[261] property and civil rights,[262] and natural resources.[263]

154. In addition to the jurisdictional framework, aboriginal and treaty rights to health are also relevant to the legal landscape. These are entrenched through section 35 of the *Constitution Act, 1982*, which states: "existing aboriginal and treaty rights of the aboriginal peoples of Canada are hereby recognized and affirmed."[264] Boyer suggests that Indigenous people may have a treaty right to practice Indigenous health in Canada.[265]

155. One of the most interesting and significant ways that the law affects Indigenous health, however, is through provincial regulation of health professionals. Provinces have used their jurisdiction to restrict the practice of health services to specific licensed professionals, thus capturing activities of traditional healers.[266]

III. Aboriginal Healers: Recognition and Regulation

156. Indigenous people have traditionally had their own healing practices. Canadian Indigenous health practices vary across the Indigenous peoples; for example, "The Anishnaabe Nation is comprised of the Algonquin, Ojibwe, Oji-Cree and Odawa Nations."[267] However, typically they are holistic processes, which focus upon "balancing of the elements of mind, body, emotion, and spirit in a person, as well as balance in that person's relationship with the earth and the natural world,

261. *Constitution Act, 1867*, 30 & 31 Victoria, c 3 (UK), s. 92(7).
262. *Constitution Act, 1867*, 30 & 31 Victoria, c 3 (UK), s. 92(13).
263. *Constitution Act, 1867*, 30 & 31 Victoria, c 3 (UK), s. 92A. For a fuller discussion of the relevance of the heads of power to indigenous health, *see* Boyer, *supra* note 250 at 93–99. For example, Boyer notes that provincial laws cannot affect Indian rights, though Indians must function under both jurisdictions depending on the circumstance.
264. *Constitution Act, 1982*, being Sch. B to the *Canada Act 1982* (UK), 1982, c 11.
265. Boyer, *supra* note 250 at 136.
266. *Ibid.*, at 99.
267. Lynn Lavallee & Jennifer Poole, "Beyond Recovery: Colonization, Health and Healing for Indigenous People in Canada" (2010) 8:2 International J of Mental Health & Addiction 271 at 273.

that is necessary for good health."[268] Indigenous healing is usually provided by recognized aboriginal healers, who perform a variety or combination of functions, such as those of a physician, psychiatrist/psychologist, family counselor and spiritual advisor.[269]

157. Indigenous healing practices are typically categorized as alternative medicines; by implication Indigenous healing practices are discussed in comparison with biomedicine, wherein biomedicine is the mainstream healing practice while Indigenous healing practices are "alternative" in nature.[270] However, Indigenous people availing such health treatments may consider Indigenous healing practices to be just as mainstream or conventional as biomedicine if such practices form part of their own cultural heritage.[271]

A. *Acceptance of Indigenous Healing Practices*

158. The official acceptance and recognition of Indigenous healing practices within the Canadian health legal framework has been a particularly sensitive issue, because of the Indigenous peoples' history in Canada and the practices' cultural significance. Historically, colonial activities attempted to eradicate Indigenous culture, and consequently the Indigenous people were statutorily prohibited from performing many of their spiritual ceremonies, particularly from 1880 up till the mid-twentieth century.[272] These measures resulted in many of the Indigenous health practices being banned, since Indigenous health practices are intertwined with spiritual and cultural customary practices.[273] A Royal Commission on Aboriginal

268. Robert Crouch et al., "Complementary/Alternative Health Care and HIV/AIDS: Legal, Ethical & Policy Issues in Regulation" (2001), online (pdf): *Canadian HIV/AIDS Legal Network* at 23 http://www.aidslaw.ca/site/wp-content/uploads/2013/04/Complimentary+Alternative+Healthcare+-+ENG.pdf; Erika Mundel & Gwen E Chapman, "A Decolonizing Approach to Health Promotion in Canada: the Case of the Urban Aboriginal Community Kitchen Garden Project" (2010) 25:2 Health Promotion International 166 at 166–167.
269. Crouch et al., *supra* note 268 at 23; Laura Norton, Chellie Goodleaf & National Indian & Inuit Community Health Representatives Organization, *Coping with HIV/AIDS in Aboriginal Communities: A 1998 Resource Manual* (NICCHRO, 1998).
270. Crouch et al., *supra* note 268 at 6–7; Peter Fisher & Adam Ward, "Complementary Medicine in Europe" (1994) 309:6947 British Medical Journal 107 at 107.
271. Crouch et al., *supra* note 268 at 7, 23.
272. For a more detailed review *see* V Douglas, *Introduction to Aboriginal Health and Health Care in Canada: Bridging Health* (New York: Springer Publishing, 2003); Waldram et al., *supra* note 238. For a discussion on the historical demise of Aboriginal midwifery during colonization *see* Dena Carroll & Cecilia Benoit, "Aboriginal Midwifery in Canada: Merging Traditional Practices and Modern Science" in Ivy Lynn Bourgeault, Cecilia Benoit & Robbie Davis-Floyd, eds., *Reconceiving Midwifery* (Montréal: McGill-Queen's University Press, 2004) at 269–271; Lavallee & Poole, *supra* note 267 at 273; AD Letendre, "Aboriginal Traditional Medicine: Where Does It Fit?" (2002) 1:2 Crossing Boundaries: An Interdisciplinary J 79; Canada, Royal Commission on Aboriginal Peoples, *Volume 3: Gathering Strength*, in *Report of the Royal Commission on Aboriginal Peoples* (online: Government of Canada, 1996) [RCAP 1996] www.bac-lac.gc.ca/eng/discover/aboriginal-heritage/royal-commission-aboriginal-peoples/Pages/final-report.aspx.
273. Waldram et al., *supra* note 238 at 147–148.

Peoples reports that "[m]any elders and healers were prosecuted."[274] In many instances, Indigenous health practices were also categorized as witchcraft and idolatry by Christian missionaries and ridiculed.[275]

159. This history influences the debate around statutory regulation of Indigenous health practices. Many aboriginal healers are skeptical of statutory regulation of Indigenous healing practices, as they "distrust … governments which they [feel] reflect[] the interests of the dominant white culture in Canada."[276] In order to achieve "[p]ersonal and societal recovery from the lasting effects of oppression and systemic racism experienced over generations,"[277] some experts argue that the approach to health must be decolonized.[278]

160. The Truth and Reconciliation Commission of Canada (TRC) was set up to address, in a unique way, the historical injustice caused by the Canadian State on Indigenous people primarily through forceful removal of Indigenous children to residential schools between the 1830s and mid-1900s. The TRC's mandate was premised on the need for acknowledging the injustices of past events to overcome existing conflict, so as to foster a stronger and healthier relationship between the Indigenous and non-Indigenous going forward. The TRC's primary duty was to gather and record peoples' experiences focusing on the victims and sharing these experiences with and educating the public. The TRC completed its work by December 2015, and the archives are now maintained by the National Centre for Truth and Reconciliation.[279]

161. The TRC explicitly recommends recognition and acceptance of Indigenous healing practices by mainstream health practitioners, "to recognize the value of Aboriginal healing practices and use them in the treatment of Aboriginal patients in collaboration with Aboriginal healers and Elders where requested by Aboriginal patients."[280]

---

274. RCAP 1996, *supra* note 272 at vol. 3, p. 105.
275. *Ibid.*
276. Crouch et al., *supra* note 268 at 75.
277. RCAP 1996, *supra* note 272 at vol. 3; Mundel & Chapman, *supra* note 268 at 171.
278. Mundel & Chapman, *supra* note 268 at 171; Juanita Sherwood & Tahnia Edwards, "Decolonisation: A Critical Step for Improving Aboriginal Health" (2006) 22 Contemporary Nurse: A J for the Australian Nursing Profession 178 at 178–190.
279. Truth and Reconciliation Commission of Canada, "TRC Findings" (Winnipeg: Truth and Reconciliation Commission of Canada, 2015) www.trc.ca/websites/trcinstitution/index.php?p=890.
280. Truth and Reconciliation Commission of Canada, *Truth and Reconciliation Commission of Canada: Calls to Action*, online (pdf) www.trc.ca/websites/trcinstitution/File/2015/Findings/Calls_to_Action_English2.pdf at 3.

B. Regulation of Indigenous Health Practices

162. In this historical background questions about the regulation of Indigenous health practitioners becomes pertinent as well as culturally sensitive, i.e., "who controls [or should control] the licensing of aboriginal healers, what standards should apply to [Indigenous] healing practices, and what is or is not an [Indigenous] healing practice."[281]

163. In Ontario, the Regulated Health Professions Act[282] specifically states that the act does not apply to "(a) Aboriginal healers providing traditional healing services or (b) Aboriginal midwives providing traditional midwifery services to Aboriginal persons or to members of an Aboriginal community."[283] This language has been interpreted to mean that the exemption applies to health services provided to all Indigenous people, whether on or off the reserves, as well as non-Indigenous people inside an Indigenous community.[284]

164. The application of this rule has some interesting consequences. In Ontario, Indigenous midwives may practice without being a member of the Ontario College of Midwives or the Ontario Midwives' Association.[285] Hence the *ex ante* regulation of midwives through the profession-specific act regulating midwives does not apply to Indigenous midwives.

165. Questions have also been raised on the extent to which *ex post* regulation through courts, i.e., under torts and criminal negligence, applicable to all allopathic and CAM practitioners, should apply to aboriginal healers. In few cases Canadian courts have held aboriginal healers criminally liable in specific circumstances. In a 1992 case, a member of the First Nation requested the elders to perform a Coast Salish Big House Tradition called the Spirit Dance on her spouse, also a member of the First Nation, to cure him of alcoholism and help remedy their marriage.[286] According to Coast Salish custom, a member of the community can be forced to go through the Spirit Dance, as the interests of the community supersede those of the individual.[287] However, the British Columbia Supreme Court awarded damages to the spouse for "assault, battery and false imprisonment" on the grounds that he lived off the reserve, he did not self-identify with the Coast Salish culture, Spirit Dance was not an "aboriginal right" under the Constitution, and his individual right, i.e., freedom from assault, battery and false imprisonment, guaranteed under Canadian

281. Lisa C Fong, "Professional Conduct Blog: Professional Regulation and Traditional Aboriginal Healing" (Sep. 7, 2015), online www.ngariss.com/professional-regulation-and-traditional-aboriginal-healing/.
282. *Regulated Health Professions Act*, 1991, SO 1991, c 18.
283. Crouch et al., *supra* note 268 at 89; Dena Carroll & Cecilia Benoit, "Aboriginal Midwifery in Canada: Merging Traditional Practices and Modern Science" in Ivy Lynn Bourgeault, Cecilia Benoit & Robbie Davis-Floyd, eds., *Reconceiving Midwifery* (Montréal: McGill-Queen's University Press, 2004) at 274–277.
284. Carroll & Benoit, *supra* note 283 at 274–277.
285. *Ibid.*
286. *Thomas v. Norris* [1992] 2 CNLR 139 (BCSC) [*Thomas*].
287. Waldram et al., *supra* note 238 at 257–258.

law had been violated.[288] In a 2001 case, an Ecuadorian shaman was invited to provide healing services to an Ontario First Nation elder. During the three-day healing ceremony the shaman instructed the elder to refrain from taking his medication for diabetes, and gave the elder herbal medicines containing *ayahuasca* and tobacco. The elder died from nicotine poisoning. The shaman was charged with criminal negligence causing death.[289]

166. The extent to which Indigenous people can "opt out" of traditional mainstream medicine and rely on aboriginal healers is particularly contested when children are involved. In 2015, controversy arose when in *Hamilton Health Sciences v. DH*[290] an Ontario judge rejected a hospital's application under the *Child and Family Services Act* to oblige an Indigenous mother to have her child undergo further chemotherapy for her cancer. The judge invoked the mother's "constitutionally protected right to pursue their traditional medicine over the applicant's stated course of treatment of chemotherapy."[291] The public reaction was strong, and some non-Indigenous academic commentators were also very dismissive of the judge's ruling. In a subsequent decision, the judge amended his ruling by allowing a motion from the Attorney General of Ontario, which endorsed a joint submission by the various parties.[292] The judgment clarified that the recognition and implementation of the right to use traditional medicines "must remain consistent with the principle that the best interest of the child remains paramount," and that an analysis of the best interest of the child must consider the importance of the recognition of this Indigenous right. The joint submission further emphasized how the various parties (hospital, parents, Indigenous community) were focused on working collaboratively to provide the best possible integrated care to the child, combining standard medicine with Indigenous healing practices.[293]

167. Although the current regulatory regime of aboriginal healers in Ontario largely exempts aboriginal healers from statutory regulation, experts and Indigenous elders/aboriginal healers are exploring whether it is appropriate or desirable for Indigenous healing to be formalized and statutorily regulated,[294] and what occupational standards should apply?[295] How should a balance be achieved between

288. *Thomas*, *supra* note 286.
289. Waldram et al., *supra* note 238 at 258–259.
290. *Hamilton Health Sciences Corp v. DH, PLJ, Six Nations of the Grand River Child and Family Services Department and Brant Family and Children's Services*, 2014 ONCJ 603 (CanLII).
291. *Ibid.*
292. *Ibid.*
293. *See* University of Saskatchewan, Indigenous Law Centre, "Hamilton Health Sciences Corp v DH" (May 7, 2015), online: *Indigenous Law Centre* https://Indigenouslaw.usask.ca/blog/2015/hamilton-health-sciences-corp-v-dh.php; *see also* Larry Chartrand, "Deciding Medical Treatment for a First Nation's Child: Is it Six Nations or Ontario Authority that should govern?" (Paper delivered at the University of Toronto Health Law Seminar Series, 2018) (unpublished, on file with authors).
294. Raymond Obomsawin, "Traditional Medicine for Canada's First Peoples" (March 2007), online (pdf): *Faculty of Land and Food Systems, Indigenous Research Partnerships* https://lfs-indigenous.sites.olt.ubc.ca/files/2014/07/RayObomsawin.traditional.medicine-1.pdf at 17; Crouch et al., *supra* note 268 at 88.
295. Carroll & Benoit, *supra* note 283 at 279; Crouch et al., *supra* note 268 at 85.

ensuring quality health-services by Indigenous practitioners, while maintaining full autonomy and control?[296] What minimum educational standards should be applied, bearing in mind that often the educational requirements are based on the model of biomedicine, and college or university education is a must?[297]

168. Recommendations have been made to ensure appropriate and better regulation of aboriginal healers. Some experts argue that to achieve decolonization of Indigenous health care, regulation must ensure: regulatory authority over Indigenous health services, self-determination and self-governance by the Indigenous community, and capacity building of aboriginal healers including determining appropriate standards of qualifications and practices for aboriginal healers.[298] Indigenous health care should be evaluated through Indigenous social determinants of health model and not those dictated by mainstream biomedicine.[299] Some experts have advocated increased research into Indigenous health services, subject to research being governed by the Indigenous principles, and the traditional knowledge is accorded adequate protection from appropriation and exploitation.[300] *Hamilton Health Sciences v. DH* described above suggest that we are at a new era in Canada with respect to how Indigenous health-care practices are dealt with: an era of more collaborative and respectful engagement between the communities and an attempt to respect at the legal and regulatory level the unique value of Indigenous health practices.

---

296. Carroll & Benoit, *supra* note 283 at 279.
297. *Ibid.*
298. K Jacklin & W Warry, "Decolonizing First Nations Health" in Judith C Kulig & Allison M Williams, eds., *Health in Rural Canada* (Vancouver: UBC Press, 2012), Ch. 20; Obomsawin, *supra* note 294 at 17; Crouch et al., *supra* note 268 at 116.
299. Jacklin & Warry, *supra* note 298.
300. Crouch et al., *supra* note 268 at iii, 109; Aman Gebru, *Intellectual Property, Traditional Knowledge, and Bioprospecting: Searching for Efficient Balance of Rights* (SJD Thesis, University of Toronto Faculty of Law, 2017) (unpublished).

Part II. The Physician-Patient Relationship

Chapter 1. General Description

§1. Rights and Duties of Physicians and Patients

I. Contract Law as a Source of Rights

A. Implied Contract

169. The early English view of the medical profession was that it was a common calling, in which the physician was seen to owe the patient a duty of care upon engaging in the practice of medicine with that patient. The nature of this duty was delictual, and the content of the duty was the exercise of proper skill and care.[301] However, with the development of contract law, the relationship between physician and patient came to be seen as contractual in nature,[302] where the requirement of the exercise of proper skill and care was seen as an implied term of the contract.[303]

170. Since it contains all of the requisite elements of a binding contract,[304] the physician-patient relationship can be characterized as contractual in nature. In the normal course, the contract reflects a mutual intention to create legal relations, namely by the purchase and delivery of medical services. The parties, the physician and the patient, are known and must have the capacity to contract and not be under any undue influence. Consideration flowing from the physician to the patient consists of the medical services, and from the patient to the physician the consideration generally would consist of payment rendered for the services.[305] However, consideration can still pass even where the patient is unable to pay fees, because the patient's mere submission to treatment by the physician has been seen as sufficient consideration for contractual relations.[306]

301. *Everard v. Hopkins* (1615), 2 Bulstrode 332, 80 ER 1164 (KB).
302. *Leighton v. Sargent* (1853), 27 NH 460, 59 AmDec 388 (NHSC).
303. *Slater v. Baker* (1767), 2 Wils. KB 359, 95 ER 860.
304. SM Waddams, *The Law of Contracts*, 2nd ed. (Toronto: Canada Law Book, 1984) at 15 ff.
305. *Matheson v. Smiley* [1932] 2 DLR 787 (Man. CA).
306. On the basis that a person has the right not to be touched, and therefore the giving up of that right is a positive act which can constitute consideration. Legal consideration requires merely an exchange of a detriment for a benefit, so the patient's submission to treatment is sufficient consideration: *Coggs v. Bernard* (1703), 2 Ld. Raym. 909, 92 ER 107 (KB); *Banbury v. Bank of Montreal* [1918] AC 626 at 657 (UKHL).

171. The terms of most contracts for medical services are not expressed or written down, but usually are implied by law to include the physician's duty to exercise proper skill and care,[307] and the obligation of confidentiality.[308] In principle, an additional implied term is the absolute warranty that materials used for performance of contractual obligations are reasonably fit for the purpose for which they are supplied.[309] On this basis, the physician is considered to have given an implied undertaking that the products supplied will be reasonably fit.[310]

172. Canadian courts have made it clear that any implied warranty that relates to medical materials does not include an absolute guarantee against defect in the substances and products used by physicians in the exercise of their medical skills. In one case before the SCC, a plaintiff contracted Human Immunodeficiency Virus (HIV) after being artificially inseminated with infected sperm; the action was based in part on a claim that there had been an implied warranty that the semen supplied during the operation would not be defective. The defendant physician was found to be under a contract to provide services rather than a contract of sale, so the *Sale of Goods Act* did not apply. Furthermore, the court found that any implied warranty applicable under the common law either did not apply in the circumstances or was limited to the imposition of reasonable care as to the product's freedom from contamination, rather than a standard of strict liability.[311] In another case where the plaintiff contracted HIV through a transfusion with contaminated blood, an Ontario court refused to find an implied warranty applicable to blood products, stating that "[t]o hold a hospital or physician to strict liability for a product such as blood may operate to discourage those responsible for our health care from exercising their professional judgment, because they are concerned about their own liability."[312] Judicial reluctance to hold physicians strictly liable for the fitness of medical products may be contrasted both with the high negligence standards applied to manufacturers of medical products,[313] and actions brought against physicians for a negligent failure to warn of potential defects in such products.[314]

307. *Davy v. Morrison* (1931) [1932] OR 1 at 6 (CA); *Gibson v. Bagnall (No. 2)* (1979), 24 OR (2d) 567 (Ont. HC).
308. *Furniss v. Fitchett* [1958] NZLR 396 at 397 (SC).
309. *Hughston v. Jost* [1943] OWN 3 (HC) in *dicta* per Hope J., *Myers v. Brent Cross Service Co.* [1934] 1 KB 46; *Dodd v. Wilson* [1946] 2 All ER 691 (KB). For additional discussion, *see* Kennedy & Grubb, *supra* note 165 at 130–132.
310. *LaFleur v. Cornelis* (1979), 28 NBR (2d) 569 (NBQB); *Dendaas (Tyler) v. Yackel* (1980), 12 CCLT 147 (BCSC); *Doiron v. Orr* (1978), 86 DLR (3d) 719 (Ont. CA).
311. *ter Neuzen, supra* note 199.
312. *Pittman Estate v. Bain* (1994), 112 DLR (4th) 257 at 334, additional reasons at (1994), 112 DLR (4th) 482, further additional reasons at (1994), 112 DLR (4th) 494, further additional reasons at (1994), 35 CPC (3d) 67 (Ont. Gen. Div.).
313. *Hollis v. Dow Corning Corp* (1996), 129 DLR (4th) 609 (SCC).
314. *Pittman Estate v. Bain* (1994), 112 DLR (4th) 257 at 334, additional reasons at (1994), 112 DLR (4th) 482, further additional reasons at (1994), 112 DLR (4th) 494, further additional reasons at (1994), 35 CPC (3d) 67 (Ont. Gen. Div.).

173. In the common law provinces tort law has surpassed contract law as the basis of suits concerning the relationship between physician and patient, since negligence and battery have been considered effective in covering most situations of breach.[315] In Quebec, contract law is more often seen as the source of rights and duties.

B. Express Contract, Specific Promises and Warranties of Cure

174. While Canadian cases on contract liability of physicians are relatively few, it has been held that an express contract between a physician and patient can exist where the physician agrees to particular terms, or warrants a particular outcome.[316] Where the treatment is not performed according to the terms expressed or outcome warranted therein, the physician may be found liable for damages to the extent of loss reasonably expected to occur in the event of a breach.[317] In general, however, the physician and patient will only rarely use a written or clearly expressed contract for the services and fees exchanged.[318] Additionally, there are limits to the terms the parties may express in a contract, in that the parties must not agree to terms contrary to public policy[319] or which waive the implied terms required by law.[320]

II. Fiduciary Duty as a Source of Rights and Duties

175. It is established law in Canada that the physician stands in the position of a fiduciary to the patient in many aspects of their relationship,[321] and thereby owes a duty of the highest order toward the patient. A fiduciary relation is characterized by a relation of trust between a person with specialized knowledge or power (in this case a physician) and a beneficiary. Fiduciary relations entail special duties of honesty, good faith, and acting in the best interest of the beneficiaries of that relation. The fiduciary duty arises whenever the physician-patient relationship is created,

315. For a discussion of elements of the tort-based relationship between physician and patient, *see* §2, Consent, and Informed Consent, *infra*. For further discussion of Quebec law, *see* Lara Khoury & Catherine Régis, "Quebec's Contributions to Health Law and Policy Debates in Canada" in Joanna N Erdman, Vanessa Gruben & Erin Nelson, eds., *Canadian Health Law and Policy*, 5th ed. (Toronto: LexisNexis, 2017).
316. *Hughston v. Jost* [1943] OWN 3 at 4 (HC); *LaFleur v. Cornelis* (1979), 28 NBR (2d) 569 at 577–579 (NBQB).
317. *See* Robertson & Picard, *supra* note 165 at 549.
318. *Ibid.*, at 547.
319. *See* Kennedy & Grubb, *supra* note 165 at 132–136.
320. *See* discussion at §1.I.A, Implied Contracts.
321. *McInerney v. MacDonald* (1992), 93 DLR (4th) 415 (SCC) [*McInerney*]; *Kenny v. Lockwood* [1932] 1 DLR 507 (Ont. CAa); *Halushka v. University of Sask.* (1965), 53 DLR (2d) 436 (Sask. CA); *Henderson v. Johnston* [1956] OR 789, affirmed (1957), 11 DLR (2nd) 19 (CA), affirmed (1959), 19 DLR (2d) 201 (SCC); *Reibl v. Hughes* (1977), 16 OR (2d) 306 at 312 (Ont. HC), affirmed [1980] 2 SCR 880; *Geffen v. Goodman Estate* [1991] 2 SCR 353 at 370. *See also Norberg v. Wynrib* [1992] 2 SCR 226, for a discussion of the unsettled issue of which aspects of the physician-patient relationship should be considered to be fiduciary in nature. *See also Stirrett v. Cheema*, 2020 ONCA 288.

even if the purpose of the relationship is not to provide care or treatment, but rather for third-party use, for example, as an insurance requirement.[322] Medical practitioners must avoid that their personal interests and professional duty come into conflict.[323] This means at a minimum that any pecuniary interest the physician has in a provision of medical services, such as a fee-splitting arrangement or rewards for cost reduction, must be disclosed to the patient.[324]

176. The recognition of the physician-patient relationship as fiduciary gives patients another legal tool to obtain compensation. It provides a basis for an equitable remedy, which is often more interesting for plaintiffs than a remedy under tort or contract. The remedy aims to restore plaintiffs in the position they would have been in if no breach of the fiduciary duty had occurred. This means that a plaintiff can be compensated for the harm suffered, but it may also involve transfer of the profits the fiduciary made as a result of the breach. Fiduciary law offers a strong basis for punitive damages.[325]

§2. Consent

I. General

A. Valid Consent to Treatment Is Required

177. In Canada, with limited exceptions, every individual's body is considered inviolate, and any medical intervention in which a physician touches the body of a patient without that patient's consent constitutes battery.[326] A patient's right to self-determination is recognized and protected by law, and it is generally paramount to a physician's obligation to provide needed medical care and to the state's interest in preserving the patient's life or health.[327]

178. The fact that serious risk or consequences may flow from a refusal of medical treatment does not vitiate the right of medical self-determination.[328] In one case, for example, a physician administered a blood transfusion to a patient who arrived in emergency in shock from blood loss. The transfusion in all likelihood saved her life. The physician was nevertheless held liable for battery because the patient was

322. *McInerney, supra* note 321.
323. *Henderson v. Johnston* (1959), 19 DLR (2d) 201 (SCC).
324. *Ibid.; Kangas v. Parker* [1976] 5 WWR 25 (Sask. QB), affirmed [1978] 5 WWR 667 (CA). For a discussion of fiduciary law and conflicts of interests, see Bernard M Dickens, "Conflicts of Interest in Canadian Health Care Law" (1995) 21 Am J L & Med 259.
325. *See* Bernard Dickens, "Medical Negligence" in Jocelyn Downie, Timothy Caulfield & Colleen Flood, eds. *Canadian Health Law and Policy*, 4th ed. (Markham: LexisNexis, 2011) 115 at 131.
326. *Malette v. Shulman* (1990), 2 CCLT (2d) 1 (Ont. CA) [*Malette*].
327. *Ibid.*
328. *Fleming, supra* note 167.

carrying a card requesting that no blood be administered to her under any circumstances due to the patient's religious beliefs.[329] Similarly, even though a respirator was necessary for the survival of a patient with an incurable neurological disorder, the patient was granted an injunction requiring her physician and hospital to comply with her instruction that the respirator be turned off.[330]

179. For consent to be valid, it must be given in the context of certain requisite conditions, which, if not met, will vitiate consent as a defense to an action for battery.[331] First, the patient must have the capacity to consent to the particular medical treatment or procedure.[332] A patient will be found to have capacity if he or she has understood the nature and effect of the treatment or of a refusal to undergo the treatment.[333] In this sense, capacity for the purpose of consent to medical treatment is distinguishable from legal capacity in the general sense. For example, an otherwise competent patient did not have capacity where it was found that the condition with which she was afflicted prevented her from fully appreciating the nature and effect of a refusal of treatment.[334]

180. The test is also applied to determine the capacity of minors. A minor will have capacity to provide valid consent if he or she is able to appreciate the nature and consequences of the treatment.[335] The test is to be applied by physicians prior to receiving consent, and often is applied even in jurisdictions where consent legislation exists. A physician may even seek a court declaration of capacity prior to treatment.[336] Where a minor with capacity consents to a medical procedure and is thereby treated, the physician will be found to have acted properly in that regard, even if the minor's parents objected to the treatment.[337] Where the minor is without

329. *Malette, supra* note 325. The Court reviewed the basic elements of battery in the medical context, and described at length the principles of patient autonomy and freedom of choice with respect to health care.
330. As a respirator is a form of medical treatment, and treatment cannot be administered without the consent of the patient: *Nancy B* (1993), 86 DLR (4th) 385 (Que. Sup. Ct.).
331. *See* Robertson & Picard, *supra* note 165 at 74; and *Reibl, supra* note 166. To a certain degree legislation has altered the common law understanding of what constitutes valid consent. For instance, *see Health Care Consent Act, 1996,* SO 1996, c 2, s. 11, where it is provided that an additional requisite element is that consent be informed. For further discussion, *see* §3, Informed Consent, *infra.*
332. *See* generally Robertson & Picard, *supra* note 165 at 74, 81; and Kennedy & Grubb, *supra* note 165 at 180–215.
333. *Ney, supra* note 168 at 53; *see also Starson v. Swayze*, 2003 SCC 32 [2003] 1 SCR 722 [*Starson*].
334. *Re W.* [1992] 4 All ER 627 (CA), where the patient suffered from *anorexia nervosa*; *see also Re SH*, 2019 CarswellOnt 6953 (WL Can) (Ont. Consent & Capacity Board).
335. *Johnston v. Wellesley Hospital* (1970), 17 DLR (3d) 139 at 144–145 (Ont. HC); *Ney, supra* note 168. *See also C.(A.), supra* note 168.
336. *Region 2 Hospital Corporation v. Walker* (1994), 385 APR 366 (NBCA).
337. *J(CS) v. Wren* (1986), 35 DLR (4th) 419 (Alta. CA), which dismissed an action against a physician after a 16-year-old with capacity sought and obtained approval for a therapeutic abortion without the approval of her parents.

capacity, however, the legal guardians of the minor must consent to any medical services provided for the minor.[338] This is also the case for adults who are found not to have capacity, and this is usually enacted in legislation.[339]

181. A second requirement for valid consent is that it be given voluntarily and without any form of coercion, duress or deceit or fraudulent misrepresentation about the procedure or treatment to be delivered.[340] A fraudulent omission can constitute a fraudulent misrepresentation, so where a physician obtained consent for an operation but concealed the true reason for the operation, the consent was vitiated.[341] Coercion may also come from the family or other persons outside the physician-patient relationship, as in the case of a patient who refused a blood transfusion as a result of the undue influence of her mother.[342] To avoid this situation, a physician should discuss treatment with the patient alone, particularly where the physician has reason to believe that the patient may be subject to compulsion.[343]

182. A third requirement of consent to medical services is that the consent be referable to both the treatment and the person administering it.[344] The patient must receive only the treatment for which consent has been given.[345] Where treatment is undertaken, a consent form may be used by hospitals to obtain a patient's consent with respect to any additional measures which may be found necessary.[346] Since consent to treatment is a consent to being touched, it refers to the person doing the touching or administering the treatment. Therefore, consent forms generally refer to many persons who will participate in the provision of the medical services. Where residents or interns will be participating, this should be specifically disclosed to the patient, since these persons may not be anticipated to be administering the treatment.[347]

183. The fourth basic element of valid consent to the provision of medical services is that the patient be informed as to the nature of the treatment, available alternatives and attendant risks.[348] The standard and extent of disclosure required before consent can be considered to be genuinely informed has changed significantly in the last several years, and now requires the physician to disclose all material risks which

---

338. *Ney, supra* note 168 at 53.
339. *See* for example, the *Adult Guardianship and Trusteeship Act,* SA 2008, c A-4.2.
340. *Norberg v. Wynrib* [1992] 2 SCR 226; *Re D and Council of College of Physicians & Surgeons of BC* (1970), 11 DLR (3d) 570 (BCSC); *Hobbs v. Kizer* (1916), 263 F. 681 (USCA 8th Ct.).
341. *Gerula v. Flores* (1995), 126 DLR (4th) 506 (Ont. CA).
342. *Re T* (1992), 4 All ER 649.
343. *See* Robertson & Picard, *supra* note 165 at 75; Somerville, Law Reform Commission of Canada, *supra* note 168.
344. Generally, *see* Robertson & Picard, *supra* note 165 at 114–121.
345. *Schweizer, supra* note 168; *Parmley v. Parmley* [1945] 4 DLR 81 (SCC).
346. *Pridham v. Nash* (1986), 33 DLR (4th) 304 (Ont. HC); *Brushett v. Cowan* (1990), 3 CCLT (2d) 195 (Nfld. CA).
347. *See* Robertson & Picard, *supra* note 165 at 119–121.
348. For discussion of this element, *see* §3, Informed Consent, *infra.*

a reasonable person in the position of the patient would want to know. Similarly, the patient has an obligation to cooperate in establishing the specifics of the complaint.[349]

B. Consent May Be Implied or Express

184. Consent to the provision of medical services is often implied by the patient's words or conduct, such as cooperatively submitting to examination or treatment.[350] The issue of whether there is implied consent also arises where consent is undoubtedly given for one procedure, but an additional or alternative procedure is performed. In such circumstances, it appears that implied consent will be found if the alternative procedure was discussed and a consent form was given.[351]

185. Consent also may be express, in either oral or written form.[352] While express written consent is not in itself determinative of the issue of whether valid consent was obtained, it can serve as evidence in support of a consent defense to an action in battery,[353] or as a waiver of the requisite explanation of risks in a negligence action.[354] Hospitals will generally obtain express written consent, particularly prior to major treatment, and reference should be made to the relevant legislation of the individual jurisdictions to determine whether express consent is a requirement.[355]

II. Specific Exceptions

A. Emergencies

186. Emergency situations are an important exception to the general requirement that consent be obtained prior to any treatment. Generally in such circumstances a physician will be permitted to treat a patient who is unable to consent, on

349. *See* Robertson & Picard, *supra* note 165 at 166, 210–212; *Hopp, supra* note 168. *See also Malinowski v. Schneider*, 2012 ABCA 125, 524 AR 231, leave to appeal to SCC refused [2012] SCCA No. 279.
350. *Malette, supra* note 325; *Reynen v. Antonenko* (1975), 30 CRNS 135 (Alta. SC); *Schweizer, supra* note 168; *Marshall v. Curry* [1933] 3 DLR 260 at 274 (NSSC); *O'Brien v. Cunard SS Co.* (1891), 28 NE 266 (Mass. SC).
351. *O'Bonsawin v. Paradis* (1993), 15 CCLT (2d) 188 (Ont. Gen. Div.); *Brushett v. Cowan* (1990), 3 CCLT (2d) 195 (Nfld. CA); *Pridham v. Nash* (1986), 33 DLR (4th) 304 (Ont. HC); *Tomeh, supra* note 172. *See also* JG Fleming, *The Law of Torts,* 6th ed. (Sydney: Law Book Co., 1983). Generally, *see* Robertson & Picard, *supra* note 165 at 60–64.
352. Robertson & Picard, *supra* note 165 at 59–64. *See also Kemp v. Vancouver Coastal Health Authority Ltd*, 2017 BCCA 229, 280 ACWS (3d) 13, leave to appeal to SCC refused, 2018 CarswellBC 641 (WL Can.).
353. *Doiron v. Orr* (1978), 86 DLR (3d) 719 (Ont. HC); *Schweizer, supra* note 168.
354. *See* Margaret A Somerville, "Structuring the Issues in Informed Consent" (1981) 26:4 McGill LJ 740.
355. *Schweizer, supra* note 168.

the premise that the treatment is necessary to save the life or preserve the health of a patient who is in immediate danger, and no alternative is available.[356] Thus, in a case where the physician removed an infected testicle during the course of a hernia operation to prevent the possible development of gangrene, an action for battery was dismissed.[357] However, where a condition is discovered during treatment for which consent has been obtained, and the physician performs a procedure in relation to that second condition out of convenience rather than necessity, the emergency exception will not apply. Therefore, where a physician, during a caesarian section, performed a tubal ligation upon discovering fibroid uterine tumors, he was found liable because a second operation after obtaining the patient's consent would have been possible, if inconvenient, and therefore the situation was not a true emergency.[358]

B. Blanket Authorizations

187. Consent to medical services, particularly in the context of a hospital, may take the form of a blanket authorization whereby the patient expresses consent for unspecified additional or alternative procedures. However, where such a blanket authorization is so broadly worded as to be vague and unspecific, it may be given little weight as evidence[359] of consent or disclosure of risks.[360]

C. Therapeutic Privilege

188. Another exception to consent which at one time was recognized in Canada is known as therapeutic privilege.[361] The rationale of this principle has been that in some situations a physician may determine that information provided to the patient may adversely affect the delivery, course or results of the treatment, and in such circumstances the physician may be justified in withholding the information.[362] Such situations would arise only in extreme cases, for example, where a severe emotional state would reduce the benefits of the treatment or would prevent the patient from rationally considering and consenting to the treatment. The mere possibility that the details of information might upset a patient or cause the patient to refuse consent would not be sufficient to justify therapeutic privilege, nor would be the fact that the patient might not understand the information.[363]

---

356. Robertson & Picard, *supra* note 165 at 68–69. Generally *see also Murray, supra* note 170 and Kennedy & Grubb, *supra* note 165 at 173.
357. *Marshall v. Curry* [1933] 3 DLR 260 (NSSC).
358. *Murray, supra* note 170. *See also* Robertson & Picard, *supra* note 165 at 70.
359. *See* discussion in §2.I.B *supra* relating to express consent.
360. *Hajgato v. London Health Assn.* (1982), 36 OR (2d) 669, affirmed (1983), 44 OR (2d) 264 (CA); *Bickford v. Stiles* (1981), 128 DLR (3d) 516 (NBQB).
361. *See* LE Rozovsky & FA Rozovsky, *The Canadian Law of Consent to Treatment* (Toronto: Butterworths, 1990) at 22–23; and Irvine, Osborne & Shariff, *supra* note 165 at 68.
362. *Reibl, supra* note 166.
363. LE Rozovsky & FA Rozovsky, *supra* note 360 at 22.

189. Since it otherwise is an abrogation of the general rule that valid consent be informed,[364] and an interference with the patient's right to self-determination, the doctrine of therapeutic privilege had been strictly construed. It had been seen as an exception to be used very infrequently in practice.[365]

190. In 1991, the doctrine was effectively eliminated from the law in Canada by a case in which a physician intentionally withheld the information that contrast media injections can cause death, because the risk of such a consequence was extremely low. The court stated that the "therapeutic privilege" exception to the doctor's duty of disclosure should not become part of Canadian law since the privilege has the potential to swallow the doctor's obligation of disclosure and thus to override the requirement for informed consent.[366] The SCC has noted that the doctrine of therapeutic privilege should only be resorted to in extreme circumstances.[367]

D. *Statutory*

191. In some circumstances, exceptions to the requirement of consent will be created by statute. The public health statutes of individual provinces[368] allow medical examinations and treatment to be conducted and performed without consent where a provincial medical officer has reason to believe the person is suffering from a communicable disease and certain requisite steps are carried out.

192. Other legislation permits treatment with the consent of someone other than the patient. Legal guardianship statutes such as child welfare and dependent adult legislation[369] have provisions for the delivery of health care without the consent of the patient where the patient is not competent to give his or her consent. Similarly, a legal guardian may be required to give consent where it is determined that a minor does not have the capacity to consent to a particular treatment.[370]

364. *See* discussion of Consent at §2.I.A *supra* and Informed Consent at §3 *infra.*
365. LE Rozovsky & FA Rozovsky, *supra* note 360 at 23.
366. *Meyer Estate v. Rogers* (1991), 2 OR (3d) 356 (Ont. Gen. Div.).
367. *McInerney, supra* note 321, LaForest J.
368. *See* for example, the *Public Health Act,* RSA 2000, c P-37.
369. *See* for example, the *Child, Youth and Family Enhancement Act,* RSA 2000, c C-12; the *Adult Guardianship and Trusteeship Act,* SA 2008, c A-4.2.
370. *Ney, supra* note 168 at 53; *see also* the *Medical Consent of Minors Act,* SNB 1976, c M-6.1.

§3. Informed Consent

I. Introduction

193. As noted above,[371] genuine consent to a treatment requires the patient to have been informed about the nature and gravity of the proposed treatment, possible alternatives to it, and the material risks involved, including those which are mere possibilities but which entail serious consequences.[372] The subject of informed consent is an area which has seen significant development in the last several years in Canada, both in the common law and in legislation.[373] While several principles have been established, several others are still evolving.

194. In general, where consent to treatment is not given by a properly informed patient, the physician's ability to rely on consent as a defense to a tort claim will be jeopardized. However, while other defects in consent caused by a failure of one of the other requisite elements[374] can vitiate consent as a defense to battery, the failure of informed consent in Canada today generally can be used only to support a claim of negligence. The courts in Canada, particularly since the landmark case of *Reibl v. Hughes*[375] in 1980, have taken the approach that no action for battery can lie if there is at least consent to the basic nature and character of the treatment.[376]

II. Standards of Disclosure

A. Prior to 1980: Physician-Based Standard

195. Prior to 1980, the standard of disclosure demanded of physicians in order for a patient's consent to be genuine was described as the professional medical disclosure standard.[377] This required the physician to give a fair and reasonable explanation of the proposed treatment including the probable effect and any special or unusual risks.[378] Whether disclosure was fair and reasonable was measured by the risks which a physician's colleagues would normally disclose about that treatment, taking into consideration the intellectual and emotional characteristics of the particular patient and the nature of the relationship between them.[379] Factors which the

371. *See* §2.1.A *supra.*
372. *Reibl, supra* note 166; *Arndt, supra* note 211; *Malinowski, supra* note 348. See in general the discussion in Trudo Lemmens, "Informed Consent" in Yann Joly & Bartha Maria Knoppers, eds., *Routledge Handbook of Medical Law and Ethics* (Abingdon: Routledge, 2015) 27-51.
373. *See* Ontario *Health Care Consent Act, 1996,* SO 1996, c 2, Sch. A; and British Columbia *Health Care (Consent) and Care Facility (Admission) Act,* RSBC 1996, c 181.
374. *See* §2.1.A *supra.*
375. *Supra* note 166.
376. Somerville, *supra* note 353; *See also Bollman (2014), supra* note 166.
377. *See* Robertson & Picard, *supra* note 165 at 161; and Laskin CJC's discussion of the decisions of the courts *infra* in *Reibl, supra* note 166.
378. *Halushka v. University of Sask.* (1965), 52 WWR 608 at 615 (Sask. CA); *Hopp, supra* note 168.
379. *Reibl v. Hughes* (1977), 16 OR (2d) 306 at 313 (Ont. HC), reversed (1978), 6 CCLT 227 at 239 (Ont. CA), affirmed [1980] 2 SCR 880.

physician was to bear in mind in determining the appropriate level of disclosure included the gravity of the patient's condition, the benefits of the proposed treatment, the nature and probability of any risks, and any questions posed by the patient.[380]

196. With the decisions of the SCC in *Reibl v. Hughes*[381] and *Hopp v. Lepp*[382] in 1980, however, the physician-based or professional medical standard was rejected as the standard for determining either disclosure or a breach of the duty to disclose. In the Court's view, to place the task of determining which risks are material in the hands of the medical profession was to turn over to the physician, rather than the trier of fact, the questions of the appropriate scope of disclosure and any consequent breach of the duty of disclosure.[383]

B. Patient Standard

197. In its decisions in *Reibl* and *Hopp,* the SCC clarified the common law standard of disclosure for informed consent in the various common law jurisdictions. It ruled that physicians have to disclose all material risks, consequences and alternatives that a reasonable person in the position of the patient would want to know. The professional standard of disclosure was therefore rejected in favor of a reasonable person standard, with a focus on the patient's specific position.[384] When this level of disclosure is satisfied, consent given by the patient in question will be determined to be informed. When health-care providers fail to disclose the information a reasonable person in the patient's position would want to know, the consent given will not be considered informed, and a finding of negligence on the part of the physician may result, if other components of the negligence test are fulfilled.[385]

198. The standard of disclosure in informed consent cases and the test for causation, discussed hereafter, have been discussed in many other cases in the courts.[386] In *Arndt v. Smith,* the majority of the SCC stated that physicians must inform their patients according to the needs of a reasonable patient who possesses "the patient's reasonable beliefs, fears, desires and expectations," along with "the specific concerns of the particular patient at the time consent was given."[387]

380. *Hopp, supra* note 168 at 79; *Male v. Hopmans* (1965), 54 DLR (2d) 592 (Ont. HC), varied on other grounds (1967), 64 DLR (3d) 105 (CA), adopting the words of a New Zealand case, *Smith v. Auckland Hosp Bd* [1964] NZLR 241, on appeal [1965] NZLR 191 (CA).
381. *Supra* note 166.
382. *Supra* note 168.
383. *Reibl, supra* note 166.
384. *Ferguson v. Hamilton Civic Hosps.* (1983), 144 DLR (3d) 214 (Ont. HC), affirmed (1985), 18 DLR (4th) 638 (CA).
385. However, before liability will be found, causation must be established: *see* §3.IV. Causation, *infra.*
386. *Hollis v. Dow Corning Corp, supra* note 313; and *Arndt, supra* note 211; *Bollman (2014), supra* note 166; *Bollman v. Soenen*, 2017 ONCA 391, 279 ACWS (3d) 649 [*Bollman (2017)*].
387. *Arndt, supra* note 211 at 54.

III. Factors to Be Disclosed

199. The duty to inform the patient requires the physician to disclose certain minimum information.[388]

A. Diagnosis

200. The physician is under a duty not only to diagnose but also to inform the patient about the diagnosis.[389]

B. Nature and Purpose of Treatment

201. The patient is entitled to know the nature of the proposed course of treatment, what will be involved, the reason the treatment is recommended and the intended result.[390] When describing the nature and purpose of the treatment, the physician also has a duty to ensure that the patient comprehends the explanation given.[391]

C. Risks and Outcomes

202. On the standard set by the SCC in *Reibl v. Hughes* and *Hopp v. Lepp,* a physician is not required to disclose all risks. The standard is that all material risks must be disclosed, and materiality is determined on the basis of whether the information would influence the person's consent to treatment, again on the basis of the reasonable person in the position of the particular patient.[392] However, even though a risk might be only a mere possibility, if the potential negative outcome is serious, then a risk should be deemed to be material.[393] Additionally, the physician should answer any specific questions about risks.[394] Where risks are minimal and are for purely elective surgery, they need not be disclosed.[395]

388. *See also* the *Health Care Consent Act, 1996*, SO 1996, c 2, Sch. A, s. 11(3).
389. *Reibl, supra* note 166; *Barr v. Hughes* (1982), 14 ACWS (2d) 112 (BCSC).
390. *See* LE Rozovsky & FA Rozovsky, *supra* note 360 at 9; *Hopp, supra* note 168 at 81.
391. *Ciarlarliello v. Schacter* [1993] SCR 119; *Smith v. Tweedale* (1995), 4 BCLR (3d) 324 (CA).
392. *Reibl, supra* note 166; *Hopp, supra* note 168; *White v. Turner* (1981), 120 DLR (3d) 269 at 282–290 (Ont. HC), affirmed (1982), 47 OR (2d) 764 (SC).
393. *Meyer Estate v. Rogers* (1991), 78 DLR (4th) 307 (Ont. Gen. Div.); *Arndt, supra* note 211; *Rayner v. Knickle* (1991), 274 APR 214 (PEICA); *Malinowski, supra* note 348.
394. *Kenny v. Lockwood* (1931) [1932] 1 DLR 507 (Ont. CA); *Videto v. Kennedy* (1981), 17 CCLT 307 (Ont. CA).
395. *Dunn v. North York General Hosp.* [1989] OJ No. 402 (Ont. HC); *Parkinson v. MacDonald* (1987), 40 CCLT 90 (BCSC); *Stewart v. Ross* (1988), 64 Sask. R. 271 (Sask. QB). But *see also Solomon v. Ali*, 2018 ONSC 3287, 295 ACWS (3d) 423.

D. Alternatives

203. The physician has a duty to inform the patient about any reasonable alternatives to the proposed treatment or test. The patient has a right to be able to compare the various reasonable alternatives and the potential consequences of those alternatives.[396]

E. Prognosis if Treatment or Test Is Declined

204. The patient has a right to be informed about the consequences of a refusal of treatment.[397]

F. Prognosis with Treatment

205. The patient is entitled to be informed about the impact and potential consequences of the proposed treatment, and the prognosis if he or she proceeds with the treatment.[398]

G. Disclosure of Conflicts of Interest

206. The fiduciary nature of the physician's relationship with the patient requires the physician to disclose to the patient any conflicts of interest the treatment may pose.[399] The existence of a remuneration arrangement whereby the physician may be seen to be in a position of conflict of interest should be disclosed to the patient.[400] Similarly, a conflict of interest arising from a physician's research interest in the treatment must be disclosed.

IV. Causation of Damage Complexities

207. While a test for informed consent which is based on the standard of the reasonable patient in the position of the plaintiff carries a greater likelihood of a finding of negligence than did the professional standard, it does not necessarily lead to

---

396. *See* LE Rozovsky & FA Rozovsky, *supra* note 360 at 10; *Zimmer v. Ringrose* (1981), 16 CCLT 51 at 60 (Alta. CA), leave to appeal to SCC refused [1981] SCCA No. 200; *Haughian v. Paine* (1986) [1987] 4 WWR 97 (Sask. CA), leave to appeal to SCC refused [1987] 6 WWR LIX (n.) (SCC); *Hopp, supra* note 168 at 81; *Solomon, supra* note 394.
397. *Reibl, supra* note 166; *Brushett v. Cowan* (1990), 69 DLR (4th) 743 (Nfld. CA); *Arndt, supra* note 211; *see* LE Rozovsky & FA Rozovsky, *supra* note 360 at 11–12.
398. *Arndt, supra* note 211.
399. *McInerney, supra* note 321.
400. *Kangas v. Parker* [1976] 5 WWR 25 (Sask. QB), affirmed [1978] 5 WWR 667 (CA); *Henderson v. Johnston* (1956), 5 DLR (2d) 524 at 533–534 (Ont. HC), affirmed (1958), 11 DLR (2d) 19 (CA), affirmed (1959), 19 DLR (2d) 201 (SCC).

a greater likelihood of liability on the part of the physician. This is because a negligence finding does not end the matter; it must also be established that any loss suffered by the patient was actually caused by the physician's negligent failure to adequately inform.[401]

208. If a court determines that a patient had not been properly informed about the material risks and alternatives relating to a particular treatment prior to having given consent, the causation test will fail if the court goes on to find that the patient would have consented even had he or she been properly informed. With *Reibl*, the Supreme Court introduced what is known as a "modified objective test" of causation. Under this test, courts have to determine if the reasonable patient in the patient's circumstances (thus with potential unique personal interests) would have consented to the treatment.[402] A trier of fact may take into account a plaintiff patient's own testimony as to the decision he or she would have made if full disclosure had been given, but such purely subjective factors would not be given final weight. Other more objective evidence as to both the plaintiff's actual state of mind at the time of consent, and the reasonableness of the plaintiff's idiosyncratic beliefs, will be more determinative in the court's analysis.[403] Still, the Supreme Court suggested that this modified objective test involves a combination of objective and subjective factors.

209. One of the factors that makes it unlikely to find causation in the context of violations of informed consent is the fact that the courts tend to presume that patients follow the advice and recommendation provided by their physicians. In other words: patients would unlikely have decided differently if the physician had given more information.[404]

210. While the Supreme Court rejected the subjective test for causality in general informed consent cases, it did introduce it in cases of informed consent failures involving the prescription of use of pharmaceuticals and medical devices (product liability cases). In the 1995 case of *Hollis v. Dow Corning Corporation*,[405] the Supreme Court first specified that the duty of disclosure of manufacturers is higher or more demanding than the duty of physicians in standard medical negligence cases, because of their "enormous informational advantage." "[I]t is reasonable and just," the Court stated, "to require manufacturers, under the law of tort, to make clear, complete and current informational disclosure to consumers concerning the

401. *Arndt, supra* note 211; *Reibl, supra* note 166; *Hopp, supra* note 168; *Kooijman, supra* note 179.

402. *Reibl, supra* note 166; *Rawlings v. Lindsay* (1982), 20 CCLT 301 at 306–309 (BCSC); *Mang v. Moscovitz* (1982), 37 AR 221 at 270–271 (QB); *Gonda v. Kerbel* (1982), 24 CCLT 222 at 223 (Ont. HC); *Kooijman, supra* note 179. *See* generally A Meagher, Marr & R Meagher, *supra* note 165 at 70–79.

403. *See* the minority concurring and dissenting judgments in *Arndt, supra* note 211; and the overturned decision of the British Columbia Court of Appeal in *Arndt v. Smith* (1995), 126 DLR (4th) 705 for endorsements of the subjective test of adequate disclosure. *See also* GB Robertson, "Informed Consent 20 Years Later" (2003) Health LJ (Spec Ed).

404. G Robertson, "Informed Consent Ten Years Later: The Impact of Reibl v Hughes" (1991) 70:3 Can Bar Rev 423 at 435.

405. *Hollis v. Dow Corning* [1995] 4 S.C.R. 634 [*Hollis*].

risks inherent in the ordinary use of their products. A high standard for disclosure protects public health by promoting the right to bodily integrity, increasing consumer choice and facilitating a more meaningful doctor-patient relationship."[406]

211. The Court then also connected this to a subjective test for causation, according to which the courts have to inquire whether a particular patient would have consented had she been informed of all the risks involved. The Court acknowledged that patients, once harmed, might rarely think in hindsight that they would still have consented had they been properly informed, which was the reason why the Court stuck to a "modified objective" test in *Reibl*. But the Court now found that "in a suit against a manufacturer for failure to warn this concern can be adequately addressed at the trial level through cross-examination and through a proper weighing by the trial judge of the relevant testimony."[407] Why this could not be done in standard medical negligence cases is not clear from the decision. The Court admitted that this imposition of a stricter standard, and a more demanding subjective test from the perspective of the manufacturer, was justified for "policy" reasons.[408]

§4. PRIVACY

I. Medical Information and Records: Confidentiality and Disclosure

A. *Introduction*

212. Generally, the term "medical record" refers to information on the health of an individual under treatment or care and includes a record of the diagnostic and treatment services provided to the individual by the health-care provider and the institution. The term is used interchangeably with the terms "patient record" or "health record."[409]

213. What must be contained in a medical record is often addressed by legislation or hospital bylaw. Provincial statutes may require a hospital board to maintain records identifying the patient, the patient's history, diagnosis, orders for treatment, treatments received, consultations, etc., although this may vary among provinces.[410]

406. *Ibid.*, at para. 26.
407. *Hollis*, *supra* note 404 at para. 46.
408. *Ibid.*
409. For a more extensive discussion of the legal issues surrounding medical records in Canada *see* LE Rozovsky & FA Rozovsky, *The Canadian Law of Patient Records* (Toronto: Butterworths, 1984) and the Royal Commission of Inquiry into the Confidentiality of Health Records in Ontario, *Report of the Commission of Inquiry into the Confidentiality of Health Information* (Toronto: Queen's Printer, 1980) (Commissioner: The Hon. Mr. Justice Horace Krever). *See also* Elaine Gibson, "Health Information: Privacy, Confidentiality and Access" in Joanna N Erdman, Vanessa Gruben & Erin Nelson, eds., *Canadian Health Law and Policy,* 5th ed. (Toronto: LexisNexis, 2017) at 207 and NJ Inions, LE Tran and LE Rozovsky, *Canadian Health Information: A Practical Legal and Risk Management Guide,* 4th ed. (Toronto: LexisNexis, 2018).
410. *See Hospital Standards Regulation*, Sask Reg 331/79, s. 12; NB Reg 92-84, s. 20, made pursuant to the *Hospital Act*; *Operation of Approved Hospitals Regulation*, Alta Reg 247/90, s. 13.

The hospital is responsible for ensuring that the attending physician or any other person providing diagnostic or treatment services to a patient keeps a record of the service provided. Hospitals may incorporate the legislative requirements into their own operating bylaws. Regulations enacted under the federal *Controlled Drugs and Substances Act* require hospitals and pharmacists to keep detailed records of the dispensing of certain controlled substances.[411] Such records may have to be maintained in a separate log and will include the name of the patient who received the narcotic, the name of the practitioner prescribing it, and other details about the prescription and its dispensing.[412]

B. *Standards of Medical Record Keeping*

214. Standards of medical record keeping may be established by current practices as maintained by provincial and federal health records associations, hospital bylaws,[413] hospital accreditation standards,[414] agencies controlling special activities such as research, and legislation. A number of provinces have enacted legislation setting forth requirements as to how and when medical information is to be recorded, who is responsible for recording it, and who signs the record. In Alberta the medical record of a hospital patient must be legible, accurate and completed and signed by the attending physician. If a patient receives out-patient services the record must be completed within twenty-four hours. A physician's patient orders must be in writing and dated and signed by the physician. The physician may dictate the orders to a nurse or other authorized person who must sign the order. The physician must then countersign the order within twenty-four hours.[415]

215. Medical records must be as accurate as possible since record keeping is one of the means of communication among health-care providers and therefore an essential part of the patient's treatment. Further, the accuracy of medical records may impact upon the legal liability of a hospital or health-care provider should a patient sue for negligence or medical malpractice.[416] Inadequate record keeping

411. The federal *Controlled Drugs and Substances Act,* SC 1996, c 19 came into force on May 14, 1997, and was enacted to consolidate Canada's drug control policy under a single piece of legislation. It repealed the *Narcotic Control Act* and Parts III and IV of the *Food and Drugs Act,* but according to s. 44 of the *Interpretation Act,* the *Narcotic Control Regulations* and relevant *Food and Drugs Regulations* are deemed to remain in force and to have been made under the new act. This will be the case until they are either repealed or explicitly replaced by new regulations enacted under the *Controlled Drugs and Substances Act.* The new Act has generally maintained existing information requirements placed on the importation, preparation, sale and disposal of restricted and controlled drugs and substances.
412. *Narcotic Control Regulations,* CRC, c 1041.
413. Alta Reg 247/90, s. 16(e).
414. *See* Accreditation Canada (formerly the Canadian Council on Health Services Accreditation). Current accreditation standards are available online: accreditation.ca/standards/.
415. Alta Reg 247/90, ss. 13–14. *See also* Sask Reg 331/79, s. 13.
416. In *Bergen v. Sturgeon General Hospital* (1984), 28 CCLT 155 (Alta. QB), inadequate record keeping was found to form part of the negligence of the hospital.

may prevent the facility or provider from being able to defend itself from such a lawsuit. Furthermore, the lack of evidence itself may form the basis of an action.[417]

C. Electronic Health Records

216. Jurisdictions across Canada are investing significant resources in the development of Electronic Health Record (EHR) systems. A national organization, Canada Health Infoway, was created in 2001 to facilitate the development and adoption of EHR systems in all provinces and territories with compatible standards and communications technologies.

217. EHR systems allow for large data banks, computerized laboratory analysis and diagnostics, and medical record linkage between systems. This may facilitate communication of patient information, potentially improve patient care, and increase cost efficiency. But it also raises a number of legal issues including: the confidentiality of health record information, the improper recording of or tampering with the information, and the unauthorized or improper dissemination of health record information.[418]

218. Since the turn of the century, numerous information and privacy laws have been enacted, many of which impact the health-care sector. These statutes typically confer rights to request access to and correct records and impose frameworks that govern collection, use and disclosure of information. While every jurisdiction in Canada has information and privacy laws that apply in the public sector (to hospitals and health authorities, in some provinces), the provinces of Alberta, Ontario, Manitoba, Saskatchewan, British Columbia, NB, Newfoundland and Labrador, Prince Edward Island, and Nova Scotia, as well as Yukon Territory and the Northwest Territories have enacted health information-specific privacy legislation as well.[419] This legislation typically applies to various health-care providers, including physicians, government health departments, and health-care facilities. Additionally, as of January 1, 2004, federal privacy legislation, the Personal Information Protection and Electronic Documents Act (PIPEDA), applies to every organization that

---

417. *See Meyer v. Gordon* (1981), 17 CCLT 1 (BCSC) and *Wipfli v. Britten* (1982), 22 CCLT 104 (BCSC), reversed in part on other grounds (1984) 13 DLR (4th) 169 (BCCA). *See also* Robertson & Picard, *supra* note 165 at 627–632.

418. LE Rozovsky & FA Rozovsky, *supra* note 408 at 85–91. *See also* Noela J Inions, Leanne E Tran & Lorne E Rozovsky, "Electronic Communications and Health Information" in *Canadian Health Information: A Practical Legal and Risk Management Guide,* 4th ed. (Toronto: LexisNexis, 2018) at 145–157; Canada Health Infoway, *Digital Health Blueprint: Enabling Coordinated & Collaborative Health Care* (Canada: Canada Health Infoway, 2016).

419. *See Health Information Act,* RSA 2000, c H-5; *Personal Health Information Protection Act, 2004,* SO 2004, c 3, Sch. A; *Personal Health Information Act,* CCSM c P33.5; *Health Information Protection Act,* SS 1999, c H-0.021; *E-Health (Personal Health Information Access and Protection of Privacy) Act,* SBC 2008, c 38; *Personal Health Information Privacy and Access Act,* SNB 1993, c P-7.05; *Personal Health Information Act,* SNL 2008, c P-7.01; *Health Information Act,* SPEI 2014, c 31; *Personal Health Information Act,* SNS 2010, c 41; *Health Information Privacy and Management Act,* SY 2013, c 16; *Health Information Act,* SNWT 2014, c 2.

collects, uses or discloses personal information, including health information, in the course of commercial activities within a province.[420] If provinces have adopted privacy legislation that is substantially similar to PIPEDA, the federal government may exempt those provinces from PIPEDA's application. As of June 2019, legislation in Alberta, Quebec, British Columbia, Ontario, NB, Nova Scotia, and Newfoundland and Labrador has been declared substantially similar.[421] In some of these provinces, it is only part of the privacy law that is declared substantially similar. In Ontario, for example, only its Personal Health Information and Protection Act is declared substantially similar, which means that when it comes to health information in the province, PIPEDA will not apply, while PIPEDA will still apply to other forms of commercial information.

§5. Secrecy

I. Provider Duty to Maintain Confidentiality

A. *Sources of the Duty*

219. Physicians are advised to fulfill their duty of confidentiality to their patients:

> by keeping identifiable patient information confidential; collecting, using, and disclosing only as much health information as necessary to benefit the patient; and sharing information only to benefit the patient and within the patient's circle of care. Exceptions include situations where the informed consent of the patient has been obtained for disclosure or as provided for by law.[422]

220. The "ethical" nature of the duty to maintain confidentiality has long been upheld by the courts in Canada, and the relationship between a doctor and a patient has been described by the SCC as being of a "fiduciary" nature.[423] The Court stated that "certain duties do arise from the special relationship of trust and confidence between doctor and patient. Among these are the duty of the doctor to act with utmost good faith and loyalty, and to hold information received from or about a patient in confidence."[424]

420. SC 2000, c 5.
421. *See* SOR/2014-219; SOR/2003-374; SOR/2004-220; SOR/2005-399; SOR/2011-265; SOR/2016-62; SI/2012-72.
422. Canadian Medical Association, *CMA Code of Ethics and Professionalism*, online (pdf): *Canadian Medical Association* https://policybase.cma.ca/documents/policypdf/PD19-03.pdf at s. 18.
423. *McInerney, supra* note 321 at 423.
424. *McInerney, supra* note 321.

B. Statutory Immunities

221. The confidential nature of the relationship between the health-care professional and the patient is also set out in a number of provincial statutes. Such legislation may impose a positive duty upon the health-care provider either to hold in confidence all patient information[425] or to release such information only if required to do so by paramount legislation or by order of a court.[426] Immunity may also be extended by legislation if disclosure of the confidential information is necessary to eliminate or reduce a "significant risk of serious bodily harm" to the patient or a third party.[427]

C. Privilege

222. In Canada, disclosures made to a physician by his or her patient during the course of treatment traditionally have not been protected by legal privilege, though a court could exercise its discretion and disallow a particular question which might elicit confidential information from a physician.[428] While the production of medical records may still be compelled, especially in criminal proceedings where an accused's right to make full answer and defense are at stake,[429] SCC cases have decided that communications made within the physician/patient relationship are at least potentially entitled to common law privilege on a case-by-case basis.[430] Any claim for privilege will be analyzed in terms of the four-part "Wigmore" test, which has long been applied in Canadian jurisprudence. The test recognizes privilege with respect to particular communications when they have originated in a confidence between two parties, confidentiality is an essential adjunct to the relationship between the parties, the relationship itself is one which in the opinion of the community should be sedulously fostered, and the interests served by protecting against disclosure outweigh the interests served by pursuit of the truth and the correct disposal of litigation.[431] A majority of the court also rejected an "all or nothing" approach to the attachment of privilege; even if a court finds against a claim of complete privilege, it may order production to be made in accordance with a partial privilege, and limit how many copies can be made or who may see the documents.[432]

223. When a party to either criminal or civil proceedings seeks to compel the production of therapeutic records for which a common law privilege is claimed, the

---

425. *See*, for example, the now repealed *Midwifery Regulation,* Alta Reg 328/94, s. 10(f).
426. *Ibid.*
427. *See* for example, *Personal Health Information Protection Act*, SO 2004, c 3, Sch. A, ss. 40, 71.
428. *See Dembie v. Dembie* (1963), 21 RFL 46 (Ont. HC) and *G v. G* [1964] 1 OR 361 (HC).
429. *R v. O'Connor* [1995] 4 SCR 411, 130 DLR (4th) 235; *R v. Carosella* (1997), 142 DLR (4th) 595 (SCC).
430. *M(A) v. Ryan* (1997), 143 DLR (4th) 1 (SCC) [*M(A)*].
431. JH Wigmore, *Evidence,* vol. 8, McNaughton rev. ed. (Boston: Little, Brown, 1961), s. 2285 at 527; *Slavutych v. Baker* [1976] 1 SCR 254, 55 DLR (3d) 224.
432. *M(A), supra* note 429 at paras. 33–34.

court must undertake a balancing of the various interests at stake. Such a balancing involves weighing numerous factors: a plaintiff or alleged victim's privacy rights; society's interest in the fair and proper disposition of litigation; and a defendant's right to fundamental justice, which requires knowledge of all information relevant to the case against him or her so that full answer and defense can be made. In the criminal context, the accused person's right to make full answer and defense is a particularly heavy factor, since personal liberty is at stake in addition to property and reputation. To determine whether privilege should attach to any particular document, the court must consider the particular circumstances of each case, as well as the document's relevance in the ongoing litigation. Continually evolving factors such as current social concerns, the development of new medical therapies, and the entrenchment of rights under the *Canadian Charter of Rights and Freedoms* may also influence how the court will weigh competing rights and interests.[433]

224. In the criminal context, an earlier SCC decision has considered the kinds of factors which legitimately could be considered by a court that is engaged in the balancing of rights and interests raised by an application for the disclosure of therapeutic records in a sexual assault case.[434] The intensely confidential nature of such records does not affect the Crown's obligation to disclose such materials to the defense when the records are already in the hands of the Crown. However, when the records remain in the possession of third parties, a constitutional right of privacy is raised. The accused must satisfy the initial threshold requirement of establishing that the records in question are relevant to the proceedings and should be produced for the court. Once this first step is passed, the judge must examine the records to determine how their disclosure or non-production would affect competing rights. The SCC found that the judge should consider the following factors:

> (1) the extent to which the record is necessary for the accused to make full answer and defence; (2) the probative value of the record in question; (3) the nature and extent of the reasonable expectation of privacy vested in that record; (4) whether production of the record would be premised upon any discriminatory belief or bias; (5) the potential prejudice to the complainant's dignity, privacy or security of the person that would be occasioned by production of the record in question.[435]

A bare majority of the Supreme Court also decided that the judge should not take account of "society's interest in encouraging the reporting of sexual offenses and the acquisition of treatment by victims" or "the effect on the integrity of the trial process," as these concerns could be addressed more appropriately through other means.[436]

433. *M(A), supra* note 429.
434. *R v. O'Connor* (1995), 130 DLR (4th) 235 (SCC).
435. *Ibid.*, at 303.
436. *Ibid.*, at 258.

225. After the decision in *R. v. O'Connor,* the federal government initiated amendments to the *Criminal Code* regarding the procedure to be followed when an accused applies for the production of personal records and the factors a court should consider in compelling or refusing production. At present, section 278.1–278.9 of the *Criminal Code* governs the production of personal records about victims and witnesses in sexual offense proceedings. The provisions place the onus on the accused to establish that the records sought are likely relevant to an issue at trial and require the trial judge to carefully scrutinize applications and determine production in accordance with a two-part process involving a consideration of both the accused's rights to full answer and defense and the victim's rights to privacy and equality. The procedure to be followed is also set out in the *Code* and includes safeguards for the victim's privacy including an *in camera* (closed) hearing, non-compellability of the victim at the hearing, a publication ban on the proceedings and the contents of the application, editing of the records (where ordered to be produced) to delete irrelevant personal information and the imposition of other appropriate conditions on production.[437] These provisions were upheld as constitutional by the SCC in *R v. Mills*.[438]

D. Liability for Breaches of Confidentiality

1. Statutory

226. Liability for a breach of confidentiality by a health-care professional may be imposed by statute. Disclosing information may be statutorily defined as unskilled practice or professional misconduct, resulting in a penalty ranging anywhere from disciplinary action to the imposition of a fine.[439] Legislation governing the operation of hospitals or other health-care facilities may also impose liability upon a person who releases or discloses information from the facility's records to an unauthorized person.[440] Some provinces have enacted "privacy" legislation which permits an individual to commence a civil suit against anyone who violates his or her privacy. What amounts to an invasion of privacy is not defined, however, but left to the court's discretion.[441] The statute may require that a violation be willful, in which case it would not apply to a negligent disclosure or breach of confidentiality.

437. For an analysis of issues raised by health records in the criminal context, *see* Wayne Renke, "The Confidentiality of Health Information in the Criminal Law" (1998) 6:3 Health L Rev 3.
438. [1999] 3 SCR 668, 180 DLR (4th) 1.
439. *See* for example, *Professional Misconduct,* Ont Reg 856/93, made under the *Medicine Act,* SO 1991, c 30.
440. *See* for example, Ontario *Hospital Management Regulation,* RRO 1990, Reg 965.
441. *See* for example, British Columbia *Privacy Act,* RSBC 1996, c 373.

2. Common Law Remedies

227. In Canada there have been very few cases addressing the wrongful or unwarranted disclosure of medical information. Notwithstanding this, there are a variety of causes of action that might be available to a patient if such disclosure should occur, including: defamation, negligence, breach of contract, breach of confidence, and breach of fiduciary duty.[442]

228. These causes of action are not mutually exclusive, and depending on the circumstances of the breach of confidentiality, a court presumably could find for the plaintiff on a number of causes. For example, where a hospital includes a plaintiff's name on an internal list of persons for whom bodily fluid precautions need to be taken, the hospital's failure to prevent the list from external circulation may constitute a negligent failure to safeguard the plaintiff's personal medical information as well as a breach of contract for the release of private information, but not constitute an act of recoverable defamation because no malice was involved.[443] Cases so far have not drawn a careful distinction between liability in contract and in tort for the failure to maintain the confidentiality of medical records.[444]

229. An action in defamation requires the patient to establish that false information that is harmful to his or her reputation has been published without consent.[445] The usefulness of this cause of action is questionable; however, as the defense of qualified privilege may serve to protect the defendant, regardless of the information's truth. Utilizing this defense the defendant is able to plead that the disclosure occurred without malicious intent and in answer to a paramount obligation, such as public health legislation requiring notification of the occurrence of an infectious disease.

230. A patient whose personal information has been disclosed without his or her consent may also bring an action claiming breach of contract. Courts have held that the physician-patient relationship is one of contract, although that contract is not normally reduced to writing. Given the historical nature of the duty of confidentiality it is probable that a court would imply a requirement of confidentiality as a term of the contract.[446]

231. Health institutions such as hospitals may also be subject to such a contractual term of confidentiality. Where this term is breached through the hospital's

442. These are discussed in detail in Sanda Rodgers-Magnet, "Common Law Remedies for Disclosure of Confidential Medical Information" in FM Steel & SM Rodgers-Magnet, eds., *Issues in Tort Law* (Toronto: Carswell, 1983) at 265.
443. *Peters-Brown v. Regina* [1996] 1 WWR 337 (Sask. QB), affirmed [1997] 1 WWR 638 (CA) [*Peters-Brown*].
444. *Ibid.*
445. *Halls v. Mitchell* [1928] SCR 125.
446. Irvine, Osborne & Shariff, *supra* note 165 at 241.

release of private information, a patient can recover damages since his or her resulting emotional distress is a foreseeable consequence of the breach.[447]

232. Similarly, an employee of a health-care provider may also have a contractual duty to safeguard confidential health information as part of their employment relationship. In one case,[448] a nurse sent an anonymous letter to a magazine about late-term abortions of fetuses with genetic defects that were performed at the hospital at which she worked. In this letter, the nurse included minutes of a staff meeting that identified where in the hospital the abortion procedures took place and also identified certain nurses and physicians who were involved in carrying out the procedures. After receiving the letter, a reporter interviewed nurses and obtained a copy of an internal staff memorandum that named two doctors who performed the abortions. The hospital initiated a court action to compel the magazine to return copies of the documents and not print identifying information. In its ruling, the court described the disclosure as "a flagrant breach" and stated that a nurse has a duty "when she commences employment … to treat as confidential, not only the information to which she has access in the hospital records but all information with respect to patients, the affairs of the hospital and the medical staff." The court also expressed concern that "a nurse—or any other employee—should not be entitled to disclose information with respect to what doctors perform what procedures. there is a very real risk to doctors who perform abortions."[449]

233. Another potential remedy is that of the tort of negligence. The rationale underlying this cause of action is that the disclosure of confidential information and the breach of confidentiality is a failure on the physician's part to maintain the standard of care to which he or she is subject. Consequently if foreseeable injuries are suffered by the patient as a result of the breach the physician will be liable.[450]

234. This duty has also been applied to hospitals and other health institutions. A hospital would likely not be held liable for distributing health information to its staff members as necessary, for example, compiling a list, for limited circulation within the hospital, of persons for whom special care was needed in the handling of bodily fluids. However, the failure to safeguard such a list from its foreseeable notice and acquisition by non-hospital staff will constitute negligence.[451]

235. One further action by which liability may be imposed upon a physician is that based upon the fiduciary nature of the physician-patient relationship. As a result of this relationship the physician is duty bound to act with utmost good faith and loyalty and to hold information received from or about a patient in confidence.[452] If

447. *Peters-Brown, supra* note 442.
448. *Calgary Regional Health Authority v. United Western Communications Ltd. (c.o.b. Alberta Report Magazine)* (1999), 75 Alta L.R. (3d) 326 (QB).
449. *Ibid.,* at paras. 7, 15–16.
450. Rodgers-Magnet, *supra* note 441 at 292–294.
451. *Peters-Brown, supra* note 442.
452. *McInerney, supra* note 321 at 423, 425.

the physician fails to perform that duty or to act in accordance with his or her fiduciary obligations, then he or she breaches the duty owed to the patient, and the court could award damages against the physician. There is recent case law to suggest that damages are an appropriate remedy for a breach of fiduciary duty and may be awarded.[453]

236. Additionally, the Ontario Court of Appeal (ONCA) has recently recognized a new common law tort of "intrusion upon seclusion," or invasion of privacy.[454] The essential elements of this cause of action are that (1) the defendant's conduct must be intentional or reckless; (2) the defendant must have invaded the plaintiff's "private affairs or concerns" without lawful justification; and (3) a reasonable person would regard the invasion as "highly offensive causing distress, humiliation or anguish."[455] It was subsequently applied in the case of a nurse improperly accessing and disclosing hospital patient records, wherein the Ontario courts clarified that the existence of the *Personal Health Information Protection Act* does not preclude a plaintiff from asserting a common law claim for intrusion upon seclusion.[456]

E. Provider Duties to Disclose Patient Information to Third Parties

1. Patient Consent

237. The duty of confidentiality or of non-disclosure that is owed by a medical practitioner to the patient may be waived by the patient. The information belongs to the patient, is normally under the patient's control, and therefore the patient may decide to make it available to others. It is a strongly recommended general practice; however, for practitioners to obtain the patient's consent or request to release the information in writing so as to protect themselves from any subsequent claim that the disclosure was unauthorized. The patient may *expressly* consent to the release of information as in a personal injury action where the injured party agrees to release medical information both to his or her lawyer as well as to the defendant's lawyer. More importantly, it has been held that when a patient puts his or her health at issue the right to confidentiality has been waived.[457] However, this waiver has also been held to be "[not] any wider than the medical matters at issue in the lawsuit" and other matters relevant to or bearing on them.[458] In some situations a

453. *See Canson Enterprises Ltd et al v. Boughton & Co et al* (1991), 85 DLR (4th) 129 (SCC) in which damages were awarded against the defendants, a firm of barristers and solicitors, as a result of their breach of the fiduciary duty they owed to their client, the plaintiff. Subsequent to *Canson*, lower courts have also awarded punitive damages for breach of fiduciary duty if warranted by the defendant's conduct. For further discussion, *see* CED 4th (online), *Damages*, "Damages in Equity" (V), at §589–594.

454. *Jones v. Tsige*, 2012 ONCA 32.

455. *Ibid.*, at para. 71.

456. *Hopkins v. Kay*, 2015 ONCA 112, leave to appeal to SCC refused, 2015 CarswellOnt 16503 (WL).

457. *Hay v. University of Alberta Hospital* [1990] 5 WWR 78 (Alta. QB).

458. *Swirski v. Hachey* [1996] 5 WWR 214 (BCSC). *See also Burgess (Litigation Guardian of) v. Wu* (2003), 68 OR (3d) 710 (Ont. SCJ).

health-care practitioner may *imply* that the patient has consented to the release of medical information, or at least the sharing of it, such as when a physician consults with other practitioners or specialists regarding the patient's care.

2. Statutory Disclosures

238. There are many statutory exceptions to the general rule of non-disclosure of patient information without consent. These reflect the balance that has been struck between the individual's personal interests and those of society. The clearest example of this is found in public health legislation which requires the disclosure of communicable diseases.[459] Public health legislation requires that the provincial medical health officer be informed when certain communicable diseases including Acquired Immune Deficiency Syndrome (AIDS)/HIV occur. Statutory disclosure requirements have been upheld under Canada's *Charter of Rights and Freedoms.* In one case, the Red Cross obtained positive AIDS results from ten-year-old frozen blood samples that had been stored and tested without donor consent. The positive results were reported to the donors and to the public health authorities, as required by the province's *Health Protection and Promotion Act.* The court found that the donors' reasonable expectation of privacy and rights to life, liberty and security of the person under the *Charter* had been violated, but the violation was not contrary to the principles of fundamental justice, and in any event, were justified under section 1 of the *Charter* as a measure necessary for the public health.[460]

239. Individuals are also obligated to notify a police officer, coroner, or medical examiner as to any facts or circumstances which may suggest that the death of an individual was not natural. In addition, a medical examiner may examine records relating to a deceased person without obtaining the consent of the deceased's representative.[461] Statutes aimed at protecting children may also require the reporting of any circumstances which indicate a child may be abused or in need of protection.[462] Some provinces have legislation requiring a physician to inform the Registrar of Motor Vehicles, or its equivalent, of the name, address and clinical condition of any individual whose condition may make it dangerous to operate a motor vehicle.[463]

240. Disclosure may be permitted for certain administrative purposes, and information may be exchanged between administrative bodies or government departments without the patient's explicit consent; however, privacy statutes are placing greater restrictions on disclosure of personal information. It may also be disclosed

459. *See* for example, the *Public Health Act,* RSA 2000, c P-37; *Public Health Act,* SBC 2008, c 28.
460. *Canadian AIDS Society v. Ontario* (1995), 25 OR (3d) 388 (Gen. Div.), affirmed (1996) 31 OR (3d) 798 (CA), leave to appeal to SCC refused (1997), 216 NR 159 (note).
461. *Coroners Act,* RSO 1990, c 37 and *Fatality Inquiries Act,* SM 1989-90, c 30 [CCSM c. F52].
462. *See* the *Child, Youth and Family Services Act,* SO 2017, c 14 and the *Child, Youth and Family Enhancement Act,* RSA 2000, c C-12.
463. *See Highway Traffic Act,* RSO 1990, c H.8, s. 203.

if it is necessary for the purposes of disciplinary or peer review proceedings.[464] Most of these statutes provide that the information is only to be disclosed to a specific individual for a specific purpose and any disclosure beyond that is prohibited.

241. Contrary to general opinion, a physician or health-care provider is not required by statute to disclose to the police medical information relating to a patient's past or potential criminal behavior, the exception being incidences of child abuse. However, statutes in some provinces require facilities or health-care professionals who treat gunshot (and sometimes stab) wounds that are not self- or unintentionally inflicted to notify local police.[465] Otherwise providing medical information to police without the consent of the patient has been held to violate the physician's common law duty of confidentiality to the patient.[466] It is questionable, however, whether a claim against the health-care provider for such disclosure would be successful if he or she did so in good faith and as a result of public safety concerns.[467]

242. While a physician's voluntary provision of information regarding his or her patient's confession of crime could well be a breach of the physician's duty of confidentiality, police use of the information itself does not necessarily violate the patient's rights. In *R. v. Spidell,*[468] a physician, under the mistaken impression that he or she was legally obligated to do so, volunteered information to the police about a patient's driving and state of intoxication. An officer arrived, observed indicia of intoxication, and requested a blood sample from the patient. The patient refused and subsequently was charged and convicted of refusing to give a blood sample. Without finally deciding whether the doctor had violated his duty of confidentiality, the court found that the patient's reasonable expectation of privacy had not been violated since "information does not become 'medical' in nature simply because it was given to a doctor."[469] It remains to be seen whether such a distinction, between "medical" information and "neutral" information, would assist any physician defending himself or herself against a civil claim for violating a common law duty of confidentiality. Clearly such a duty is more obviously violated where a physician

---

464. *See Hospitals Act,* RSA 2000, c H-12, s. 24.
465. *See* for example, *Gunshot and Stab Wound Mandatory Disclosure Act,* SA 2009, c G-12; *Mandatory Gunshot Wounds Reporting Act, 2005,* SO 2005, c 9. Alberta's *Health Information Act,* RSA 2000, c H-5, s. 37.3, permits but does not require a custodian to disclose health information without consent to a police service where the custodian reasonably believes that the information relates to the possible commission of a criminal offense and that the disclosure will protect the health and safety of Albertans.
466. *R v. Dersch* [1993] 3 SCR 768, 85 CCC (3d) 1.
467. *See* Sharpe, *supra* note 129 at at 187–191. *See also* Wayne Renke, "The Confidentiality of Health Information in the Criminal Law" (1998) 6:3 Health L Rev 3 at 3–11; and Irvine, Osborne & Shariff, *supra* note 165 at 252–257.
468. *R v. Spidell,* 1996 NSCA 162, 107 CCC (3d) 348, leave to appeal to SCC refused (1997), 161 NSR (2d) 80 (note).
469. *Ibid.,* at 358.

or other health worker turns over specific medical information,[470] or is acting as an active agent of the state in gathering information or evidence from a patient.[471]

3. Duty to Warn Third Parties

243. Traditionally, a health-care provider was not obligated to warn third parties or the police of a possible danger posed by a patient. There is now a trend in the common law, however, toward the imposition of a duty to warn third parties. Physicians have also taken steps to recognize at least an ethical, if not legal, duty to warn third parties.[472] This trend has been influenced by the well-known U.S. case of *Tarasoff v. the Regent of the University of California*[473] in which a patient revealed his intention to kill a young woman to his psychologist, and then acted on his intention. The psychologist did not advise the individual of the threat, even though he alerted the university police and thus realized that there was a real likelihood that the patient would carry out the murder. The Court agreed with the family's claim that the psychologist had a duty to warn[474] the deceased of the danger (and not just the University authorities) and held that the duty was owed as a result of the existence of three criteria:

(1) the danger was immediate;
(2) the victim was identifiable;
(3) the danger was foreseeable and predictable given the behavior of the patient.

244. This case has been referred to in Canada, although not specifically applied.[475] In *Smith v. Jones*, the Supreme Court, referencing extensively to the case, ruled that public safety outweighed confidentiality obligations embedded in the solicitor-client and doctor-patient relation. The case was brought by a psychiatrist who was acting as an expert for the defense of a person accused of aggravated sexual assault of a sex-worker. As such, the case arose out of concerns for solicitor-client privilege. The accused had confided his intent to kidnap, rape and murder more sex-workers once released. The psychiatrist wanted to alert the court about the dangerousness of the accused. The Supreme Court ruled that there was an option (thus not a firm duty) to warn if: (1) there is an imminent risk; (2) to an identifiable person *or group of persons* (which seems to go further than *Tarasoff*); (3) of serious bodily harm or death.

---

470. *R v. Dersch* (1993), 85 CCC (3d) 1 at para. 22 (SCC).
471. *R v. Dorfer* (1996), 104 CCC (3d) 528 (BCCA).
472. *See Code of Ethics of the Canadian Medical Association.*
473. *Tarasoff v. The Regent of the University of California et al.* 551 P. 2d 334 (Calif. 1976).
474. For further discussion of duty to warn in Canadian health law, *see* Gibson, *supra* note 408 at Ch. 9. *See also* Elaine Gibson, "Privacy Protection and the Confidentiality of Psychiatric Health Care Records" in Jennifer A Chandler & Colleen M Flood (eds.), *Law and Mind: Mental Health Law and Policy in Canada* (Toronto: LexisNexis Canada Inc, 2016) at 170–183.
475. *See Wenden v. Trikha* (1991), 116 AR 81 (QB); *Smith v. Jones* [1999] 1 SCR 455.

245. The Quebec Court of Appeal dealt in *Liss v. Watters* (also referred to as *Watters v. White*) with an interesting case about the duty to warn about a genetic risk.[476] In this case, two physicians had diagnosed an infant patient with a debilitating neurological disease inherited through a gene carried by the boy's mother. The physicians had not informed family members, except for one of the child's parents, of the risk that they or another relative might pass the disease on to their children. Thirty years later, the boy's second cousin had a child with a sex-linked neurological disease with similar symptoms. The woman and her husband sued the physicians, alleging that if the relatives had been informed of the earlier diagnosis, she would have known of the risks of having a sick child and would have terminated her pregnancy. The trial judge had ruled that the duty to inform patients of genetic risks includes close relatives of those with a heritable genetic condition, and awarded the parents CAD 6,000,000 for losses connected to the birth of their child.[477] The Court of Appeal overturned the decision and found that informing the extended family members that they may be carriers of the disease would have disclosed privileged information about the infant patient's condition, thus violating the duty of confidentiality owed by a physician to their patient. The Court noted that while it was important for the family members to have learned of the diagnosis, "asserting this is a far cry from saying that [the physician] was obliged to see that [an extended family member] was informed, or that she had an entitlement to know the risks associated with the diagnosis, at the expense of the duty of confidentiality." In reaching these conçlusions, the Court of Appeal recognized that there "is a narrow category of exception whereby non-consensual disclosure is justified by considerations of public health, urgency or imminent danger," that it was "far from plain that the imperative to inform [the family member]" was in the order of imminent danger in this case, and that, as scholars have observed, "the imminence of danger criterion is not easily transposable to the genetic risk circumstance where, temporally, the threat faced is generally not of the moment."[478]

246. Some statutes impose an explicit obligation or duty to warn third parties. In Alberta, the *Health Information Act* permits but does not require any custodian of health information to disclose such information without consent upon a reasonable belief that disclosure will avert or minimize a risk of harm to the health or safety of a minor, or an imminent danger to the health or safety of any person.[479]

---

476. *Liss v. Watters*, 2012 QCCA 257, leave to appeal to SCC refused (2012), 439 N.R. 394 (note) [*Liss CA*]. For a good discussion, *see* Ma'n H. Zawati & Adrian Thorogood, "The Physician Who Knew Too Much: A Comment on *Watters v White*" (2014) 21 Health LJ 1. *See also* Trudo Lemmens, Lori Luther & Michael Hoy, "Genetic Information Access, a Legal Perspective: A Duty to Know or a Right Not to Know, and a Duty or Option to Warn?" *Encyclopedia of Life Sciences* (Chichester: John Willey & Sons, Ltd, 2015).

477. *Liss v. Watters*, 2010 QCCS 3309, rev'd 2012 QCCA 257, leave to appeal to SCC refused (2012), 439 N.R. 394 (note).

478. *Liss CA*, *supra* note 475. *See also* Zawati & Thorogood, *supra* note 475.

479. *Health Information Act*, RSA 2000, c H-5, s. 35(1)(m).

4. AIDS Confidentiality and Reporting

247. In Canada no distinction is drawn between AIDS and other communicable diseases. A health-care worker is obligated to report the occurrence of the disease to the Medical Officer of the province.[480] Such statutory reporting requirements, involving the release of confidential health information without a patient's prior consent or knowledge, have been upheld under the Canadian *Charter of Rights and Freedoms*.[481]

5. Quality of Care and Outcome Data

248. Medical records contain information relevant to investigations concerning the competency of health-care workers, the quality of care being delivered, the allocation of resources, and the success/failure (outcomes) of treatment. To a certain extent it is necessary that this information be made available to government and administration for the purpose of managing the health-care system. This is more relevant to the provincial governments as it is the responsibility of the provincial governments to maintain health-care insurance plans or medicare programs. Consequently, all provinces have legislation which allows for the release of certain information by the health-care worker or health facility for the purpose of obtaining payment for the service or treatment rendered to the patient. In addition, the legislation authorizes the release, for specified purposes, of information between government departments and the health-care provider, and between the government department and various disciplinary committees. The statutes usually impose a penalty if a person knowingly discloses information for purposes other than those expressed therein.[482]

§6. Complaints

249. If patients have a complaint regarding health-care workers' conduct or treatment they have several options. They may complain to the workers' professional association or the appropriate statutory regulating body. Alternatively, they may commence a civil action against the worker for negligence, breach of contract, or breach of fiduciary duty.[483]

480. *See* for example, *Communicable Diseases Regulation*, Alta Reg 238/1985, Sch. 1.
481. *Canadian AIDS Society v. Ontario* (1995), 25 OR (3d) 388 (Gen. Div.), affirmed (1996), 31 OR (3d) 798 (CA), leave to appeal to SCC refused (1997), 216 NR 159 (note).
482. *See* for example, the *Health Information Act*, RSA 2000, c H-5, s. 102; *Hospitals Act,* RSA 2000, c H-12; and the *Alberta Health Care Insurance Act,* RSA 2000, c H-5.
483. *See* Control over the Practice of Medicine, Part I, Chapter 3 *supra.*

§7. ACCESS TO MEDICAL RECORDS

I. Ownership of Records

250. Medical records contain information about the patient as revealed by the patient, and information that is acquired and recorded on behalf of the patient. The physician, institution or clinic that compiled the medical record owns the physical record and the patient is not entitled to the records themselves. However, as the records contain information that is highly private and which goes to the personal integrity and autonomy of the patient, the information remains the patient's own, to communicate or retain as he or she sees fit. The confiding of the information to the physician for medical purposes gives rise to an expectation that the patient's interest in and control of the information will continue. As a result, the patient has a qualified right of access to the information contained in the medical record.[484] Most provincial jurisdictions have enacted legislation requiring hospitals to maintain records regarding the treatment rendered to patients. These records are considered to be the physical property of the hospital.[485]

A. *Patient Access*

251. As a general rule patients have a right of access to their medical records. Correspondingly, the physician has an obligation to provide the information upon request. However, the right of access is not absolute. The fiduciary relationship between physician and patient is founded on trust and confidence. The physician is therefore obligated to act in the best interests of the patient. If the physician reasonably believes it is not in the patient's best interests to inspect his or her own medical records, the physician may deny access to the information. This discretion must be exercised only in extreme circumstances. In the ordinary case, records should be disclosed upon the request of the patient unless there is a significant likelihood of a substantial adverse effect on the physical, mental or emotional health of the patient, or harm to a third party.[486] The onus is on the physician to justify a denial of access. The general rule of access is also subject to the superintending jurisdiction of the court.[487] This statement of common law is now codified in statute

484. *McInerney, supra* note 321 at 423.
485. *See* for example, *Hospitals Act,* RSA 2000, c H-12, s. 24; *Hospital Act,* RSBC 1996, c 200, s. 51, and Saskatchewan *Health Facilities Licensing Regulation,* RRS c H-0.02, Reg 1 (1999).
486. *See Tuck v. Lam* (1988), 57 Alta. L.R. (2d) 323 (QB); *Butler v. Waterford Hospital* (1990), 80 Nfld. & PEIR 310 (Nfld. TD); *Choboter v. Reimer* (1983), 49 BCLR 59 (CA).
487. *McInerney, supra* note 321 at 423. *See also* Robertson & Picard, *supra* note 165 at 635–638.

law in jurisdictions with information and privacy legislation that applies to health-care providers.[488] The physician's common law discretion in the area of patient access to medical records is also recognized in the *Canadian Medical Association Code of Ethics and Professionalism.*[489]

B. Third-Party Access

252. It is generally accepted that in the absence of legislation, medical records are not to be disclosed to a third party without the express consent of the patient.[490] However, most jurisdictions in Canada have legislation which provides for access to medical records by certain individuals or which allows the hospital or physician to divulge the record for specific purposes. The records may be provided to a discipline committee, the child welfare authorities, the Worker's Compensation Board, or a provincial hospital insurance authority, for example.[491] These individuals may access the records without the patient's consent and without fear of recourse provided the information is utilized for the specified statutory purpose.

253. This type of access is also provided to the provincial Minister of Health. The Minister of Health in the Province of Alberta has the power to request that a hospital provide him or her with the medical records of its patients for the purposes of assessing the standard of care furnished to patients, improving hospital or medical procedures, medical research or for any other purpose considered by the Minister to be in the public interest.[492] Other government officials, such as medical examiners and coroners, may also have legislated access to a person's medical records. This information is not to be published, released or disclosed in any manner that would be detrimental to the personal interests, reputation, or privacy of a patient or the health-care provider.[493]

II. Retention of Medical Records

254. The requirements for retaining medical records may vary according to facility, practitioner and province. Hospitals in Alberta are required to keep diagnostic and treatment service records for a minimum period of ten years, and X-ray films for a minimum period of five years from the patient's discharge date. In addition, if the patient is a minor the records must be kept for a period of two years after

---

488. *See* for example, the *Health Information Act,* RSA 2000, c H-5, s. 11(1), and the *Personal Health Information Protection Act,* SO 2004, c 3, Sch. A, s. 52.
489. Section 19 directs physicians to "provide the patient or a third party with a copy of their medical record upon the patient's request, unless there is a compelling reason to believe that information contained in the record will result in substantial harm to the patient or others."
490. *Canada (Solicitor General) v. Ontario (Royal Commission of Inquiry into Confidentiality of Health Records)* [1981] 2 SCR 494.
491. *See Hospitals Act,* RSA 2000, c H-12, s. 24.
492. *Ibid.*
493. *See The Fatality Inquiries Act,* CCSM c F52 and the *Coroners Act,* RSO 1990, c C.37.

the patient reaches the age of eighteen years.[494] In British Columbia, the length of time for which a hospital record must be kept depends on the categorization of the records as primary (to be kept for ten years from the date of most recent discharge), secondary (to be retained for six years from the date of the treatment or services) or as transitory (to be retained for one year from the date of final completion of the patient's health record by the attending practitioner).[495]

255. Legislation which regulates a specific profession may also impose requirements for the retention of records. For example, in Nova Scotia, pharmacists are required to retain a patient's record for at least ten years following the date of their last transaction with that patient or ten years after the patient attains the age of majority, whichever is longer.[496]

256. In the absence of legislative guidelines, limitation periods for commencing an action against a hospital or health-care provider become relevant in determining how long a medical record should be retained. The limitation periods for actions against hospitals vary from province to province,[497] as they do for actions against doctors and other health-care professionals.

257. New information technologies have made the retention of medical records more convenient and cost-effective. Health institutions increasingly replace paper records with computer-based records and routinely store information in electronic forms from which a copy can be produced, a practice that is expressly allowed for by statute in some provinces.[498]

III. Discovery of Records

258. Medical records which document a patient's medical condition and treatment may be relevant in lawsuits involving the patient, such as actions for personal injuries against a third party and malpractice actions against a health-care provider. If the records are necessary to obtain a full understanding of the case, the patient may be required to produce them through the discovery process. In Canada, the parties to an action are entitled to full disclosure of the case which they have to meet. A party may be compelled to produce records, through the rules of civil procedure and an application to the court for disclosure, if he or she does not disclose the

494. *Operation of Approved Hospitals Regulation*, Alta. Reg. 247/90, s. 15.
495. *Hospital Act Regulation*, BC Reg 121/97, ss. 13–14.
496. *Qualification and Professional Accountability Regulations,* N.S. Reg. 144/2003, s. 37(1).
497. *See* paras. 104 and 105 for further discussion of limitation periods.
498. *See* for example, Ont. Reg. 114/94, s. 20.

records voluntarily.[499] The court will balance the right of the plaintiff patient to confidentiality against the right of a defendant to review all the relevant information concerning the plaintiff's claims.[500]

IV. Medical Records as Evidence

259. Because medical records are usually made at the time and in direct relation to specific medical acts, they are often important evidence in medical malpractice actions, personal injury claims, and criminal proceedings. They may be admitted into evidence with the consent of all parties, or the party wishing to use them may subpoena them. A plaintiff in a personal injury action may utilize the records as documentation of the injuries suffered and may voluntarily disclose them. Alternatively, and in the absence of the plaintiff's consent, the defendant may seek a court order compelling the production of the medical records relating to the plaintiff's injury on the basis that they are relevant evidence.[501]

260. The general rule is that if the medical record is made contemporaneously by someone who has personal knowledge of the matters being recorded, and who is under a duty to make the entry, then it should be received in evidence as prima facie proof of the facts stated therein. This does not, however, preclude a party from challenging the accuracy of the records or entries.[502]

261. Under Canadian common law, physician-patient communications traditionally have not been covered by legal privilege. That is, the court was free to compel medical treatment records and notes for production as if they were any other relevant document, despite the obviously confidential and trust-like nature of information received in the physician-patient relationship.[503] However, it was within the court's discretion to exclude any irrelevant evidence, and before producing the required records, a party to the action could black out confidential information that did not specifically relate to the subject matter of the litigation.[504] The SCC has indicated that the rules of privilege are flexible enough to accommodate current legal and social realities, so that at least a partial privilege may attach on a case-by-case basis to physician-patient communications, especially therapeutic psychiatric records in the context of a civil action.[505] A party to an action may still apply to the

499. *See* Ontario *Rules of Civil Procedure*, RRO 1990, Reg. 194, R. 30 and *Alberta Rules of Court*, Alta. Reg. 124/2010, Part 5.

500. *See* for example, *St. Louis et al v. Feleki et al.* (1990), 75 DLR (4th) 758 (Ont. Ct. Gen. Div.); *Hay v. University of Alberta Hospital* (1990), 69 DLR (4th) 755 (Alta. QB), and *P.(M.N.) (Next Friend of) v. Whitecourt General Hospital* [2001] 8 WWR 107 (Alta. QB)

501. *See* Inions, Tran & Rozovsky, *supra* note 408 at 53–72.

502. *Ares v. Venner* [1970] SCR 608.

503. *Evans v. Kent General Insurance Corp.* (1991), 78 DLR (4th) 428, leave to appeal to SCC refused (1991), 108 NSR (2d) 90 (note). *See also R v. O'Connor* [1995] 4 SCR 411, 130 DLR (4th) 235; *L.L.A. v. A.B.* [1995] 4 SCR 536, 130 DLR (4th) 422; and *R v. Carosella* [1997] 1 SCR 80, 142 DLR (4th) 595.

504. Inions, Tran & Rozovsky, *supra* note 408 at 53–72.

505. *M.(A.), supra* note 429. Also *see* Part II, s. 5 on Privilege.

court to compel production of any document, including therapeutic records, which may be relevant to issues that are central in the action, or to the testimonial competence or credibility of a witness.[506] However, the court may now apply the "Wigmore" criteria[507] to analyze whether partial privilege will attach to particular communications so as to limit or entirely prohibit their accessibility.

V. Alteration or Spoliation of Records

262. Of further concern is the alteration of records. If liability is at issue, for example, a negative inference may be drawn from any indication that someone has tampered with a record.

§8. Medical Fees

263. In Canada the provinces are responsible for maintaining a provincial health insurance plan that covers all medically necessary or required services. The physicians and other primary health-care providers bill the provincial health-care department for the services which they provide to the patient. The fees which they are able to charge the patient are established by the government and are set forth in legislation.[508] Physicians are not permitted to directly bill a patient for services unless they opt out of the provincial health-care plan, to the extent that the province allows private for-profit service of medically necessary services.

264. Some physicians operate private clinics offering such services as abortion and eye surgery. Patients attending these clinics are usually charged a facility fee even though the physicians' fees are paid by the government. Private clinics have been operating in a number of provinces, but the future of this practice is uncertain. Such clinics are seen by some to be a violation of the principles of the federal funding legislation set forth in the *Canada Health Act*[509] and contrary to the underlying philosophy of the Canadian medicare system.

506. *See R v. Carosella* [1997] 1 SCR 80, 142 DLR (4th) 595 (SCC).
507. Wigmore, *supra* note 430 at 527.
508. *See* for example, the *Alberta Health Care Insurance Act,* RSA 2000, c A-20; the *Medical Benefits Regulation,* Alta. Reg. 84/2006.
509. *Canada Health Act*, RSC 1985, c C-6.

Chapter 2. The Physician-Patient Relationship in Specific Terms

§1. The Minor Patient

I. Parental Authority to Make Health-Care Decisions

265. Some provinces have enacted legislation setting the age of consent to medical treatment. This age may vary, although the most common age is that of sixteen years.[510] Other provinces continue to rely upon the common law.[511] At common law in order for there to be valid consent to treatment four elements must be present. The consent must be voluntary and genuine. The individual must have the mental capacity to understand the nature of the treatment, and understand and appreciate the risks, the alternatives, and the consequences. The consent must be informed in that the individual has received all relevant information and has been able to understand and appreciate it. Finally, the consent must be referable to a specific provider and a specific treatment.[512] If these elements are satisfied, the consent will be considered valid regardless of the age of the patient.

266. With respect to minors the issue is whether they have the capacity to consent to medical treatment. In very young children or infants it is presumed that they do not and that the legal guardian must consent to the treatment on the child's behalf. In most circumstances, but not all, the legal guardian will be the parent. Health practitioners should therefore ensure that they obtain consent to treatment from a person authorized to give it. Proceeding with treatment without the legal guardian's consent, other than in the case of an emergency, constitutes battery. If the minor is capable of fully appreciating the nature of the illness and the consequences of the medical treatment then he or she can give a legally effective consent. In such a case, the child is considered to be a mature minor and capable of making his or her own decisions.[513]

---

510. *See* for example, *Medical Consent of Minors Act,* SNB 1976, c M-6.1, s. 2; *Health Care Directives Act,* CCSM, c H27, s. 4(2); *Substitute Decisions Act, 1992,* SO 1992, c 30, s. 2(2); and *Advance Health Care Directives Act*, SNL 1995, c A-4.1, s. 7, all of which state that a person who is 16 years of age or over is presumed capable of giving or refusing consent to health care. In New Brunswick, a child under 16 may consent to medical treatment where an opinion from a physician, dentist, nurse practitioner, midwife, or nurse is obtained attesting that the minor understands the nature and consequences of the treatment and that the treatment is in the best interests of the child. *See Medical Consent of Minors Act,* SNB 1976, c M-6.1, s. 3. In British Columbia, a child of any age may consent to health care as long as the health care provider has explained to the child and been satisfied that the child understands the nature and consequences of the health care, and has made reasonable efforts to determine and has concluded that it is in the infant's best interests. *See Infants Act*, RSBC 1996, c 223, s. 17.
511. The provinces of Alberta, Saskatchewan, Nova Scotia, and Prince Edward Island continue to rely on the common law, which requires that a determination of competency and capacity to consent be made in each case.
512. For a general discussion of the elements of a valid and informed consent *see Reibl, supra* note 166 and *Hopp, supra* note 168. *See also Watson v. Dr. Shawn Soon*, 2018 ONSC 3809 for a summary of case law in Ontario.
513. *See Johnston v. Wellesley Hospital* [1971] 2 OR 103 (HC) and *C.(J.S.) v. Wren* [1987] 2 WWR 669 (Alta. CA).

II. Limitations on Parental Authority to Make Health-Care Decisions for Their Children

267. The philosophy underlying the mature minor rule is that although parental decision-making rights regarding a child continue to exist, the degree of control that parents exercise over a child must decrease as the child matures.[514] Even for immature minors and infants, however, the parental authority to make decisions regarding medical treatment is not absolute. First, the courts retain their *parens patriae* jurisdiction and can intervene to protect a child when the decision of the parent may not be in the child's best interest. Second, all provinces and territories have child welfare legislation that allows for a child to be declared in need of protection. The child then becomes a ward of the court or of the province or territory.[515] The courts have intervened when parents have refused to authorize life-saving treatment for their child because of religious beliefs (Jehovah Witness' who refuse blood transfusions for their children, for example).[516] However, in a decision regarding an operation involving a higher degree of risk and uncertainty of outcome, the court refused to intervene as it found the decision of the parents to be not so overtly offensive and against the interests of the child that the state should countermand the parents' choice. It appears that if the decision of the parents is within the bounds of current medical practice and is recognized by the medical community as being acceptable in the circumstances, the court will not interfere with the decision of the parent.[517]

268. It is generally accepted that parents can only authorize non-therapeutic treatment if it has no permanent deleterious effect on a child, such as circumcision. Parents cannot authorize the sterilization of their minor children unless it is for therapeutic purposes.[518] The consent of a minor to an *inter vivos* organ donation is generally considered invalid because neither the parents nor the courts should be allowed to deprive a child of a vital organ when he or she does not have the intelligence or maturity to appreciate the act. In some provinces, legislation prohibits live organ donation by children, although the age at which consent may be given varies.[519] The provinces of Alberta, Manitoba and Prince Edward Island permit

514. *See* generally Irvine, Osborne & Shariff, *supra* note 165 at 37–53; *See* Joan M Gilmour, "Legal Capacity and Decision Making" in Joanna N Erdman, Vanessa Gruben & Erin Nelson, eds., *Canadian Health Law and Policy,* 5th ed. (Toronto: LexisNexis, 2017) at 357–358.
515. *See Region 2 Hospital Corp v. Walker* (1994), 385 APR 366 (NBCA). Examples of legislation include: *The Child and Family Services Act,* SS 1989–90, c C-7.2, ss. 11, 17; and *Child, Youth and Family Services Act, 2017,* SO 2017, c 14, ss. 74(2), 101.
516. *See* for example, *B.(R.) v. Children's Aid Society of Metropolitan Toronto* [1995] 1 SCR 315; and *Re D* (1982), 22 Alta. L.R. (2d) 228 (Alta. Prov. Ct.).
517. *See Saskatchewan (Minister of Social Services) v. P.(F.)* [1990] 4 WWR 748 (Sask. Prov. Ct.).
518. *E. (Mrs.) v. Eve* [1986] 2 SCR 388 .
519. *Human Tissue Gift Act,* RSBC 1996, c 211, s. 3(1) (19 and older); *Human Tissue Act,* RSNL 1990, c H-15, s. 4(1) (19 and older); *Human Tissue Gift Act,* RSNB 2014, c 113, s. 3(1) (19 and older); *Human Tissue Gift Act,* CCSM c H180, s. 9(1) (18 and older); *Human Tissue Gift Act, 2015,* SS 2015, c H-15.1, s. 6(1) (age of majority); *Trillium Gift of Life Network Act,* RSO 1990, c H.20, s. 3(1) (16 and older).

inter vivos donation by minors, provided certain statutory conditions are met.[520] In Alberta, such donation requires the consent of a guardian (if the minor is under 16 years of age) as well as the unanimous approval of an independent assessment committee, which must ensure that: the minor agrees to the donation without coercion or inducement and understands the nature and consequences of the donation; only regenerative tissue or organs are to be donated, if the minor is under 16 years of age; the donation poses minimal risk to the minor; and all adult members of the recipient's immediate family have been eliminated as donors.[521] The law is divided on the issue of medical research. Parents may be able to give consent on behalf of their children where the research offers a reasonable hope of benefit to the child; however, it is less likely where the research is non-therapeutic.[522]

III. A Minor's Right to Forgo Life-Sustaining Treatment for Religious Reasons

A. The General Rule

269. Whether or not a minor is able to exercise a right to forgo life-sustaining treatment will depend upon the circumstances of the case. As stated in the foregoing, the court will intervene to protect a child if his or her parents refuse to authorize medical treatment. There is precedent, however, for a court to respect the wishes of the parents if they are reasonable, within the bounds of current medical practice, and recognized by the medical community as acceptable in the circumstances.[523] Courts have also considered the maturity of the minor and the chance of success of the proposed treatment.[524]

270. Respecting a minor's decision to forgo life-sustaining treatment will depend on a minor's maturity and age. If the child is seen to be a mature minor as the term has been described then his or her wishes should be respected. In a NB decision the court upheld the right of a 16-year-old, diagnosed with leukemia, to refuse blood transfusions.[525] As the child was a mature minor, was sufficiently mature to understand the nature of the treatment and the consequences of refusing it, the court held that his wishes were to be respected even though the proposed treatment would be in his best interests. In Alberta, however, a court ruled that the wishes of a mature minor in need of protection under that province's child welfare

520. *Human Tissue and Organ Donation Act,* SA 2006, c H-14.5; *Human Tissue Act,* CCSM, c H180, ss. 10–11; *Human Tissue Donation Act,* RSPEI 1988, c H-12.1, ss. 6–7. In Manitoba and Prince Edward Island, such a donor must be 16 years of age or over.

521. *Human Tissue and Organ Donation Act*, SA 2006, c H-14.5, s. 5.

522. *See* Gordon Duval, "The Regulation of Health Research Involving People" in Joanna Erdman, Vanessa Gruben & Erin Nelson, eds., *Canadian Health Law and Policy,* 5th ed. (Toronto: LexisNexis, 2017) at 252.

523. *Saskatchewan (Minister of Social Services) v. P.(F.)* [1990] 4 WWR 748 (Sask. Prov. Ct.).

524. *See Re K.(L.D.) (Children's Aid Society of Metropolitan Toronto v. K.)* (1985), 48 RFL (2d) 164 (Ont. Prov. Ct.); *Walker (Litigation Guardian of) v. Region 2 Hospital Corp.* (1994), 116 DLR (4th) 477, 150 NBR (2d) 366 (NBCA); and *C.(A.), supra* note 168.

525. *Walker (Litigation Guardian of) v. Region 2 Hospital Corp.* (1994), 385 APR 366 (NBCA).

legislation need not be taken into account.[526] The SCC upheld the constitutionality of sections of Manitoba's *Child and Family Services Act* that permitted the non-consensual treatment of mature minors under, but not over, 16 years of age.[527]

B. Statutory Exemptions for Spiritual Healing

271. In Canada a competent adult may refuse life-sustaining medical treatment on the basis of religious or spiritual beliefs. Recent court decisions have also upheld a mature minor's right to do so.[528] However, as a general rule, the court will intervene and override a parent's decision to refuse life-sustaining treatment with respect to infants and immature minors. The hospital or medical practitioner will involve child welfare services, who will then seek to have the child declared in need of protection so that the necessary treatment may be provided.[529] There are no statutory exemptions which may be used to justify the refusal of treatment. The *Criminal Code* imposes a legal duty on a parent to provide the necessaries of life, which includes medical aid to a child under the age of 16 years. Failure to do so constitutes a criminal offense.[530] Religious or spiritual beliefs are not a lawful excuse and the fact that they are not does not offend the *Canadian Charter of Rights and Freedoms* which protects religious freedom.[531] Indeed, *not* providing the child with the required treatment would in some situations violate the child's rights, even when the parents have refused to authorize the treatment in question.[532]

IV. Special Rules for Infants with Life-Threatening Conditions

272. In Canada there are no special rules for infants with life-threatening conditions. Each case depends upon its circumstances. In the past, the court has intervened to protect an infant from decisions of the parents which were not oriented

526. *B.H. (Next Friend of) v. Alberta (Director of Child Welfare)*, 2002 ABQB 371, affirmed 2002 ABCA 109. *See also C.U. (Next Friend of) v. Alberta (Director of Child Welfare)*, 2003 ABCA 66.
527. *See C.(A.), supra* note 168.
528. But *see also B(S.J.) (Litigation Guardian of) v. British Columbia (Director of Child, Family & Community Service)*, 2005 BCSC 573 (provincial child protection legislation empowered court to authorize blood transfusion deemed medically necessary despite objection by mature minor).
529. *See* for example, *Children's Aid Society of Niagara Region v. S.(M.)*, 2011 ONSC 4718; *Children's Aid Society of Toronto v. P.(L.)*, 2010 ONCJ 320; *M.(V.) v. British Columbia (Director of Child, Family & Community Service)*, 2008 BCSC 449; *Re D.(T.T.)* (1999), 171 DLR (4th) 761 (Sask. QB); *Re R.K.* (1987), 79 AR 140 (Prov. Ct.); *Wintersgill v. Minister of Social Services* (1981), 131 DLR (3d) 184 (Sask. U.F.C.).
530. *Criminal Code,* RSC 1985, c C-46, s. 215. *See R v. Brooks* (1902), 5 CCC 372 (BCSC).
531. *Canadian Charter of Rights and Freedoms,* Part I of the *Constitution Act, 1982*, being Sch. B to the *Canada Act 1982* (UK), 1982, c 11, s. 2(a). *See also R v. Tutton* (1985), 18 CCC (3d) 328 (Ont. CA), affirmed on other grounds [1989] 1 SCR 1392.
532. *New Brunswick (Minister of Health and Community Services) v. B.(R.)* (1990), 70 DLR (4th) 568 (NBQB).

toward saving the life of the child at almost any cost.[533] It may be argued that this position is changing and that the courts are now prepared to review the parents' decisions in light of their beliefs.[534]

273. In the earliest Canadian decision on point, *Child and Family Services of Central Manitoba v. L.(R.),* it was held that, where, in the opinion of physicians, continued treatment was medically futile, a Do Not Resuscitate order might be placed on an infant's chart without either parental consent or court order.[535] Subsequent rulings have held that Ontario legislation grants both guardians and child welfare officials the authority to provide or refuse consent to the cessation of life-sustaining treatment in infants—this power must, however, be exercised in the infant's statutorily defined "best interests." Where parents of an eight-month-old infant in a persistent vegetative state failed to take into account the "best interests" criteria set out in the province's *Health Care Consent Act,* the Ontario Consent and Capacity Board directed them to consent to the gradual discontinuation of mechanical ventilation.[536] Similarly, the Alberta courts have also allowed medical professionals to withdraw life-sustaining treatment in favor of palliative care where it was in the best interests of the child against the objections of parents.[537] On the other hand, parents of a brain-injured 3-month-old infant succeeded in their application for an injunction temporarily prohibiting his health-care team from removing such life support to allow time for an independent medical assessment.[538]

§2. Patients with Mental Health Issues

I. Decisional Capacity

A. *Competency, Decisional Capacity and the Notion of Variable Capacity*

274. The ability of an individual to consent to or refuse medical treatment is determined by that individual's mental capacity. If a person is not mentally capable of making a decision and of understanding the consequences of that decision then he or she does not have the capacity necessary to provide a valid consent. The question of an individual's competence arises in relation to many of life's events other than health care, including the making of a will and entering into a contract. Although a person may not be legally competent for the purpose of one activity he or she may be for another. A patient who is suffering from depression or delusions

533. *See British Columbia (Superintendent of Family and Child Service) v. D.(R.)* (1983), 42 BCLR 173 (SC).
534. *See Saskatchewan (Minister of Social Services) v. P.(F.)* [1990] 4 WWR 748; and *R v. Cyrenne, Cyrenne and Cramb* (1981), 62 CCC (2d) 238 (Ont. Div. Ct.).
535. (1997), 154 D.L.R. (4th) 409 (Man. C.A.).
536. *See E.J.G. (Re),* 2007 CanLII 44704. *See also Children's Aid Society of Ottawa-Carleton v. M.C.* (2008), 301 D.L.R. (4th) 194 (Ont. Sup. Ct.).
537. *See Alberta (Director, Child, Youth and Family Enhancement Act) v. L.(D.),* 2012 ABQB 562, affirmed 2012 ABCA 275; and *Chalifoux v. Alberta Health Services,* 2014 ABQB 624.
538. *See May v. Alberta Health Services,* 2010 ABQB 213.

may be able to appreciate the nature and consequences of the proposed medical treatment and yet may not be competent for the purpose of giving evidence or entering into a contract.[539] In one case, an individual was found to be incapable of consenting to psychiatric treatment but was found to be capable of managing his own financial affairs.[540]

B. The Presumption of Capacity

275. The common law in Canada presumes that an individual has capacity (often also referred to as "competency") unless legislation or a court order specifies otherwise. This applies to all persons, including children and the mentally ill. The law also presumes that an individual is mentally capable of consenting to medical treatment. This presumption may of course be rebutted by evidence that the individual is not capable of appreciating the nature and consequences of the treatment. The evidence required to rebut the presumption of competency would depend upon the circumstances of each case.[541]

276. This presumption is upheld in most mental health legislation which requires that a patient, whether voluntary or involuntary, must consent to treatment unless a determination is made that the patient is not mentally competent.[542] Further, Ontario, Prince Edward Island, and Manitoba have enacted statutes recognizing that a person has the capacity to make a health-care decision if he or she is able to understand the information that is relevant to making a decision and is able to appreciate the reasonably foreseeable consequences of a decision.[543] In addition, the legislation specifically acknowledges that a person may have capacity respecting some treatments and not others.[544]

539. *See* Sharpe, *supra* note 129 at 75–78. *See also* GB Robertson, *Mental Disability and the Law in Canada,* 2nd ed. (Toronto: Carswell, 1994); Law Commission of Ontario, *Legal Capacity, Decision-Making and Guardianship: Final Report* (Toronto: Law Commission of Ontario, March 2017); Sheila Wildeman, "Consent to Psychiatric Treatment: From Insight (Into Illness) to Incite (A Riot)" in Jennifer A Chandler & Colleen M Flood, eds., *Law and Mind: Mental Health Law and Policy in Canada* (Toronto: LexisNexis Canada Inc, 2016) at 81.
540. *Khan v. St. Thomas Psychiatric Hospital* (1992), 87 DLR (4th) 289 (Ont. CA).
541. *Ibid.,* at 467–488; Rozovsky, *supra* note 165 at 7–12.
542. *See Mental Health Act,* RSO 1990, c M-7 and *Howlett v. Karunaratne* (1988), 64 OR (2d) 418 (Ont. Dist. Ct.).
543. *The Health Care Directives Act,* CCSM c H27, s. 2; *Health Care Consent Act, 1996,* SO 1996, c 2, Sch. A, s. 4(1); *Consent to Treatment and Healthcare Directives Act,* RSPEI 1988, c C-17.2, s. 7(1).
544. *Health Care Consent Act, 1996,* SO 1996, c 2, Sch. A, s. 15; *The Health Care Directives Act,* CCSM c H26, s. 6(2); *Consent to Treatment and Healthcare Directives Act,* RSPEI 1988, c C-17.2, s. 7(3).

C. Judicial Considerations of Questions of Capacity

277. The issue of a patient's capacity usually arises when the patient, or substitute decision maker, disagrees with or refuses the treatment that the physician orders. This is particularly frequent in the context of treatment for mental illness. Mental health legislation usually establishes procedures for the determination of mental capacity. That determination may then be challenged in a hearing before a review board, whose decisions are subject to review by the courts.[545] The wishes of a capable person are to be respected even when they lead to choices that others find ill-advised or even irrational. The obligation of a physician to determine mental capacity exists, however, whether or not the patient agrees with the physician and consents to the proposed treatment plan. The common law right to medical self-determination is displaced only when a patient is determined to be incapable of consenting.[546] Further, if the attending physician is aware of the patient's wishes regarding treatment that were expressed when capable, those wishes must be considered.[547]

D. Legal Tests of Capacity

278. There is no formal legal test of capacity, although health-care consent legislation does provide some guidelines.[548] For patients to be deemed mentally capable in Ontario, they must:

(a) be able to understand the information that is relevant to making a decision about the treatment; and
(b) be able to appreciate the reasonably foreseeable consequences of a decision or lack of decision.[549]

279. A person is not mentally capable unless both elements are present. It is important to note, however, that assessments with respect to capacity in this context relate to the patient's ability to understand, not his or her actual understanding. According to the Supreme Court, this means that a person cannot be deemed incapable if he or she lacks information about his or her condition, or holds different views with respect to the diagnosis and treatment.[550]

545. *See* for example, the *Mental Health Act*, RSO 1990, c M.7; and the *Mental Health Act*, RSA 2000, c M-13. Both the *Health Care Consent Act, 1996*, SO 1996, c 2, Sch. A and the *Substitute Decisions Act, 1992*, SO 1992, c 30, have established procedures for the review of a decision of incompetency. *See also Howlett v. Karunaratne* (1988), 64 OR (2d) 418 (Ont. Dist. Ct.); *Khan v. St. Thomas Psychiatric Hospital* (1992), 7 OR (3d) 303 (CA); and *Starson, supra* note 332.
546. *Fleming, supra* note 167.
547. *Ibid.*, and *see Sevels v. Cameron* [1995] OJ No. 381 (Gen. Div.).
548. As the legislation varies from province to province, the legislation specific to the province in which the issue arises should be reviewed.
549. *See Health Care Consent Act, 1996,* SO 1996, c 2, Sch. A, s. 4(1) as discussed in *Starson, supra* note 332.
550. *See Starson, supra* note 332 at para. 14.

280. If a patient has the ability to understand the information relevant to making a treatment decision and has the ability to appreciate the consequences of their decisions, then he or she has the mental competency to make a decision regarding treatment. A physician must review all of the evidence available in making such an assessment. This would include any history of mental illness and any evidence of delusions that could affect the patient's ability to understand the treatment and the consequences of consenting to or refusing treatment. Although a physician will normally consider the patient's refusal to consent to a recommended treatment plan in determining mental competency, it should not in itself be a determinant consideration.[551] In assessing whether a patient truly understands and appreciates the situation so as to make an informed decision, the following factors should be considered: the patient's level of consciousness, lucidity and coherency; whether alcohol or drugs, including pain-killers, have been ingested; and the degree of pain that the patient is experiencing.[552]

281. In Nova Scotia, the determination of the capacity to consent to care, in both general and psychiatric hospitals, is set out in legislation. A psychiatrist is required to examine the patient and consider whether the patient understands:

(1) the condition for which the treatment is proposed;
(2) the nature and purpose of the treatment;
(3) the risks involved in undergoing the treatment;
(4) the risks involved in not undergoing the treatment, and
(5) whether or not the patient's ability to consent is affected by his or her condition.[553]

282. The legislation in Alberta is similar to that of Ontario. In order to be deemed mentally competent a person must be able to understand the subject matter relating to the decisions and be able to appreciate the consequences of making the decisions.[554]

II. Informed Consent and the Right to Refuse Treatment

283. It is well settled in Canada that a capable patient has the right to refuse medical treatment.[555] If a patient is not mentally capable, however, then she cannot consent to or refuse treatment. Further, at common law only that treatment which is immediately necessary to preserve the patient's life or health may be performed in the absence of the patient's consent.[556] As it is recognized that a mentally ill patient

551. *Khan v. St. Thomas Psychiatric Hospital* (1992), 77 OR (3d) 303 (CA).
552. *Ibid.*, at 7.
553. *Hospitals Act*, RSNS 1989, c 208, s. 52(2).
554. *See Mental Health Act*, RSA 2000, c M-13, s. 26.
555. *Starson*, *supra* note 332; *Fleming*, *supra* note 167; and *see also Malette*, *supra* note 325.
556. *C.(A.)*, *supra* note 168; *Malette*, *supra* note 325. *See also* Alberta Law Reform Institute, *Advance Directives and Substitute Decision Making in Personal Health Care* (Report for Discussion No. 11) (Edmonton, 1991) at 6–10.

may be capable for the purpose of health-care decision-making, it may be presumed that a mentally ill patient who is capable has the right to refuse treatment even in life-threatening situations. Further, if a capable patient made a health-care decision to refuse treatment in particular circumstances or to refuse a type of treatment and then made those wishes known to the health practitioner, then those wishes are to be respected if the patient subsequently becomes incapable.[557]

284. An issue arises if the mentally ill patient is a formal patient or has been civilly committed to a psychiatric facility. Although there is no presumption of incapacity to consent merely because of committal, some provinces do not allow mentally ill patients to refuse treatment. The relevant statutes in British Columbia and Newfoundland and Labrador expressly provide for the treatment of formal patients who are capable, notwithstanding their refusal to consent.[558] The legislation in Manitoba requires that a determination of competency be made and protects the competent individual's right to refuse treatment.[559] In other provinces patients deemed competent have only a qualified right to refuse treatment. They may refuse treatment, but their decision may be overridden by a review panel if the panel determines that the treatment is in the best interests of the patient.[560] It is suggested that any legislation which limits a competent person's right of self-determination and his or her ability to refuse treatment, whether that person is a voluntary or involuntary patient in a psychiatric facility or other institution, would not withstand a challenge under the *Canadian Charter of Rights and Freedoms.*

557. *See Fleming, supra* note 167; *Rasouli (Litigation Guardian of) v. Sunnybrook Health Sciences Centre*, 2013 SCC 53; *The Health Care Directives Act,* CCSM c H27, s. 7; and *Health Care Consent Act, 1996,* SO 1996, c 2, Sch. A, s. 26.
558. *Mental Health Act,* RSBC 1996, c 288, s. 31; *Mental Health Care and Treatment Act,* SNL 2006, c M-9.1, s. 35.
559. *Mental Health Act,* CCSM, c M110, s. 27(1).
560. *See* Robertson, *supra* note 538 at 479–486; JE Gray, MA Shone & PF Liddle, *Canadian Mental Health Law and Policy*, 2nd ed. (Toronto: LexisNexis, 2008) at 23–24; *Mental Health Act,* RSA 2000, c M-13, s. 29(3)(b); *Mental Health Act,* RSY 2002, c 150, s. 23(2), (4).

Chapter 3. Specific Activities

§1. Abortion

I. The Constitutional Framework

285. In *R. v. Morgentaler*,[561] a 5–2 decision, the SCC held that section 251 of the Criminal Code unjustifiably infringed or denied the rights and freedoms guaranteed by section 7 of the *Canadian Charter of Rights and Freedoms.* Section 251 had made procuring or attempting to procure a miscarriage an offense punishable by life imprisonment. An exculpatory clause permitted "therapeutic abortions," those done in compliance with complex procedural requirements described in the section. The delays, arbitrariness and unfairness inherent in the administrative process were held to infringe pregnant women's rights to security of the person under section 7 of the Charter. State interference with bodily integrity and serious state-imposed psychological stress constituted a breach of security of the person. The court therefore ruled that section 251 was an unreasonable limit on Charter rights and declared the statute invalid under section 52(1) of the *Constitution Act,* 1982.

286. The Court's decision left open the possibility that other means of regulating abortion could be constitutionally valid. The primary objective of section 251 had been the protection of the fetus as a potential life, while the protection of the woman's life and health was an ancillary objective. The Court held that these are substantial concerns in a free and democratic society, but the means chosen in section 251 were not reasonable and demonstrably justified, as required by section 1 of the *Charter. Obiter* statements in the judgment provide some indication of what restrictions the court might find to be reasonable: a law that required a higher standard of danger to maternal health in the later months of pregnancy, for the abortion to be legal, might meet this proportionality test. The state's interest in protecting the fetus might be given greater weight during the later stages of gestational development. However, in the years since the decision in *Morgentaler*, the federal Parliament has yet to pass a bill to recriminalize or otherwise regulate abortion. No federal party has indicated any interest in opening the debate around abortion by proposing new legislation.

287. While some provinces have attempted to limit access to abortion services, the courts have found these efforts to be unconstitutional on the basis that they were *ultra vires* the province.[562]

288. In addition to the direct criminalization of abortion, the recognition of fetal rights via negligence laws or the court's *parens patriae* jurisdiction could also potentially affect women's access to abortion. Canadian decisions have recognized that constitutional issues concerning pregnant women's rights are inherently raised

561. [1988] 1 SCR 30.

562. *See* Vanessa Gruben, "Regulating Reproduction" in Joanna Erdman, Vanessa Gruben & Erin Nelson, eds., *Canadian Health Law and Policy,* 5th ed. (Toronto: LexisNexis, 2017) at 402.

with the recognition of fetal rights, but have avoided developing a conclusive position on the legal interaction between women's rights, the state's interest in the fetus, and tortious liability.[563] In *Winnipeg Child and Family Services (Northwest Area) v. G. (D.F.)*,[564] the SCC refused to authorize the detention and mandatory treatment of a woman who was five months pregnant and addicted to glue-sniffing. There was no indication that abortion had been sought or considered by the woman. The province had sought a court order for the purpose of protecting the unborn fetus and argued for the court's intervention on the basis of either the court's inherent *parens patriae* jurisdiction or the mother's negligent failure to exercise a duty of care toward the fetus. A majority of the SCC found that the court's *parens patriae* jurisdiction did not encompass unborn children, and neither English common law nor Quebec civil law recognized the fetus as a legal person with rights of action. An extension of either the court's own *parens patriae* jurisdiction or the existing law of negligence would be a major change, with ramifications for the pregnant woman's fundamental choices and constitutional rights. Such changes should be left to legislative enactment, and not the common law.

289. In *Winnipeg Child and Family Services (Northwest Area) v. G.(D.F.)*, the majority did recognize that a child, once born, could sue in tort for injuries suffered before birth, though damages would be assessed only as from the date of birth.[565] However, subsequently the SCC decided in *Dobson (Litigation Guardian of) v. Dobson* that while there is a sufficient relationship between a child who suffered prenatal injuries and its negligent mother to establish a duty of care, this duty should not be imposed for public policy reasons.[566] Imposing such a duty on mothers would negatively impact on the relationship between mothers and their children and on the family unit as a whole. Such a duty would limit a pregnant woman's right to privacy, bodily integrity and autonomous decision-making.

II. Particular Limitations and Restrictions on Abortions

A. *Limitations on Government Funding*

290. In Canada, medical treatment is insured by the provinces. Provincial statutes provide that "medically required" health services are insured. Under the *Canada Health Act*,[567] the government of Canada makes transfer payments to the provinces to compensate for insured health services paid for under provincial health insurance plans.[568] Unfortunately, none of these statutes define "medically

563. *See Winnipeg Child and Family Services (Northwest Area) v. G.(D.F.)* [1997] 3 SCR 925, 152 DLR (4th) 193; *Dobson (Litigation Guardian of) v. Dobson* [1999] 2 SCR 753, reversing (1997), 148 DLR (4th) 332 (NBCA).
564. (1997), 152 DLR (4th) 193 (SCC).
565. *Winnipeg Child and Family Services (Northwest Area) v. G.(D.F.)* [1997] 3 SCR 925, 152 DLR (4th) 193 at 205 [cited to DLR].
566. *Dobson (Litigation Guardian of) v. Dobson* [1999] 2 SCR 753.
567. RSC 1985, c C-6.
568. For a more complete description of the health insurance system, *see* General Introduction, §2.

required," which has left an area of uncertainty. Since the 1988 Supreme Court decision of *R. v. Morgentaler*,[569] several provinces have attempted to restrict the performance of abortions and the funding of abortions.

1. Restrictions on Funding of Abortions outside Hospitals

291. In 1993, the Supreme Court struck down Nova Scotia's *Medical Services Act* and *Medical Services Designation Regulation,* which prohibited the performance of abortions anywhere other than an approved hospital and denied insurance coverage for abortions performed outside a hospital. The Court ruled[570] that the legislation was *ultra vires* the legislature because it was in pith and substance criminal law, which is within the exclusive legislative authority of the Parliament of Canada.[571]

292. After learning of a doctor's intent to establish a free-standing abortion clinic, NB enacted legislation under which performing abortions outside hospitals was considered professional misconduct. This legislation gave the Minister of Health the power to request the suspension of the license of any doctor who had performed or was likely to perform abortions outside a hospital. The trial and appeal courts both ruled that the legislation was *ultra vires* the province because the conduct being regulated—the establishment of free-standing abortion clinics—was something the province regarded as socially undesirable conduct and thus fell within the ambit of the criminal law.[572]

293. Fully funded clinic abortions are not available in all provinces. Actions have been brought against provinces that refuse to fund abortions performed in free-standing clinics. One such action was successful. The regulation enacting the restriction was found not to be authorized by its governing statute.[573] A second action was dismissed by the Prince Edward Island Court of Appeal. The court found that the regulation defining abortions as basic medical services only when they were performed in hospitals was valid.[574] In 2002, Dr. Henry Morgentaler launched an action against the province of NB with respect to their continued refusal to fund abortions performed in free-standing clinics, alleging that the *Medical Services Payment Act and Regulations* contravened both the *Canada Health Act* and the *Canadian Charter of Rights and Freedoms.* He was granted public interest standing to challenge the law but died before the case was resolved.[575]

569. [1988] 1 SCR 30.
570. *R v. Morgentaler* [1993] 3 SCR 463.
571. *Constitution Act, 1867* (UK), 30 & 31 Vict, c 3, s. 91(27).
572. *Morgentaler v. New Brunswick (Attorney-General)* (1994), 117 DLR (4th) 753, affirmed (1995), 121 DLR (4th) 431 (CA), leave to appeal to SCC refused.
573. *Lexogest Inc v. Manitoba (A.G.)* (1993), 10 DLR (4th) 523 (Man. CA).
574. *Morgentaler v. Prince Edward Island (Minister of Health and Social Services)* (1996) 139 DLR (4th) 603 (PEICA).
575. *Morgentaler v. New Brunswick*, 2009 NBCA 26. *See also* Gruben, *supra* note 561 at 403.

294. These cases do not stand for the proposition that the provinces can never enact legislation that will restrict access to, or funding for, abortions. However, the legislation must have a health-care purpose, which will bring it within provincial authority under the Constitution.[576] If the impugned legislation is a regulation, it must be clearly authorized by its governing statute. Certainly the courts will give close scrutiny to any provincial legislation affecting abortion. Even if otherwise properly enacted, the legislation might not survive a Charter challenge.[577]

295. Access to the procedure is restricted in those provinces that do not fund abortions performed in free-standing clinics. In the Province of Manitoba, a class action lawsuit contended that a government decision to exclude private clinic abortion services from provincial health insurance violates the *Canadian Charter of Rights and Freedoms.*[578] However, the government subsequently reversed its rule to provide funding and the class action does not appear to have proceeded.

B. *Regulation of Medical Techniques and Facilities for Use in Performing Abortion*

1. Techniques

296. Neither Parliament nor the provincial Legislatures have attempted to regulate surgical techniques for performing abortions. Physicians who perform abortions in an unsafe or unrecognized manner may be liable to disciplinary proceedings by their provincial College of Physicians and Surgeons, to a patient's action for negligence, or to a criminal prosecution.

297. However, the federal government does regulate drugs manufactured or distributed in Canada, including abortifacients. The Therapeutic Products Directorate in the Health Protection Branch of Health Canada has the mandate to give or withhold approval for the manufacture or distribution of drugs in Canada.

a. RU-486

298. RU-486, also known as mifepristone, is an early abortion-inducing drug. It is effective at seven to nine weeks of pregnancy. Its use in Canada has been approved by the Therapeutic Products Directorate as a component of Mifegymiso, which is a combination drug containing mifepristone and misoprostol. In 2017,

576. *Constitution Act, 1867* (UK), 30 & 31 Vict, c 3, s. 92.
577. For further analysis, *see* M.L. McConnell, "Abortion: Provincial Legislation—Control over Health Care: *R. v. Morgentaler*" (1994) 73 Can Bar Rev 417 at 417–430.
578. *See Jane Doe 1 v. Manitoba,* 2008 MBQB 217.

requirements for physicians to be registered and complete an education program in order to prescribe Mifegymiso were lifted.[579]

b. Methotrexate and Misoprostol

299. Some physicians in Canada are using a combination of these two commonly available drugs to induce abortion. The research methods regarding these drugs, and the use of the drugs for a purpose for which they were not licensed, are currently the source of some controversy.

300. There are advantages to this method over surgical abortion. It can be done earlier in pregnancy (six to nine weeks), the abortion takes place at home, and it is inexpensive (the drugs cost only about CAD 10). However, the method has a rather high 5% failure rate, and some patients would find the uncertainty and the wait of up to two weeks for the conclusion to be unacceptable.

301. Although the drugs are legal, they have not been licensed for use as abortifacients under the *Food and Drugs Act*.[580] In general, physicians should not prescribe drugs for purposes for which the drugs are not licensed. The exception is an ethically reviewed and approved research protocol. Any other use may render a physician liable to professional discipline by the province's College of Physicians and Surgeons and to a civil action for negligence should a patient be harmed.

2. Facilities

302. The Supreme Court's ruling in *R. v. Morgentaler*[581] indicates that the courts will closely scrutinize any restrictive regulation of abortion facilities. In *Morgentaler,* the court struck down Nova Scotia's *Medical Services Act* and *Medical Services Designation Regulation,* which prohibited the performance of abortions anywhere other than an approved hospital and denied insurance coverage for abortions performed outside a hospital. The Court ruled that the legislation was *ultra vires* the legislature because it was in pith and substance criminal law, which is within the exclusive legislative authority of the Parliament of Canada.[582]

303. Guidelines for performing abortions in non-hospital medical surgical facilities exist. According to those of the College of Physicians and Surgeons of British Columbia: terminations dated up to fourteen weeks gestation may be performed by a specialist obstetrician/gynecologist or a qualified general practitioner who has

579. Health Canada, *Health Canada updates prescribing and dispensing information for Mifegymiso* (RA-65034, Nov. 7, 2017), online www.healthycanadians.gc.ca/recall-alert-rappel-avis/hc-sc/2017/65034a-eng.php.
580. RSC 1985, c F-27.
581. [1993] 3 SCR 463.
582. *Constitution Act, 1867* (UK), 30 & 31 Vict, c 3, s. 91(27).

approval from the Non-Hospital Medical/Surgical Facilities Committee; terminations performed in an accredited non-hospital facility dated beyond fourteen weeks and up to and including sixteen weeks gestation may only be performed by a specialist obstetrician/gynecologist who has approval from the Non-Hospital Medical/Surgical Facilities Committee; and terminations beyond sixteen weeks gestation may only be performed in an accredited hospital.[583]

C. *Record Keeping Requirements*

304. Canadian courts have not been asked to rule on particular record keeping requirements for abortion facilities. There has been no federal or provincial legislation in this area. The Colleges of Physicians and Surgeons in the provinces have guidelines for record keeping, but they are the same for abortion facilities as for other medical facilities.[584]

D. *Consent or Notification Requirements*

305. In principle, the requirements for consent to abortion are the same as for any therapeutic procedure.[585] In practice,[586] physicians tend to exercise particular caution in providing full disclosure of information and risks and in ascertaining that the patient has capacity to consent, or if the patient lacks capacity, that a valid consent can be obtained from the appropriate substitute decision maker.

1. Parental Consent or Notification

306. Parental consent to abortion is required only if the patient is in law an immature minor.[587] Several provinces have enacted statutes that specify when a minor has the capacity to consent to medical treatment.[588] For minors whose circumstances do not fit the statutory description, and for minors in provinces without statute law on point, the common law will apply. The common law applies in Alberta.

583. *See* College of Physicians and Surgeons of British Columbia, *Resource Manual: Abortion* (Vancouver: College of Physicians and Surgeons of British Columbia, 2009).
584. *See McInerney, supra* note 321, and provincial health legislation (e.g., the *Health Information Act*, RSA 2000, c H-5).
585. For further discussion, *see* Chapter 1, §2, Informed Consent, *supra.*
586. *See* Irvine, Osborne & Shariff, *supra* note 165 at 71; and Robertson, *supra* note 538 at 165–166. Consider also Bernard M Dickens & Rebecca J Cook, "Dimensions of Informed Consent to Treatment" (2004) 85 International J Gynecology & Obstetrics 309; Bernard M Dickens & Rebecca J Cook, "Patients' Refusal of Recommended Treatment" (2015) 131 International J Gynecology & Obstetrics 105; Bernard M Dickens & Rebecca J Cook, "Types of Consent in Reproductive Health Care" (2015) 128 International J Gynecology & Obstetrics 181.
587. *See* Chapter 2, §1, The Minor Patient, *supra.*
588. *See Substitute Decisions Act, 1992,* SO 1992, c 30, s. 2(2); *Medical Consent of Minors Act,* SNB 1976, c M-6.1, s. 2; *Infants Act,* RSBC 1996, c 223, s. 17.

307. In *J.S.C. v. Wren*,[589] the Alberta Court of Appeal ruled that a "normal intelligent 16-year-old" was capable of consenting to an abortion, despite her parents' objections. The parental right to determine whether their minor child will have medical treatment terminates when the child achieves a sufficient understanding and intelligence to enable her to fully understand what is proposed.[590] "Understand" includes understanding obligations to parents, as well as medical matters.[591]

308. In some cases, hospital practice may be more conservative than the law would require. An example of this "ultra-conservative approach" may be found where hospital consent forms require parental consent for any treatment of patients under the age of majority.[592]

2. Spousal or Partner Consent or Notification

309. At common law, the father of a fetus has no authority to prevent a mother from having an abortion.[593] To date, neither the federal or provincial governments have attempted to regulate access to abortion by requiring that the woman's husband (or the father of the fetus) consent to, or be given notice of, the woman's intent to have an abortion. It is probable that the courts would find such legislation to be unconstitutional, as an infringement of pregnant women's Charter rights and freedoms.[594]

§2. Sterilization

I. Introduction

310. A useful definition of sterilization is "any surgical operation or other medical procedure or treatment that ends or is likely to end the ability to procreate."[595] This definition includes any technique that permanently ends reproductive capacity. It could include, for example, non-surgical techniques that may be developed in the future. This section reviews three categories of sterilization: therapeutic, eugenic, and non-therapeutic (contraceptive).

---

589. *C. (J.S.) v. Wren* [1987] 2 W.W.R. 669, 49 Alta L.R. (2d) 289 (CA) [*Wren*].
590. *Gillick v. West Norfolk and Wisbech Area Health Authority* [1985] 3 WLR 830 [1985] 3 Al ER 402 (HL), applied in *Wren, supra* note 588.
591. *Wren, supra* note 588.
592. *See* Irvine, Osborne & Shariff, *supra* note 165 at 51.
593. *Tremblay v. Daigle* [1989] 2 SCR 530.
594. *Canadian Charter of Rights and Freedoms*, Part I of *the Constitution Act, 1982*, being Sch. B to the *Canada Act 1982* (UK), 1982, c 11; e.g., s. 2(a) (freedom of conscience); s. 7 (security of the person), and s. 15(1) (right to equal protection and equal benefit of the law without discrimination based on, *inter alia,* sex or physical disability).
595. Alberta, Institute of Law Research and Reform, Report for Discussion No. 6, *Sterilization Decisions: Minors and Mentally Incompetent Adults* (Edmonton: The Institute, 1988) at 13.

A. Competent Adults

311. A mentally competent adult may choose to be sterilized, whether for contraceptive or therapeutic purposes. Further, there is no legal requirement for spousal consent, or even notification, before the sterilization of a married person. If a statute to that effect were ever enacted, it would fall to a challenge under the *Canadian Charter of Rights and Freedoms*.[596]

B. Incompetent Adults

312. It is possible for a person with a mental disability to give a valid consent to sterilization, even if that person has been declared to be "mentally incompetent" by a court. Capacity for legal decision-making, including consent to health care, is always measured in reference to the particular legal issue in question. Total legal incapacity, arising from mental disability, does not exist in Canadian law.[597]

313. However, sterilization has generally permanent and important effects upon the patient and upon the patient's future life. A fairly high level of understanding would be required for a valid consent. For instance, a mentally ill female patient seeking a contraceptive sterilization must understand the nature and consequences of the surgery, and the connection between sexual intercourse, pregnancy and childbirth.[598]

314. In most provinces, the guardian of an incompetent person has authority analogous to that of a parent. As does a parent's, the guardian's authority to give consent to health care exists only in the absence of the ward's capacity to do so. In Alberta, an order granting a guardian authority to act and make decisions respecting an adult's health care may only be made if the court is satisfied that: the adult does not have the capacity to make decisions about health care; less intrusive and less restrictive alternative measures than the appointment of a guardian have been considered or have been implemented and would not likely be or have not been effective to meet the needs of the adult; and it is in the adult's best interests to make the order.[599]

315. The balance of this discussion will address decision-making on behalf of a person who is clearly mentally incompetent to give a valid consent to health care.

596. As a possible infringement of freedom of belief (s. 2(b)), security of the person (s. 7), or equality (s. 15(1)).
597. Robertson, *supra* note 538 at 2–3.
598. Irvine, Osborne & Shariff, *supra* note 165 at 370.
599. *Adult Guardianship and Trusteeship Act,* SA 2008, c A-4.2, s. 26(6).

1. Therapeutic Sterilization of the Mentally Incompetent

316. Therapeutic sterilization is that which is indicated to protect the life or health of the subject. Sterilization for some purposes is clearly therapeutic: for instance, to remove uterine or ovarian cancer. In these cases, the guardian's authority (and responsibility) is, clearly, to consent to the procedure. However, in Canadian law the scope for therapeutic sterilization of the mentally incompetent is narrow.

317. The British Columbia Court of Appeal decision in *Re K.*[600] was later referred to by the SCC as "at best dangerously close to the limits of the permissible."[601] The ward in *Re K.* was a 10-year-old, severely mentally handicapped girl, who had a phobic aversion to the sight of blood. The object of the sterilization was to prevent the onset of menses. The Court of Appeal reversed the trial decision, allowing the sterilization to proceed immediately. The Court ruled that it was an error to focus on the rights of the mentally handicapped generally, rather than on the best interests of the ward. The only question for the Court was this: "Is it in the best interests of the ward to undergo surgery to avoid the risk of suffering which may result if the operation is not performed?" The Court emphasized that the proposed operation was purely therapeutic, to protect K. from increased trauma and from the risk of inhibiting her progress in other areas.

318. Although it did not overrule *Re K.*, the decision in *Re Eve* did cast some doubt upon the range of its precedential value. *Eve* clearly indicates that "therapeutic sterilization" must be construed narrowly.

2. Non-therapeutic Sterilization of the Mentally Incompetent

319. In the absence of clear statutory authority, a guardian cannot consent to medical procedures that have no therapeutic benefit for the ward. In *Re Eve,*[602] the SCC ruled that a court cannot, at common law, authorize a non-therapeutic sterilization of a mentally incompetent person. Unfortunately, the distinction between a therapeutic and a non-therapeutic sterilization is sometimes unclear. In order to understand the basis for the ruling in *Eve,* and the current law, it is necessary to review the historical background.

320. Eugenics is the now-discredited theory, popular in the early twentieth century, that the human race could be improved by selective breeding. Its goal was to improve the human race by eliminating hereditary diseases. A branch of social Darwinism, eugenicism held that biological inheritance caused many ills ranging from mental illness to pauperism to social deviance. The solution sought by eugenics was

600. *Re K; K v. Public Trustee* (1985), 19 DLR (4th) 255 [1985] 4 WWR 724, 63 BCLR 145 (CA).
601. *Re Eve* (1986), 31 DLR (4th) 1 (*sub nom. E. v. Eve)* [1986] 2 SCR 388 [*Re Eve*] at para. 93.
602. *Re Eve, supra* note 600.

to make it impossible for "deviants" and "defectives" to procreate. Eugenics received widespread support in North America and Europe in the early twentieth century.[603]

321. Alberta enacted a eugenic sterilization law in 1928;[604] British Columbia followed in 1933.[605] The other provinces did not enact legislation, and records now are scant, but it is believed that hundreds of involuntary sterilizations were performed over the years.[606]

322. Alberta's Act authorized a four-member Eugenics Board to order the sterilization of mental hospital inmates. The consent of a parent, spouse or guardian was required, except in the case of Huntington's Chorea. In 1937, the Board's authority was extended to mental defectives, with no family consent requirement. The amendment placed children, especially, at risk of sterilization.[607] Sterilization was made a condition of release from the institution. Statistics developed from Eugenics Board records show that females, Indigenous peoples, Métis, and Eastern Europeans were over-represented among those sterilized.[608]

323. For many good reasons, eugenics theory has been discredited and eugenic sterilization laws have been repealed. Alberta's eugenics statute was repealed in 1972;[609] British Columbia's in 1973.[610] They were brought to consideration again, in the course of the Supreme Court judgment in *Re Eve*.[611] More recently, Alberta's statute came under fresh scrutiny in *Muir v. The Queen in Right of Alberta*.[612]

324. In 1955, at the age of 10, Ms. Muir had been declared "retarded" and committed to Alberta's Provincial Training School for Mental Defectives. This was done without testing or other criteria to support her admission. In 1959, she tested as subnormal on an intelligence test. On the order of the Eugenics Board, she was sterilized. She was told the operation was an appendectomy. She did not discover the sterilization until years later, when she was married and living in the community. The operation proved to be irreversible and she was unable to adopt children.

603. In Canada, two royal commissions (British Columbia, 1925; Ontario, 1938) and several respected political figures recommended the enactment of a eugenic statute. (G.B. Robertson, testimony Jun. 27, 1995, *Muir v. The Queen in Right of Alberta* (Action 890320759, Alta. QB).)
604. *Sexual Sterilization Act,* SA 1928, c 37.
605. *Sexual Sterilization Act,* SBC 1933, c 59.
606. A McLaren, *Our Own Master Race: Eugenics in Canada 1885–1945* (Toronto: McClelland and Stewart, 1990).
607. From 1939 to 1953, 30% of the patients sterilized were between the ages of 10 and 15. *See* Irvine, Osborne & Shariff, *supra* note 165 at 367.
608. *See* Alberta, Institute of Law Research and Reform, *Sterilization Decisions: Minors and Mentally Incompetent Adults,* Report for Discussion No. 6 (Edmonton: The Institute, 1988) at 30; A McLaren, *Our Own Master Race: Eugenics in Canada 1885–1945* (Toronto: McClelland and Stewart, 1990).
609. SA 1972, c 87.
610. SBC 1973, c 79.
611. *Re Eve*, *supra* note 600.
612. [1996] 4 WWR 177 (Alta. QB).

325. The Alberta government has settled claims with respect to wrongful sterilization under the eugenics laws. In 1999, the government paid approximately 246 claimants USD 325,000 each, in addition to their legal costs. It also settled with approximately 600 other claimants, who were classified as "dependent adults." They received approximately USD 100,000 each. The government also issued an apology to the victims.[613]

326. According to the provisions of the *Sexual Sterilization Act*[614] then in force, the surgery should not have been authorized before the patient was proposed for release. Ms. Muir left the facility, without being officially discharged, six years after the surgery. The province admitted liability for the wrongful sterilization, but contested the other issues and left the *quantum* to the court. The court awarded the maximum amount of damages for pain and suffering resulting from the wrongful sterilization—CAD 250,280. An aggravating feature of the sterilization was that it branded the plaintiff, physically and mentally, as a "moron." The court awarded aggravated damages of CAD 115,000. The court also awarded damages for wrongful confinement, with interest from 1965 (the date the confinement ended), totaling CAD 265,500. The overall award in the case was CAD 740,780.

3. Non-therapeutic Sterilization Before *Eve*

327. Aside from sterilizations performed in furtherance of eugenic goals, other involuntary sterilizations of disabled or mentally ill individuals were done. Before *Eve* was decided in 1986, it was not uncommon for physicians, at the request of parents or institutions, to perform sterilizations upon persons who lacked the mental capacity to consent.[615] For example, in 1976, nearly 300 "mentally retarded" minors were sterilized, according to a study of health insurance billings.[616] The Supreme Court was certainly conscious of this dark history of involuntary sterilization when it made its ruling in *Re Eve.*[617] The Court considered eugenics laws at some length, although no one was alleging that Eve's sterilization was for the public good, or advocating sterilization of the incompetent as a general social policy.

613. *See also D.E. (Guardian ad litem of) v. British Columbia,* 2005 BCCA 134.
614. SA 1928, c 37, as amended.
615. Irvine, Osborne & Shariff, *supra* note 165 at 370–371. *See* generally Robertson, *supra* note 538.
616. Community and Social Services Ministry, cited in Irvine, Osborne & Shariff, *supra* note 165 at 370–371.
617. *Re Eve, supra* note 600.

II. Legal Limitations on Sterilization of the Mentally Incompetent

A. *Constitutional Limitations*

328. The application of the *Canadian Charter of Rights and Freedoms*[618] to the sterilization of the mentally incompetent has not been examined extensively by the courts. Charter issues had been the basis of the decision of the Court of First Instance in *Re K.*,[619] but the appeal court had reversed the decision on other grounds.[620] Charter arguments were before the Court in *Re Eve*;[621] however, the Supreme Court decision was made on the basis of the *parens patriae* jurisdiction.

329. There are three relevant protections under the Charter. Section 7 protects the right to life, liberty, and security of the person. Section 12 prohibits cruel and unusual treatment or punishment. Section 15 protects equality rights and includes a prohibition of discrimination based on mental or physical disability. The rights and freedoms guaranteed by the Charter are subject "to such reasonable limits prescribed by law as can be demonstrably justified in a free and democratic society."[622] Legislatures may expressly declare that a statute is in force notwithstanding Charter provisions protecting fundamental freedoms, legal rights, or equality rights.[623] (To date, this "notwithstanding" provision has seldom been used.) The court may provide a remedy for those whose rights have been infringed or denied.[624]

B. *Parens Patriae Jurisdiction*

330. The *parens patriae* jurisdiction of superior courts is exercised for the benefit of infants and other persons with a disability, including mentally incompetent adults. The jurisdiction has been called "broad, sweeping and expansive."[625] It adapts to a changing society and new situations. It is unlikely ever to be replaced by statute. It is available to fill in gaps in protective legislation such as child welfare legislation. Because the jurisdiction is a protective one, it can only be exercised for the benefit of the person being protected. It cannot operate to protect the interests of

618. *Canadian Charter of Rights and Freedoms*, Part I of *the Constitution Act, 1982*, being Sch. B to the *Canada Act 1982* (UK), 1982, c 11.
619. *Re K; K v. Public Trustee* [1985] 3 WWR 204, 60 BCLR 209 (SC).
620. (1985) 19 DLR (4th) 255 [1985] 4 WWR 724, 63 BCLR 145 (CA), leave to appeal to SCC dismissed on jurisdictional grounds (1985), 19 DLR (4th) n. 1255 [1985] 4 WWR 757, 62 BCLR XLI.
621. *Re Eve*, *supra* note 600.
622. Section 1.
623. Section 33.
624. Section 24.
625. Alberta, Institute of Law Research and Reform, *Sterilization Decisions: Minors and Mentally Incompetent Adults,* Report for Discussion No. 6 (Edmonton: The Institute of Law Research and Reform, 1988) at 50.

others (such as society, parents, or institutions) at the expense of the ward.[626] "[T]he discretion is to do what is necessary for the protection of the person for whose benefit it is exercised."[627]

331. In *Re Eve*,[628] the SCC ruled that the *parens patriae* jurisdiction cannot be used to authorize non-therapeutic sterilization. In the words of the Court:[629]

> The grave intrusion on a person's rights and the certain physical damage that ensues from non-therapeutic sterilization without consent, when compared to the highly questionable advantages that can result from it, have persuaded me that it can never safely be determined that such a procedure is for the benefit of that person.

332. The Court defined "therapeutic sterilization" rather narrowly:

> sterilization may, on occasion, be necessary as an adjunct to treatment of a serious malady, but ... this, of course, does not allow for subterfuge or for treatment of some marginal medical problem.[630]

The only reason given for seeking a sterilization for *Eve* was to avoid the hardship a pregnancy would cause *Eve* and her mother. The purpose was contraceptive and thus, clearly, non-therapeutic. The Court also referred to the case of *Re K.*[631] as "at best dangerously close to the limits of the permissible."[632]

333. As noted above, *Re K.* involved a severely mentally handicapped 10-year-old, who had a phobic reaction to blood.[633] In this case the Court allowed sterilization for the purpose of avoiding menses. In coming to this conclusion the Court noted that the proposed operation was purely therapeutic and that "it was in the best interest of the ward to undergo a surgery."

334. Case law research for all Canadian jurisdictions discloses few recent cases in this area. The order in *Re E.M.H.*[634] approved the performance of a procedure which would in effect result in sterilization. However, the purpose of the procedure was to eliminate the ward's menstrual flow, not to prevent conception.

626. For an analysis and history of the *parens patriae* jurisdiction, *see Re Eve*, *supra* note 600 at 14–21.
627. *Re Eve*, *supra* note 600.
628. *Ibid.*
629. *Ibid.*, at 32.
630. *Re Eve*, *supra* note 600.
631. *Re K; K v. Public Trustee* [1985] 3 WWR 204, 60 BCLR 209 (SC), reversed [1985] 4 WWR 724, 63 BCLR 145, 19 DLR (4th) 255 (CA), leave to appeal to SCC dismissed on jurisdictional grounds [1985] 4 WWR 757, 62 BCLR XLI, 19 DLR (4th) n. 1255.
632. *Re Eve*, *supra* note 600.
633. *Re K; K v. Public Trustee* (1985) 19 DLR (4th) 255 [1985] 4 WWR 724, 63 BCLR 145.
634. [1995] SJ No. 220 (QB) (QL).

335. The subject was a 12-year-old with a moderate to severe mental disability, left-sided hemiparesis and a seizure disorder. She did not understand the menstrual cycle, and became very upset and lost bladder control for the ten-day duration of menstrual flow. She was then unable to participate in her usual activities and her education and training were also interrupted. The prognosis was that her understanding of and reaction to menses would never improve.

336. In these circumstances, the court had little difficulty in authorizing the performance of an endometrial ablation, which would destroy the endometrium by cauterization, thus preventing future menstruation. The court found the treatment to be therapeutic and a commensurate response to the child's serious condition. The court, however, refused to authorize a tubal ligation whose only purpose was contraceptive. In any case, as the court had noted earlier in the judgment, "the reality is that [fertility] would be rare … so improbable as to be impossible."[635]

337. Since the *parens patriae* jurisdiction is not available for non-therapeutic sterilizations, it follows that if they are to be permitted at all, it must be by legislation enacted for that purpose.[636] The protective *parens patriae* jurisdiction is carefully guarded by the courts. They will not assume it has been removed by legislation. Any legislation permitting non-therapeutic sterilization must be written in clear and unequivocal language.[637]

338. However, in 2018, the Alberta Court of Queen's Bench authorized a non-therapeutic sterilization for a dependent adult who sought a vasectomy for contraceptive purposes, with the support of his guardians, who brought substantial evidence of his understanding of what a vasectomy was and its consequences as well as his strong desire for one. Thus, while the court recognized that it could not exercise its *parens patriae* jurisdiction to authorize a non-therapeutic sterilization, it found the authority to do so under the relevant statute, which carved out non-therapeutic sterilization from the "health-care" decisions that could be made by a guardian, but not from the broad and inclusive definition of a "personal matter."[638]

C. Provincial Limitations

339. Substitute decision-making legislation in certain provinces and territories explicitly precludes guardians and other substitute decision makers from consenting to the non-therapeutic sterilization of represented adults. Manitoba's law, for example, lists "sterilization that is not medically necessary for the protection of the vulnerable person's health" among the matters to which the power of a substitute

635. *Ibid.*, at para. 8.
636. *Re Eve*, *supra* note 600.
637. *Ibid.* at 32–33.
638. *G.T.M. v. D.A.M.*, 2018 ABQB 450.

decision maker for personal care does not extend.[639] Alberta's *Adult Guardianship and Trusteeship Act* excludes "sterilization that is not medically necessary to protect health" from the definition of that "health care" with respect to which a guardian may be granted authority to act and make decisions.[640]

340. In Saskatchewan, Nunavut and the Northwest Territories, guardians and other substitute decision makers may be granted the authority to consent to such, but only upon special court order.[641]

341. In Ontario, the procedure is one on which "the law relating to giving or refusing consent on another person's behalf" is preserved.[642] There, and in those provinces and territories that have not legislated otherwise, the common law, as stated in *Re Eve,* governs: neither court nor substitute decision maker may consent to the non-therapeutic sterilization of an incapable adult.

III. Other Forms of Contraception

A. *Introduction to Other Forms of Contraception*

342. Contraception is any practice, drug or device intended to prevent pregnancy despite sexual intercourse. The federal government regulates all contraceptive drugs and devices manufactured in or imported to Canada.

B. *Federal Regulatory Requirements*

1. Authority of the Health Protection Branch

343. The federal *Food and Drugs Act*[643] regulates the advertisement, labeling, packaging, distribution, manufacturing, importation, and sale of medical devices, including contraceptive devices, within Canada. The act is administered by the Department of Health, which uses a mixture of internally designated inspectors and accredited third parties for compliance monitoring. The *Medical Devices Regulations*[644] have been enacted pursuant to sections 3(3), 30(1) and 37(1) of *the Food and Drugs Act.* These regulations were designed to harmonize Canada's medical devices' requirements with those of other nations participating in the "Global Harmonization Taskforce" (the U.S., European Union, Japan and Australia), which aims

639. *Vulnerable Persons Living with a Mental Disability Act,* CCSM c V90, s. 61(b). *See also Consent to Treatment and Health Care Directives Act,* RSPEI 1988, c C-17.2, s. 12(b); *Decision Making, Support and Protection to Adults Act,* SY 2003, c 21, s. 16(a).
640. SA 2008, c A-4.2, s. 1(r)(v).
641. *Adult Guardianship and Co-decision making Act,* SS 2000, c A-5.3, s. 22(5); *Health Care Regulations,* Nu. Reg. 050–97, s. 1; *Health Care Regulations,* NWT Reg. 050–97, s. 1.
642. *Substitute Decisions Act, 1992,* SO 1992, c 30, s. 66(14).
643. RSC 1985, c F-27.
644. SOR/98–282.

to converge the regulatory practices in each of these participating countries to enhance product safety and quality, facilitate international trade, and promote technological innovation. The *Medical Devices Regulations* now allow Canada to recognize medical devices that have already been assessed by a regulatory body in a participating country and to place them directly on the market. The regulations use a licensing scheme to establish quality systems requirements, pre-market scrutiny and post-market surveillance as the means of assessing and controlling the safety and efficacy of medical devices on the Canadian market.

344. The *Medical Devices Regulations*[645] cover medical devices whose purposes range from contraception to genetic testing to investigational testing involving human subjects. Medical devices are classified according to the risk presented by the device. If a given contraceptive device is given a Class I (lowest risk) rating, its manufacturers generally do not have to be licensed under the act before their products can be imported and sold in Canada, though the person who actually imports and sells the device may require an establishment license, and the contraceptive devices will be subject to labeling requirements and advertising restrictions under the regulations.[646] The manufacturers of Class I devices are still held accountable for ensuring and proving that their products are safe and effective. Manufacturers of all other classes of medical devices must apply for and obtain a license from the Minister of Health, and meet mandatory record keeping and reporting requirements.

2. Penalties

345. Any attempt to produce, distribute or import an unapproved drug or device can result in the seizure of the drug or device, as well as in civil or criminal[647] penalties.

3. Process for Approval

346. New contraceptive drugs and devices must go through the approval process of the Health Protection Branch before they can be placed on the market. Use in other countries is not directly relevant to approval in Canada; however, studies completed elsewhere may be probative of the safety and efficacy required for approval. The approval process begins with the manufacturer conducting animal and laboratory studies to identify therapeutic uses and risks of a new compound, or new uses of an existing compound. If these studies demonstrate that the drug has a therapeutic effect and an acceptable level of risk, the manufacturer may obtain permission from the Therapeutic Products Directorate, Health Protection Branch to

645. SOR/98–282 (May 7, 1998).
646. For instance, s. 24 of the current regulations allows the advertising of most types of contraceptives, by any means except the direct distribution of samples door-to-door or via mail.
647. *Food and Drug Act,* RSC 1985, c F-27.

conduct clinical trials. If all three required levels of clinical trials show that the drug is effective and safe, the manufacturer files a New Drug Submission (NDS). The Therapeutic Products Directorate reviews the NDS in detail to assess whether to approve the drug for use in Canada. Upon approval, the drug receives a Notice of Compliance, and the approved dosages and indications are set. If a manufacturer wants to promote the drug for other uses or dosages, it must submit evidence that the drug is effective and safe for use in those conditions.[648]

4. Emergency Contraceptive Pill

347. Levonorgestrel, an emergency contraceptive treatment, can be used up to seventy-two hours after unprotected intercourse to reduce the possibility of pregnancy. In 2008, the National Association of Pharmacy Regulatory Authorities authorized access to levonorgestrel at pharmacies without a doctor's prescription.

§3. Reproductive Technologies

348. Reproductive technologies include infertility treatments such as fertility drugs, and in vitro fertilization (IVF) and assisted insemination and their variants. Surrogacy arrangements, which may or may not make use of new reproductive technologies, are also discussed here, as is the status of frozen pre-embryos (zygotes).

349. New reproductive technologies are responses by medicine and science to the problem of human infertility. Infertility is generally defined by the failure to conceive after a certain period of unprotected sexual intercourse.[649] In Canada, the period of time used to define infertility is one year for women under the age of 35, and six months for women over the age of 35.[650] Around 16% of Canadian couples experience infertility.[651]

350. There is little or no case law in Canada concerning any of these technologies. Developments in reproductive technologies raise medical, legal, social and ethical concerns. An indication of the growth of issues in this area is the number of formal inquiries that have been funded. A high-profile inquiry in Canada was the

---

648. Canada, Royal Commission on New Reproductive Technologies, *Proceed with Care: Final Report of the Royal Commission on New Reproductive Technologies* (Ottawa: Minister of Government Services Canada, 1993) at 404–405.
649. Government of Canada, *Fertility* (online: Government of Canada, May 28, 2019) www.canada.ca/en/public-health/services/fertility/fertility.html (Government of Canada, *Fertility*); Consider also Canada, Royal Commission on New Reproductive Technologies, *Proceed with Care: Final Report of the Royal Commission on New Reproductive Technologies* (Ottawa: Minister of Government Services Canada, 1993) at 182 (hereinafter RCNRT).
650. Government of Canada, *Fertility, supra* note 648.
651. *Ibid.*

Royal Commission on New Reproductive Technologies, appointed by the federal government in 1989.[652] The terms of reference for the inquiry were to:

> inquire into and report on current and potential medical and scientific developments related to new reproductive technologies, considering in particular their social, ethical, health, research, legal and economic implications and the public interest, recommending what policies and safeguards should be applied.[653]

351. After four years of study, the Royal Commission released its report in 1993. Among the recommendations, the Royal Commission on New Reproductive Technologies included in its report, several concerned statutory prohibitions and offenses relating to reproduction and reproductive technologies. The Report has been criticized for offering no analysis of Parliament's constitutional authority to enact such legislation, and no consideration of the principles of criminal jurisprudence that could justify the prohibitions.[654]

352. To address some of the recommendations of the Royal Commission, in 1995, the federal Minister of Health introduced a voluntary moratorium on many of the activities the Royal Commission had found problematic, including: commercial surrogacy agreements; buying and selling of eggs, sperm and embryos; egg donation in exchange for IVF; egg retrieval from cadavers and fetuses for donation, fertilization and research; and sex selection of a child for non-medical reasons. An advisory committee was established the following year to help monitor compliance by researchers and health professionals, although the chair of the Royal Commission was reported as stating that compliance with the voluntary moratorium was poor.[655]

353. In 1996, the federal government introduced legislation, Bill C-47, *an act respecting human reproductive technologies and commercial transactions relating to human reproduction,* which proposed a series of prohibitions based on the voluntary moratorium. Although approved by the House of Commons Standing Committee on Health, the Bill died on the order paper with the dissolution of the federal Parliament in spring 1997. Two other bills, Bill C-56, an act respecting assisted human reproduction, and Bill C-13, an act respecting assisted human reproduction and related research, also died on the Order Paper—in 2002 and 2003, respectively.

652. Order in Council, PC 1989–2150.
653. *Ibid.*
654. Patrick Healy, "Statutory Prohibitions and the Regulation of New Reproductive Technologies under Federal Law in Canada" (1990) 40 McGill LJ 905. *See also* M Eichler, "Frankenstein Meets Kafka: The Royal Commission on New Reproductive Technologies" in G Basen, M Eichler & A Lippman, eds., *Misconceptions: The Social Construction of Choice and the New Reproductive and Genetic Technologies* (Hull, Quebec: Voyageur Pub, 1993) vol. 1 at 196.
655. Healy, *supra* note 653 at 943.

354. Bill C-6, the *Assisted Human Reproduction Act,* passed third reading in the Senate, and received Royal Assent in March 2004.[656] The sections which remain, following the 2010 Supreme Court decision and the 2012 amendments which repealed large portions of the act, have been fully in force as of June 9, 2020.[657]

355. Under the act, the following practices are prohibited: creating a human clone for any purpose (i.e., reproductive or therapeutic purposes); identifying the sex of an embryo created for reproductive purposes, except for medical reasons such as sex-linked disorders; creating human/non-human combinations for reproductive purposes; paying a woman a financial incentive to be a surrogate mother (commercial surrogacy); paying a donor for their sperm or eggs, or providing goods or services in exchange; and, selling or buying human embryos, or providing goods or services in exchange.[658]

356. In its original form, the act authorized the regulation of assisted human reproduction activities and related research including: the collection, alteration, manipulation or treatment of any human reproductive material for the purpose of creating an embryo (e.g., IVF); the collection of donors' medical information; and, the storage, handling and use of reproductive materials and embryos.[659]

357. The act also established the Assisted Human Reproduction Agency, an organization separate from Health Canada that reports directly to the Minister of Health. A 2010 decision of the SCC curtailed its legislated powers.[660] It was subsequently dismantled in 2012.[661]

358. In 2008, in a reference to that province's Court of Appeal, the Attorney General of Quebec challenged the constitutionality of certain provisions of the *Assisted Human Reproduction Act.* The following question was posed:

> Are sections 8 to 19, 40 to 53, 60, 61 to 68 of the *Assisted Human Reproduction Act,* S.C. 2004, c. 2, *ultra vires* the Parliament of Canada in whole or in part under the *Constitution Act, 1867*?[662]

---

656. SC 2004, c 2.
657. SI/2019-38 (2019) C Gaz II, 4038. Sections 45–58 came into force as of Jun. 9, 2019; s. 10 came into force as of Feb. 4, 2020; s. 12 came into force on Jun. 9, 2020.
658. *Ibid.*, ss. 5(1)(a), (e), (g)–(j), 6, 7.
659. *Ibid.*, ss. 10, 14–19.
660. *See Reference re Assisted Human Reproduction Act,* 2010 SCC 61 [2010] SCJ No. 61. *See* T Lemmens et al., eds., *Regulating Creation: The Law, Ethics, and Policy of Assisted Human Reproduction* (Toronto: University of Toronto Press, 2017), in particular the chapters: B. Dickens, "A Historical Introduction to the Supreme Court's Decision on the *Assisted Human Reproduction Act*" at 23–33 and T Lemmens & A Flavelle Martin, "Introduction" at 1–20.
661. *Jobs, Growth and Long-term Prosperity Act,* SC 2012, c 19, ss. 741–745.
662. *In the matter of a Reference by the Government of Quebec pursuant to the Court of Appeal Reference Act, R.S.Q., c R-23, concerning the constitutional validity of sections 8 to 19, 40 to 53, 60, 61 and 68 of the Assisted Human Reproduction Act, S.C. 2014, c. 2,* 2008 QCCA 1167, 298 DLR (4th) 712.

Finding the impugned sections lacked a legitimate federal criminal law purpose, the Quebec Court of Appeal answered the question in the affirmative.[663]

359. In late 2010, an appeal to the SCC was allowed in part. By a narrow majority, the following sections were struck down: sections 10, 11 and 13 (controlled activities, including IVF); sections 14 through 18 (privacy and access to information); subsections 40(2) through 40(5) (issuance of licenses for certain controlled activities); and subsections 44(2) and (3)(entry and management of premises by inspectors). The validity of the following sections was upheld: sections 8 and 9 (consent requirements for use of reproductive materials and in vitro embryos); section 12 (reimbursement of donor, surrogate and in vitro embryo maintenance and transport expenditures); section 19 (public availability of Agency information); and section 60 (punishment for contraventions of prohibitions). As well, subsections 40(1), (6) and (7) (issuance of licenses for controlled activities generally); sections 41 through 43 (amendment, renewal and suspension of licenses); subsections 44(1) and (4) (Agency's power to mitigate threats to human health or safety); sections 45 through 53 (inspection and enforcement); section 61 (punishments for contraventions of other than prohibited acts); and section 68 (non-application of provisions where equivalent provincial laws in force) were upheld to the extent that they relate to constitutionally legitimate provisions.[664] Currently, Quebec is the only provincial or territorial jurisdiction to have legislated with respect to reproductive technologies.[665]

I. Fertility Drugs

360. Fertility drugs are hormones that affect the reproductive system. They are the most common treatment for infertility, being used alone or in support of more complex treatments such as IVF.[666]

361. There are about a dozen fertility drugs on the market in Canada. Clomiphene citrate and human menopausal gonadotropin (hMG) have been among the most commonly used. They are prescribed to induce ovulation. Both entered the market in the 1960s, before the current testing and approval process was in place. There is very little reliable data available on their effectiveness and the risks that may be associated with their use. The most common known risks associated with ovulation induction drugs are ovarian hyperstimulation syndrome and multiple births. Severe ovarian hyperstimulation syndrome can be life-threatening. Women

663. *Ibid.*, at para. 146.
664. *See Reference re Assisted Human Reproduction Act,* 2010 SCC 61 [2010] 3 SCR 457.
665. *An Act Respecting Clinical and Research Activities Relating to Assisted Procreation,* CQLR, c A-5.01. *See also* Gruben, *supra* note 561 at 424–426.
666. RCNRT, *supra* note 648 at 387.

receiving these drugs must be monitored closely, with careful regulation of dosages. Multiple pregnancies raise significant health risks for women and for fetuses and children.[667]

362. Treatment and prescription practices in connection with fertility drugs also raise concerns. Possible over-use, or use without a complete diagnosis of the cause of a couple's infertility problems, raises issues of medical ethics and legal risk.[668]

II. Artificial Insemination

363. Artificial (or assisted) insemination (AI) is a long-known, and relatively non-technical, means of conception for women who do not have a fertile male partner. AI includes all forms of insemination without intercourse, using partner or donor sperm.

364. In Assisted Insemination Homologous (AIH), the male partner's sperm is used. AIH can improve the chances of conception when the male partner has a low sperm count (oligospermia) or poor sperm motility or when the woman has an immune reaction to the male's sperm. AIH raises legal issues that are not significantly different from those that may be associated with any medical procedure. While Donor Insemination (DI) also raises all the usual potential for legal liability,[669] it also raises new significant legal issues.

365. Where sperm is donated by someone other than the patient's spouse or sexual partner, various testing and quarantine requirements must be met before it can be used for insemination. Specifically, pursuant to the recently brought-into-force section 10 of the *Assisted Human Reproduction Act*, sperm or ovum collected from a donor who is not the patient's spouse or sexual partner cannot be used unless the gametes have been: (a) tested and "obtained, prepared, preserved, quarantined, identified, labelled and stored" and quality assessed in accordance with the regulations; and (b) "screened and tested" and the "donor's suitability" assessed in accordance with the regulations.[670] The *Safety of Sperm and Ova Regulations* provide further guidance on the requirements related to donor screening for infectious and

667. *Ibid.,* at 398–399.
668. *Ibid.,* at 390.
669. *See ter Neuzen, supra* note 199, in which a physician was found liable in negligence after performing an artificial insemination procedure in which his patient contracted HIV through infected donor sperm.
670. *Assisted Human Reproduction Act*, S.C. 2004, c 2, s. 10; *See also* discussion regarding the impact of these policies on LBGTQ people in S Marvel et al., "Listening to LGBTQ People on Assisted Human Reproduction: Access to Reproductive Material, Services, and Facilities" in T Lemmens et al., eds., *Regulating Creation: The Law, Ethics, and Policy of Assisted Human Reproduction* (Toronto: University of Toronto Press, 2017) at 325–358.

genetic diseases, physical exams, and testing for infectious (and possibly, genetic) diseases, and to quarantine periods and processes.[671]

366. DI severs social and genetic fatherhood. This fact could encourage attempts to vary existing social, legal and financial networks of parental rights/ responsibilities. For example, the Ontario case *M.L. v. J.C.*[672] involved a dispute over the parentage of a child born by DI between three adults involved in her conception. M.L. and J.C. agreed to assist each other in conceiving two children. M.L. would provide semen to J.C. and her spouse S.N., and each woman would carry a child. One would be for M.L., and the other would be for J.C. and S.N. When S.N. appeared to be pregnant, J.C. was also inseminated and became pregnant. However, only J.C. carried a child to term, and the parties disagreed on who would get the child, having not produced any written agreement. At the time of the trial, the child lived five days per week with J.C. and S.N., and two days per week with M.L. Ultimately, the court ruled that there was no valid surrogacy agreement according to the statutory requirements in Ontario and declared all three adults to be the child's legal parents. It granted sole custody to J.C. (joint custody would create conflict between M.L. and J.C. based on their different parenting styles and home environments), required M.L. to be consulted on major decisions, and split parenting time relatively equally in a schedule giving the child an average of three days per week with M.L. with alternating weekends.

367. Similar issues have also been raised in cases with more prosaic circumstances of conception. In *Johnson-Steeves v. Lee*,[673] a mother applied for an order that, among other things, would deny the child's father access to their jointly conceived child. The plaintiff argued that she had entered a binding "paternity agreement" with the father, in which he had agreed to act as a sperm donor and give financial support while not interfering with her raising of the child. Alternatively, the plaintiff argued that the defendant was only a biological father to her child, and not a social father entitled to access. The plaintiff also raised a constitutional issue, and claimed that a right to choose one's own family structure (i.e., single-parent) was protected under the guarantee of liberty contained in section 7 of the *Charter of Rights and Freedoms.* The court ultimately decided that access to his father was in the child's best interests, and the child's right to access could not be bargained away by either of his parents. Even though the court in *Johnson-Steeves v. Lee* did not fully canvass all the novel legal issues before it, the case certainly indicates how potential challenges to current common law and statutory definitions of family and parental responsibility could be supported by the use of DI and other reproductive technologies that sever biological and social fatherhood.

671. *Safety of Sperm and Ova Regulations*, SOR/2019-192; "Health Canada Directive: Thechnical Requirements for Conducting the Suitability Assessment of Sperm and Ova Donors" (published Jun. 26, 2019, effective Feb. 4, 2020), online (pdf): Health Canada https://www.canada.ca/content /dam/hc-sc/documents/services/publications/drugs-health-products/technical-directive-sperm-ova-donors/technical-directive-sperm-ova-donors.pdf. *See also* the (now repealed) *Processing and Distribution of Semen for Assisted Conception Regulations*, SOR/96-254.

672. 2017 ONSC 7179.

673. (1997), 29 RFL (4th) 126 (Alta. QB), affirmed (1997) 33 RFL (4th) 278 (Alta. CA).

368. DI severs social and genetic fatherhood. Provincial family law statutes set out the legal rights and obligations of a parent in relation to maternity, paternity, filiation, custody, access and support. Some jurisdictions, such as Yukon, the Northwest Territories, Alberta, British Columbia, Ontario, Newfoundland, and Quebec, have enacted legislation that expressly protects the interests of DI children, recipients and donors.[674]

369. The Royal Commission of New Reproductive Technologies concluded that DI families and donors are not adequately protected by existing family law, and recommended enacting legislation which would address the rights, responsibilities, and legal status of donors, male partners of donor recipients, and legal mothers.[675]

370. The Royal Commission of New Reproductive Technologies also recommended that full records be kept of all sperm donors, insemination and DI births. As with adoption records, this would allow DI children to identify and trace genetically caused health problems, prevent related persons from marrying or conceiving a child unknowingly, and enable recipient families and DI children to know about the child's biological background. Attempts to obtain a judicial recognition of the right to receive information about one's biological background and origin have failed in Canada.[676] In *Pratten v. British Columbia (Attorney General)*, the courts were not convinced by the plaintiff's argument that any right to know one's genetic origins is significant enough to warrant free-standing constitutional protection.[677] The plaintiff's other argument, that British Columbia's *Adoption Act* discriminates against DI children by failing to include them in provisions providing access to certain information about birth parents to adopted persons, succeeded at trial but was overturned on appeal. The Court of Appeal found instead that the impugned provisions were directed toward remedying disadvantage faced by adoptees, thus qualifying them as ameliorative legislation protected by section 15(2) of the *Charter* and not obligating the legislature to provide comparable benefits to DI children.[678]

371. With technological advances in recent years, some individuals conceived by DI have been able to learn about their genetic history and discover previously unknown biological relatives through the use of direct-to-consumer genetic testing kits (like those made available by Ancestry.com or 23andMe). In several cases, DNA testing has revealed that from the 1970s through the 1990s, some physicians used their own sperm to inseminate unsuspecting patients without their consent.

---

674. *Children's Law Act*, RSY 2002, c 31, s. 13; *Children's Law Act*, SNWT 1997, c 14, ss. 2(1.1), 3(3), 5.1, 8.1; *Family Law Act*, SA 2003, c F-4.5, ss. 5.1–8.2; *Family Law Act*, SBC 2011, c 25, ss. 20, 24, 27–31; *Children's Law Reform Act*, RSO 1990, c C.12, ss. 5–11; *Children's Law Act*, RSNL 1990, c C-13, s. 12; and *Vital Statistics Act, 2009*, SNL 2009, c V-6.01, s. 5; Arts. 538–542 CCQ.
675. RCNRT, *supra* note 648 at 467–468.
676. *See* the discussion in Michelle Giroux & Cheryl Milne, "The Right to Know One's Origins, the *AHRA Reference,* and *Pratten v. AGBC:* A Call for Provincial Legislative Action" in T Lemmens et al., eds., *Regulating Creation: The Law, Ethics, and Policy of Assisted Human Reproduction* (Toronto: University of Toronto Press, 2017) at 124–144.
677. 2012 BCCA 480, reversing 2011 BCSC 656, leave to appeal to SCC refused.
678. *Ibid.,* at para. 42.

Cases of "fertility" or "insemination" fraud have been discovered across the globe, including in the Netherlands, the U.S., and Canada and, while only a handful of physicians have been identified as having engaged in this conduct, this small group of physicians has collectively fathered a significant number of children.[679] While hundreds of children and families have been adversely affected by fertility fraud, without laws explicitly making it illegal for a physician to use his own sperm in DI cases, the legal consequences for this conduct have been unclear.[680] Some physicians in the U.S. have been convicted on criminal charges for actions *related* to the fertility fraud (e.g., mail, travel and wire fraud, perjury, obstruction of justice), while other physicians, both in the U.S. and elsewhere, have faced civil suits. Some of these physicians have also faced disciplinary proceedings for breaching the ethical standards and fiduciary obligations of the profession and have either surrendered their medical licenses or had them revoked by their governing professional bodies.[681]

372. In the one case of fertility fraud so far discovered in Canada, both civil and regulatory proceedings were eventually engaged against the physician. Dr. Norman Barwin is currently the subject of a class action lawsuit filed by former patients and their children alleging that over seventy-five children were conceived using the wrong sperm (either a different donor than the one chosen by the patient or using the sperm of a donor rather than the patient's husband's sperm), with eleven of these cases involving the use of Barwin's own sperm. The plaintiffs in the class action allege that Barwin's conduct constitutes breach of contract, medical battery, negligence, and breach of trust and fiduciary duty and are seeking general and punitive damages, including compensation for pain and suffering and loss of enjoyment of life and for various expenses including for investigating biological ancestry and relatives and completing their medical backgrounds and for counseling and other medical treatment related to the discovery of the fertility fraud.[682] In addition, in June 2019, Barwin's medical license was revoked by the Ontario College of Physicians and Surgeons after a discipline committee found that he engaged in professional misconduct both by using his own sperm and using the wrong sperm to inseminate numerous patients. Barwin was also ordered to pay costs to the College of CAD 10,730 within thirty days. In their decision, the committee found that Barwin's misconduct was "of the most egregious kind" and that he had "completely violated his patient's trust, as well as their bodies," and described his actions as, among other things, "reprehensible and abhorrent," "despicable," "mindboggling"

679. Jody Lynee Madeira, "Uncommon Misconceptions: Holding Physicians Accountable for Insemination Fraud" (2019) 37:1 Law & Ineq 45.

680. Notably, in the United States a couple of states have recently introduced legislation addressing fertility fraud (*see* Dov Fox, I. Glenn Cohen & Eli Y. Adashi, "Editorial: Fertility Fraud, Legal Firsts, and Medical Ethics" (2019) 134:5 Obstetrics & Gynecology 918.

681. Madeira, *supra* note 678.

682. *Davina Dixon, Daniel Dixon & Rebecca Dixon v. Dr. Norman Barwin,* Ontario Superior Court of Justice, Court File No. 16-70454CP (Fresh As Amended Statement of Claim dated Nov. 1, 2016, amended Oct. 29, 2019); Amanda Pfeffer, "Disgraced Fertility Doctor's Clinic Broke Federal Rules as Far Back as 1999, Inspection Reports Reveal," *CBC News* (Jan. 6, 2020), online https://www.cbc.ca/news/canada/ottawa/disgraced-fertility-doctor-s-clinic-broke-federal-rules-as-far-back-as-1999-inspection-reports-reveal-1.5411100.

and "atrocious." The committee also issued a public reprimand denouncing Barwin's misconduct. In the reprimand, the committee lamented that "at this time, all we can do is revoke [Barwin's] licence to practice medicine and to deliver this reprimand," but took "some solace in the fact that [Barwin is] no longer in a position to cause further harm."[683]

373. There has been some litigation in Canada regarding physicians' refusal to perform AI for some individuals. For example, in one case, an obstetrician/ gynecologist was found to have violated human rights legislation by refusing to perform AI for a lesbian couple.[684] In January 2004, a lawsuit was filed against a fertility specialist who refused to perform AI for an HIV-positive couple.[685] Although it is reported that the specialist initially agreed to perform the procedure, he eventually refused after his clinic's ethics committee advised against it due to concerns about future legal liability if the child born as a result of AI contracted HIV from the infected mother.[686]

374. The processing and distribution of semen used in assisted conception were previously governed by regulations under Canada's *Food and Drugs Act.*[687] Applying only to the semen of donors who are not recipient spouses or sexual partners, these were the subject of more than one legal challenge.[688] The processing and distribution of donor sperm and ova for use in assisted reproduction, where the recipient is not a spouse or sexual partner of the donor, is now governed by regulations under the *Assisted Human Reproduction Act.*[689]

III. In Vitro Fertilization (IVF) and Related Procedures

375. IVF involves removing eggs from a woman's ovaries, fertilizing them in a laboratory, and returning the resulting pre-embryos (zygotes) to her body, in the hope that they will implant, resulting in pregnancy. Variants of IVF include Gamete Intra-Fallopian Transfer, Zygote Intra-Fallopian Transfer, and direct egg/sperm transfer. Embryos in excess of those required for immediate implantation (three embryos are considered optimum) may be frozen (cryo-preserved) for later use.

---

683. *Ontario (College of Physicians and Surgeons of Ontario) v. Barwin*, 2019 ONCPSD 39.
684. *Korn v. Potter* (1996), 134 DLR (4th) 437 (BCSC); Consider also Marvel et al., *supra* note 669.
685. *See* M Cardwell, "HIV+ Couple Sues Clinic over Insemination Refusal" (2004) 40:4 Medical Post 8, online: Canadian Business & Current Affairs Database (ProQuest).
686. *Ibid.*; *See also* discussion in Marvel et al., *supra* note 669 about the exclusion of HIV-positive men for anonymous third-party sperm donation and surrogacy.
687. *See Processing and Distribution of Semen for Assisted Conception Regulations,* SOR/96–254, as repealed by *Safety of Sperm and Ova Regulations*, SOR/2019-192, s. 93.
688. *See Susan Doe v. Canada (Attorney General)*, 2007 ONCA 11, affirming (2006), 79 OR (3d) 586 (SCJ); *Jane Doe v. Canada (Attorney General)* (2005), 75 OR (3d) 725 (CA), affirming (2003), 68 OR (3d) 9 (SCJ).
689. *Safety of Sperm and Ova Regulations*, SOR/2019-192; *See also* "Guidance Document: Safety of Sperm and Ova Regulations" (published Aug. 30, 2019, effective Feb. 4, 2020, revised May 28, 2020), online (pdf): *Health Canada* https://www.canada.ca/content/dam/hc-sc/documents/programs /consultation-safety-sperm-ova-regulations/consultation-safety-sperm-ova-regulations-en.pdf

376. Informed consent is an issue in this area. At some IVF clinics, patients may find misleadingly optimistic calculation of success rates, along with a lack of information about risks to physical and mental health created by participation in IVF. To date, there has been no litigation by IVF participants.

377. IVF using a heterosexual couple's own eggs and sperm creates no issues as to legal parentage. However, if a couple, or a woman without a male partner, uses an egg donor or a sperm donor, the legal issues are similar to those that arise in relation to DI.

378. There has been some controversy over who may be considered an appropriate recipient of IVF. Many clinics have required patients to sign agreements stating that upon their divorce, or the death of one partner, the clinic will destroy their cryo-preserved embryos. Some clinics also have limited access to IVF on the basis of social factors such as marital or economic status or sexual orientation.[690]

379. Lack of public health-care funding for IVF has resulted in a constitutional challenge in one Canadian province. In *Cameron v. Nova Scotia*,[691] an infertile couple argued the provincial government violated their rights to equality under section 15 of the *Canadian Charter of Rights and Freedoms* by not funding IVF services. Although the majority of the Nova Scotia Court of Appeal found the government's refusal to fund the service discriminated against infertile persons, the Court held that the refusal was justified due to the cost of providing the service, as well as concerns regarding its efficacy and safety.

IV. The Status of Frozen Pre-embryos

380. As a result of IVF and related assisted conception techniques, there may be pre-embryos (zygotes) or eggs (ova) in excess of those needed for immediate implantation. These pre-embryos or eggs may be disposed of by the clinic, stored for the patient's own future use, donated to other infertile couples, or donated for research.

381. The Royal Commission on New Reproductive Technologies recommended that guidelines for pre-embryo and egg donation in licensed clinics should ensure that:[692]

690. For statistics, *see* S Ikonomidis & F Lowy, "Access to *in vitro* Fertilization in Canada" (1994) 16 J SOGC 50, cited in L Shanner, "The Right to Procreate: Where Rights Claims Have Gone Wrong" 40 McGill LJ 823 at 827. *See also* Sarah Hudson, "Great Expectations: Access to Assisted Reproductive Services and Reproductive Rights" in Trudo Lemmens et al., eds., *Regulating Creation: The Law, Ethics, and Policy of Assisted Human Reproduction* (Toronto: University of Toronto Press, 2017) 389; and Marvel et al., *supra* note 669.

691. 1999 NSCA 14, 177 DLR (4th) 611, affirming (1999), 172 NSR (2d) 227 (SC), leave to appeal to SCC refused [1999] SCCA No. 531 (QL).

692. RCNRT, *supra* note 648 at 1028–1029.

- no designated donation of eggs or zygotes occurs;
- egg retrieval solely for the purpose of donation not be performed;
- post-menopausal women are not eligible to receive donated eggs or zygotes;
- donor anonymity is protected;
- donors are tested to prevent the transmission of infectious diseases; and
- donors are not compensated in any way (including by receiving access to IVF at reduced cost).

Zygotes would be disposed of in accordance with the wishes of the gamete donors, expressed in writing before the gamete retrieval. Zygotes would be stored for no more than five years from the date of freezing, and zygotes stored for a couple's own use only would be disposed of upon the death of one partner or upon their divorce.

V. Surrogacy

382. In a pre-conception arrangement, also called surrogacy or surrogate motherhood, a woman undertakes to bear a child to be raised by others who have commissioned the surrogacy. A pre-conception arrangement may be commercial or non-commercial. It may be purely gestational, as when an embryo created from the egg and sperm of the commissioning couple is implanted in another woman for gestation and birth. In a genetic-gestational arrangement, artificial insemination is used to impregnate the gestational mother with the commissioning father's sperm.

383. The Royal Commission on New Reproductive Technologies recommended that pre-conception arrangements should be discouraged. They have the potential to make a commodity out of reproduction and children, and can exploit women's vulnerability due to race, poverty, or powerlessness.

384. To discourage commercial pre-conception arrangements, the Royal Commission on New Reproductive Technologies proposed criminal prosecutions for intermediaries, and making payments for pre-conception arrangements illegal. To protect the interests of children born through non-commercial pre-conception arrangements, the Royal Commission on New Reproductive Technologies proposed legislation to establish that a child's legal mother is the woman who gave birth to the child, and that the best interests of the child should be determinative of custody disputes.

385. Section 6 of Canada's *Assisted Human Reproduction Act* prohibits the payment or offer of consideration to a surrogate mother or surrogate intermediary. In June 2020, section 12 of the same act, which governs the reimbursement of work-related income loss and other expenditures incurred by surrogate mothers, also entered into force.[693] Specifically, section 12 provides that, except as stipulated in

693. SC 2004, c 2. *See also Reimbursement Related to Assisted Human Reproduction Regulations*, SOR/2019-193.

the regulations, no person may reimburse a surrogate mother for an expenditure incurred by her in relation to her surrogacy. Further, no expenditures may be reimbursed without receipts and a surrogate mother may not be reimbursed for any loss of work-related income incurred during her pregnancy unless a "qualified medical practitioner certifies, in writing, that continuing to work may pose a risk to her health or that of the embryo or foetus" and the reimbursement is made in accordance with the regulations.[694] The *Reimbursement Related to Assisted Human Reproduction Regulations*, which also came into force on June 9, 2020, set out a list of expenditures which may be reimbursed to a surrogate mother in relation to her surrogacy, including expenditures for travel, dependents or pets, counseling services, legal services, drugs or devices, products or services provided or recommended by authorized health-care providers, midwife or doula services, groceries, maternity clothes, telecommunications, prenatal exercise classes, health, disability, travel or life insurance coverage, as well as those related to the delivery or to obtaining or confirming medical or other records. The regulations also set out the documentary and record keeping requirements for reimbursement of expenses and for reimbursement for loss of work-related income.[695]

§4. Organ Transplants

386. At common law in Canada, a person had no right to control the disposition of his body after death. He could provide for the *post-mortem* donation of his body or organs, but his next-of-kin was not legally bound to honor his wishes. However, all of the provinces have enacted Human Tissue or Human Tissue Gift Acts. (In Quebec, the legislation is contained in the Civil Code.) In all provinces, the legislation states that an informed and competent adult may in writing consent to the removal of the tissue specified from his body and to its implantation in another living person.

387. Shortage of available organs for transplant, at times resulting in death for patients awaiting transplant, remains a chronic problem. Under the provincial Human Tissue Gift Acts and Quebec Civil Code, expressed consent is required for *post-mortem* organ removal for transplantation. The organs are removed only if the donor previously signed an organ donor card, or if the family permits the removal. Public education campaigns and training medical people to approach family members could increase donations.

388. Provincial Human Tissue Gift Acts do not generally apply to the donation of regenerative tissue, including "skin, bone, blood, blood constituent or other tissue that is replaceable by natural process of repair."[696] The common law applies to

694. *Assisted Human Reproduction Act*, S.C. 2004, c 2, s. 12.

695. *Reimbursement Related to Assisted Human Reproduction Regulations*, SOR/2019-193.

696. *See Human Tissue Gift Act*, RSBC 1996, c 211, s. 1; *Human Tissue Gift Act, 2015*, SS 2015, c H-15.1, s. 1; *Human Tissue Gift Act*, RSNB 2014, c 113, s. 1; *Human Tissue Gift Act*, RSNS 1989, c 215, s. 1; *Human Tissue Act*, RSNL 1990, c H-15, s. 1.

that which is excluded from the legislative regime. Any competent adult may choose to donate regenerative tissue at common law. In Manitoba, Prince Edward Island and Quebec, the legislation defines tissue to include regenerative as well as non-regenerative tissue.[697] In Manitoba and Prince Edward Island, the legislation excludes "spermatozoa or ova, an embryo or fetus, or blood or blood constituents."[698]

389. Alberta, Manitoba, Prince Edward Island and Quebec legislation permits organ and regenerative tissue donations by minors provided certain requirements are met. In other provinces, common law principles would apply.

390. The donating of organs from persons who have received MAiD also raises complicated legal and ethical issues. As discussed more fully later in this chapter, MAiD has recently become legal in Canada and, if a recently proposed federal Bill is passed by the government, it will soon be available to persons both who are nearing the end of their natural lives and those who are not. While organ donation after death is a common and life-saving practice in Canada, where decisions regarding MAiD and organ donation are combined, there is a risk that conflicts of interest may arise and that a vulnerable patient's decision to pursue MAiD may be influenced (or coerced) by internal or external pressures related to organ donation. These concerns must be balanced against the patient's autonomy and their right to make decisions regarding organ donation. Some authors have argued that the potential problems raised by combining MAiD and organ donation can be managed through various policies and practices, such as ensuring that the decision to proceed with MAiD is separate from, and precedes, the decision to donate, and maintaining separation between the health-care teams providing MAiD, donation, and organ retrieval/transplant services.[699]

§5. Safety of the Blood Supply

391. Thousands of Canadians, most of them hemophiliacs, became infected with HIV or hepatitis C through blood transfusions and medical treatments with contaminated blood products during the 1980s. (There is also at least one instance of a woman being infected with HIV as the result of an artificial insemination with contaminated semen.)[700] The Canadian Red Cross operated the blood system until 1998 when a new corporate entity, the Canadian Blood Services (CBS), was established. The CBS is a not-for-profit charitable organization charged with managing the blood and blood products supply for Canadians. The CBS Board of Directors is

697. *Human Tissue Gift Act*, SM 1987-88, c 39, s. 1; *Human Tissue Donation Act*, SPEI 1992, c 34, s. 1; Art. 22 CCQ.

698. *Ibid.*

699. James Downar et al., "Deceased Organ and Tissue Donation after Medical Assistance in Dying and Other Conscious and Competent Donors: Guidance for Policy" (2019) 191:22 CMAJ E604; Johannes Mulder, "Facilitating the Wishes of Patients who Choose both MAiD and Organ Donation" (2019) 191:22 CMAJ E595.

700. *ter Neuzen, supra* note 199.

comprised of thirteen directors appointed by the provincial and territorial ministers of health, as follows: one Chair; four regional nominees; six nominees from the medical, scientific, technical, business, and public health sectors; and two nominees with relevant consumer experience.[701]

392. The Canadian Red Cross did not begin testing blood products for HIV until November 1985. (Major blood suppliers in the U.S. had begun testing in March 1985.) In July 1993, federal health authorities admitted that the government knew before July 1984 that blood products for hemophiliacs were contaminated with HIV, but said that there were at that time no alternative blood products available. Canada did not begin screening blood for hepatitis C until 1990. In September 1993, the provinces and territories announced a compensation plan for people who contracted HIV from contaminated blood. (Nova Scotia announced its plan in May 1993.) By 2002, a settlement agreement was reached between the federal, provincial, and territorial governments and lawyers for class action plaintiffs that provides compensation to those individuals who were infected with hepatitis C through the Canadian blood system between January 1, 1986, and July 1, 1990.

I. Krever Inquiry

393. In 1993 the federal government appointed Justice Krever of the ONCA to head a Commission of Inquiry on the Blood System in Canada (now called the Krever Inquiry). Although initially scheduled to conclude in May 1996, the inquiry's final report was not tabled until November 21, 1997.[702] Some of the delay was attributable to individual attempts to prevent the inquiry's findings and evidence from being used in future liability actions against implicated individuals. While the report does single out certain named individuals who had key decision-making authority, the inquiry's main account is one of systemic failure; the lack of any institutional or organizational policy of accountability for the safety of Canada's national blood supply resulted in the "unprecedented public health disaster." The report's six main sections focus on the following: uses for blood and derivative blood products and the risks of use; organizational relationships and roles in the Canadian blood system during the 1980s; the emergence of AIDS as a global health threat and the Canadian blood system's response; measures taken by seven other countries to safeguard their blood supply; the safety of plasma derivatives; and the "major systemic problems that contributed to the contamination of the blood supply in the 1980s."

394. In its final section, the Krever Report makes fifty recommendations for a future national blood system. The first, and most controversial, recommendation

701. Canadian Blood Services, "Our Board of Directors," online: blood.ca/en/about-us/governance/our-board-directors.

702. Canada, Commission of Inquiry on the Blood System in Canada, *Final Report* (Ottawa: Minister of Public Works and Government Services Canada, 1997).

calls for the provinces and territories to devise and immediately implement statutory no-fault compensation schemes for persons who suffer serious, adverse consequences through the administration of blood components or products. The next recommendation establishes five governing principles for the Canadian blood system: blood is a public resource; blood and plasma donors should not be paid except in rare circumstances; Canada must collect sufficient quantities of whole blood, plasma and platelets to meet national domestic needs; Canadians should have free and universal access to blood components and products; the safety of the blood system is paramount. The remaining recommendations address issues of funding, surveillance and structural accountability, and stress the need for developing clear lines of administrative responsibility for the safety of Canada's blood supply. A number of the report's final recommendations already had been implemented by the time the Krever Inquiry submitted its Final Report.

395. The CBS historically had a policy that excluded blood donations from men who have had sex with another man any time since 1977, the year in which the spread of HIV began through countries such as the U.S. and Canada. A gay male blood donor challenged this exclusionary policy as unlawful discrimination under the *Canadian Charter of Rights and Freedoms.* An Ontario court dismissed this challenge in 2010, ruling that CBS is not subject to the Charter, since it is a private corporation and its policy development and operational activities are not controlled by the government.[703] However, the policy has since been changed to a time-based deferral, which is currently set at three months.[704]

II. Criminal Liability

396. In a landmark 1998 ruling, the SCC ruled that a person with HIV can be criminally liable for assault for failing to inform a sexual partner of the infection.[705] This decision established a legal obligation on a person with HIV to disclose their infection before engaging in behaviors that create a "significant risk of serious bodily harm" for another person. In *R. v. Mabior*, the Supreme Court clarified that the threshold for criminal liability is a "realistic possibility of transmission," which is not met if the accused had a low viral count at the time of sexual relations and condom protection was used.[706] In 2009, an HIV-positive man was convicted of murder (in addition to convictions for sexual assault) as two of his past sexual partners had died from AIDS-related conditions. In 2011, this man was declared a dangerous offender (described as an "offender whose risks cannot be predicted or controlled in the community [and who] must be segregated from their potential victims and society") and sentenced to an indeterminate period of incarceration for

703. *Canadian Blood Services v. Freeman* [2010] O.J. No. 3811, 2010 ONSC 4885 (Ont. SCJ).
704. "Blood Donation Waiting Period for Men Who Have Sex with Men Reduced to Three Months" (May 8, 2019), online: *Canadian Blood Services* blood.ca/en/news-and-events/newsroom/blood-donation-waiting-period-for-men-who-have-sex-with-men-reduced-to-three-months.
705. *R v. Cuerrier* [1998] 2 SCR 371. *See also R v. Williams* [2003] 2 SCR 134.
706. *R v. Mabior*, 2012 SCC 47 at para. 4.

multiple assault convictions.[707] According to a 2019 report from Canadian HIV/AIDS Legal Network, in the last thirty years at least 197 people have been charged with criminal offenses in Canada related to failure to disclose their HIV-positive status.[708]

III. Civil Liability

397. Persons infected with HIV from blood transfusions, and their families, have launched a number of lawsuits against doctors, hospitals, the federal government and the Canadian Red Cross Society.

398. In *Sutherland v. Canadian Red Cross Society*[709] the court dismissed an application for certification as a class action against the defendants under the *Class Proceedings Act, 1992*.[710] The court ruled that the claims of class members did not raise common issues. It would be prejudicial to deny the defendants' full right of discovery and the opportunity to third-party potential indemnitors. There would potentially be different third parties for each of the hundreds of class members. The claims were highly individual as to time, state of the art, and limitation period. Proof of causation would be required in each case. Without class status, the class members would still have access to justice via the provincial compensation package.

399. In *Pittman Estate v. Bain*,[711] the court awarded over CAD 500,000 to a woman whose husband had become infected with HIV during surgery and unknowingly passed the virus on to her. Liability was assessed at 40% against the husband's family doctor and at 30% each against the Red Cross and the Hospital. The Red Cross and the hospital were found negligent in not tracing donors with greater urgency. The Red Cross was negligent in not monitoring the hospital's tracing program, as was the hospital in not following up on the doctor's response to their notice. Both were negligent for failing to ensure that the doctor had sufficient information to enable him to give an adequate warning to the husband. The doctor was negligent in failing to disclose the fact that the husband may have been infected with HIV.

400. In *ter Neuzen v. Korn*[712] a jury awarded CAD 883,000 to a woman who became infected with HIV as a result of an artificial insemination performed by the defendant physician. On the defendant's appeal and the plaintiff's cross-appeal, the appeal was allowed in part and a new trial was ordered; the plaintiff's cross-appeal

707. *R v. Aziga*, 2011 ONSC 4592.
708. "The Criminalization of HIV Non-Disclosure in Canada: Current Status & The Need for Change" (April 2019), online (pdf): *Canadian HIV/AIDS Legal Network* www.aidslaw.ca/site/the-criminalization-of-hiv-non-disclosure-in-canada-report/?lang=en. *See also R v. Armour Pharmaceutical Co.* [2007] O.J. No. 3733, 226 C.C.C. (3d) 438 (Ont. Sup. Ct.).
709. (1994), 17 OR (3d) 645 (Ont. Gen. Div.).
710. SO 1992, c 6.
711. (1994), 112 DLR (4th) 257 (Ont. Gen. Div.).
712. (1991), 64 BCLR (2d) 125 (BCSC).

was dismissed.[713] The ground on which the jury's decision rested could not be determined and a new trial was necessary. The plaintiff's appeal from this decision was dismissed by the SCC.[714]

401. In *Walker Estate v. York-Finch General Hospital*,[715] the SCC dismissed an appeal by the Canadian Red Cross Society (CRCS) from the Ontario courts' finding of negligence in its donor-screening procedures between 1983 and 1985, when the three plaintiffs received blood tainted with HIV from the CRCS (all three were infected; two developed AIDS and died before the resolution of the case). By late March 1983, CRCS' own medical directors had come to a consensus based on mounting evidence that AIDS could be transmitted by blood that it would be appropriate to ask donors symptom-specific questions to screen out potential carriers. However, the CRCS did not do so until May 1986, and only in fact revised its donor-screening pamphlet to describe men who have had sex with men since 1977 as a high-risk group in November 1985. In its ruling, the Supreme Court found that the CRCS breached the standard of care in failing to do either of those things and was thereby negligent in failing to screen out the two infected donors who provided the tainted blood received by the plaintiffs. The applicable measure in damages had already been settled prior at an undisclosed sum.

IV. Problems of Supply

402. In the wake of the blood supply contamination scandal, blood donations dropped, leading to supply shortages and campaigns to reassure the public that they will not contract a disease by donating blood and various efforts to avoid future contamination with known or new infectious agents. Confidence in the blood supply system has again risen, but the CBS remains vigilant in regard to public education, rigorous testing, and recalling blood where concerns about possible contamination exist.

403. In February 1996, the Red Cross recalled 8,000 vials of blood products that were possibly infected with Creutzfeldt-Jakob disease, a potentially fatal brain disease. The Red Cross notified hospitals across Canada that the blood products should be used only if absolutely necessary and only with the consent of the patient. The initiation of the recall raised numerous medical, legal and economic issues, since the chances and consequences of contracting Creutzfeldt-Jakob disease through the use of blood or organ donations are markedly different than the transmissibility of HIV and other diseases.[716]

---

713. (1993), 103 DLR (4th) 473, 6 WWR 647, 81 BCLR (2d) 39 (CA).

714. *Supra* note 199.

715. 2001 SCC 23, affirming (1999), 169 DLR (4th) 689 (Ont. CA), reversing in part (1997), 39 CCLT (2d) 1 (Ont. Gen. Div.).

716. *See* Douglas M Sawyer & Timothy M Caulfield, "Creutzfeldt-Jakob Disease and Blood Transfusion: Policy Issues" (1997) 6 Health L Rev 12, and Gordon DuVal, "Creutzfeldt-Jakob Disease: The Problem of Recipient Notification" (1997) 25:1 JL Med & Ethics 34.

404. In September 2003, the CBS withdrew certain blood products collected in Saskatchewan due to concerns that the blood could expose recipients to West Nile virus (WNV). WNV, which was first detected in Canada in 1999, is transmitted to humans by mosquito bites, and although most people infected with the virus have no or minor flu-like symptoms, a small number of those infected may develop potentially fatal brain swelling. More recently, CBS issued a voluntary recall of blood products collected in Regina between October 2, 2011 and October 3, 2012 after it was discovered that one part of the donor-screening process in Regina was not performed according to standard procedures. The blood products had undergone routine testing and the risk to recipients was considered remote, but they were withdrawn regardless for failing the quality control standard.[717]

405. The CBS policy permits directed donations made by a parent to a minor child.[718] A directed donation is one given by one donor specifically and exclusively for one recipient, such as a family member. The CBS states that directed donations cost significantly more than regular donation and the question of whether they offer greater safety is open to debate. Each province and territory currently sets its own policy on the availability of directed donations.

§6. Research Involving Human Beings

I. The Governance of Research Involving Human Research Subjects in Canada

A. *Dual Sources of Governance*

406. Research involving human subjects includes research conducted directly with living human participants as well as research conducted with human biological materials (e.g., tissues, organs, blood, DNA, cells) or materials related to human reproduction (e.g., embryos, fetuses).[719] Canada does not have a comprehensive scheme of legislation to regulate research on human subjects. Instead, research on human subjects is principally controlled by a patchwork of policies and guidelines

---

For discussion of cost impacts of blood supply safety, *see* for example, Kumanan Wilson & Paul C Hebert, "The Challenge of an Increasingly Expensive Blood System" (2003) 168:9 CMAJ 1149, online www.cmaj.ca/; (search for article).

717. "Blood Collection Agency Issues Recall of Regina Donations," *CBC News* (Oct. 5, 2012), online www.cbc.ca/news/canada/saskatchewan/blood-collection-agency-issues-recall-of-regina-donations-1.1131718.

718. In 1996, a Quebec Supreme Court judge ordered the Red Cross to allow a couple to donate blood for their infant son's heart surgery. *See Quintal c Société Canadienne de la Croix-Rouge* [1996] QJ No. 517 (QL).

719. Consider Canadian Institutes of Health Research, Natural Sciences and Engineering Research Council of Canada, and Social Sciences and Humanities Research Council of Canada, *Tri-Council Policy Statement: Ethical Conduct for Research Involving Humans* (Ottawa: Secretariat on Responsible Conduct of Research, 2018) [TCPS 2] at 6, 13, 195, 198.

(lacking the clear force of law), and, to a lesser extent, health and privacy legislation and regulations, the common law and, in Quebec, the *Civil Code*.[720] There are two major sources of governance for research on human subjects in the health context in Canada namely: (a) Canada's federal research funding agencies; and (b) Health Canada, Canada's federal drug and health product regulatory agency.[721] Specifically, research on human subjects that is funded by one of Canada's federal research agencies (e.g., the Canadian Institutes of Health Research (CIHR)) has to comply with the research ethics rules set out in the *Tri-Council Policy Statement: Ethical Conduct for Research Involving Humans (TCPS 2)*.[722] Research undertaken in the context of the drug or medical device approval system, largely clinical trials, must comply with the regulations and guidelines administered by Health Canada. While these two regulatory schemes comprise the main sources of laws and governance for research on human subjects, depending on the nature and subject matter of the research, various other regulatory schemes may also apply, including those established at common law or, in the case of Quebec, in the civil law and those established in specific pieces of legislation.

1. Canadian Research Agencies and the Tri-Council Policy Statement (TCPS 2)

407. The responsibility for developing and implementing ethical guidelines in Canada for research involving human participants (outside of the drug and medical device context) has been given jointly to Canada's three federal research agencies, the CIHR, the Natural Sciences and Engineering Research Council of Canada (NSERC), and the Social Sciences and Humanities Research Council of Canada (SSHRC).[723] Each of these three agencies promotes and funds research according to their respective legislative mandates, with the CIHR having legal responsibility for:

> promoting, assisting and undertaking research that meets the highest international scientific standards of excellence and ethics and that pertains to all aspects of health, including biomedical research, clinical research and research respecting health systems, health services, the health of populations, societal and cultural dimensions of health and environmental influences on health.[724]

---

720. *See* DuVal, *supra* note 521 at 234–235.
721. Trudo Lemmens & C Tess Sheldon, "The Governance of the Safety and Efficacy of Psychopharmaceuticals: Challenges and Opportunities for Reform" in J A Chandler & C M Flood, eds., *Law and Mind: Mental Health Law and Policy in Canada* (Toronto: LexisNexis Canada Inc., 2016) 223 at 225.
722. TCPS 2, *supra* note 718. The term "Tri-Council" refers to the three major federal funding agencies: the Canadian Institutes of Health Research, the Natural Sciences and Engineering Research Council of Canada, and the Social Sciences and Humanities Research Council of Canada.
723. TCPS 2, *supra* note 718 at 3; *Social Sciences and Humanities Research Council Act*, RSC 1985, c S-12; *Natural Sciences and Engineering Research Council Act*, RSC 1985, c N-21; *Canadian Institutes of Health Research Act*, SC 2000, c 6.
724. *Canadian Institutes of Health Research Act*, SC 2000, c 6, s. 4(e). *See also* TCPS 2, *supra* note 718 at 3.

408. CIHR, SSHRC, and NSERC provide the majority of federal funding for research conducted through Canadian universities and hospitals.[725] As a condition of funding, all three federal research agencies require compliance with the *Tri-Council Policy Statement: Ethical Conduct for Research Involving Humans (TCPS 2)*.[726] Compliance with the *TCPS 2* is mandatory both for research projects directly funded by one of the agencies, as well as research conducted at an institution which is eligible for funding from one or more of the agencies. The power of the federal funding agencies within federally funded institutions is based on an institutional contract signed by the institutions in which they commit to respecting the *TCPS 2* for all of its research involving human subjects. As essentially all major universities and hospitals in Canada receive federal funding from CIHR, SSHRC, and/or NSERC, this means that all research with human subjects undertaken at or in association with these institutions will be subject to the *TCPS 2*.[727]

409. The *TCPS 2* underwent substantial revision in 2009–2010 and the second edition was published in late 2010. It was revised again in 2014, and subsequently in 2018, to make additional changes. The funding of research is tied to compliance with the *TCPS* 2. As the CIHR provides a substantial amount of resources for medical research, and as it has provided the only federal statement of research guidelines in the biomedical area, the *TCPS 2* exercises substantial authority over the way human subjects are involved in medical research protocols. Further, the *TCPS 2* serves as a benchmark even for non-CIHR funded research. As there are no laws or regulations in Canada governing research involving human subjects, non-CIHR funded research generally adheres to the CIHR guidelines.

410. CIHR (as well as SSHRC and NSERC) applicants and administrators undertake that any research carried out with funds from the federal research agencies will respect all of the agencies' requirements for ethical conduct of research as expressed in the *TCPS* 2.[728] The signatures on the application commit both the applicant(s) and the institution to specific responsibilities. They are jointly responsible for adherence to the general conditions governing the award of a research grant as outlined in the respective agencies' policies and guidelines for grants and awards, including adherence to the *TCPS 2*, and the administration of the funds according to accepted practices.[729] One of the central and fundamental requirements in the *TCPS 2* is that ethics review and approval be obtained from a Research Ethics Board (REB) before any proposed research involving human participants

725. DuVal, *supra* note 521 at 235.
726. TCPS 2, *supra* note 718.
727. DuVal, *supra* note 521 at 235.
728. Canadian Institutes of Health Research, *Canadian Institutes of Health Research (CIHR) Application Administration Guide* (Ottawa: *CIHR*, Nov. 15, 2019) [CIHR Application Administration Guide]; TCPS 2, *supra* note 718 at 3; Canadian Institutes of Health Research, Natural Sciences and Engineering Research Council of Canada, and Social Sciences and Humanities Research Council of Canada, *Tri-Agency Framework: Responsible Conduct of Research* (Ottawa: Secretariat on Responsible Conduct of Research, 2016) [Tri-Council Framework: Responsible Conduct of Research].
729. *See* for example, CIHR Application Administration Guide, *supra* note 727.

commences.[730] Failure to comply with the requirements in *TCPS 2*, or any of the federal research agencies' other policies, may result in the agency exercising some form of "recourse," namely terminating future payments or seeking a refund of funds already paid.[731]

411. The three major funding agencies established a Framework for the Responsible Conduct of Research, which aims at promoting and ensuring that research integrity standards are respected.[732] The framework contains rules for the administration of grants, the performance of research, and the reporting of results. It also has a procedure for complaints, which largely relies on institutional responsibility: when a complaint is made to the Panel on the Responsible Conduct of Research, it is largely left to the institutions to investigate these complaints and to report back to the Panel.

2. Health Canada: Clinical Trials for Drugs and Medical Devices

412. The majority of the clinical trials submitted to Health Canada to support the approval of a pharmaceutical product or medical device are conducted or funded by pharmaceutical and biotechnology companies.[733] Clinical trials for drugs, medical devices, and other health-care products submitted to Health Canada are primarily governed by a combination of regulations and guidance and policy documents. In governing clinical trials, Health Canada enforces applicable regulations under Federal laws, such as the *Food and Drug Regulations* and the *Medical Devices Regulations*.[734]

413. Health Canada has also developed various complex technical regulations, "guidance documents," and policies related to the governance of clinical trials involving human subjects. While these administrative documents may play an important role in regulating clinical trials in Canada, it is important to note that the guidance and policy documents do not carry the "force of law."[735] The regulation of clinical trials for drugs, medical devices and other health-care products is highly technical and the exact requirements will depend on the nature of the product, among other factors. While it is beyond the scope of this chapter to describe these requirements in detail, a brief overview is provided.[736]

---

730. TCPS 2, *supra* note 718, at Art. 2.1.
731. Tri-Council Framework: Responsible Conduct of Research, *supra* note 727.
732. *Ibid.*
733. DuVal, *supra* note 521 at 249.
734. *Food and Drug Regulations*, C.R.C., c 870; *Medical Devices Regulations*, SOR/98-282; *Natural Health Products Regulations*, SOR/2003-196; DuVal, *supra* note 521 at 249.
735. Matthew Herder, "Pharmaceutical Regulation in Canada" in J N Erdman, V Gruben & E Nelson, eds., *Canadian Health Law and Policy*, 5th ed. (Toronto: LexisNexis Canada Inc., 2017) at 183; Health Canada, *Guidance Document for Clinical Trial Sponsors: Clinical Trial Applications* (Ottawa: Ministry of Health, adopted Jun. 25, 2003, revised date, Mar. 17, 2016) at i.
736. For a more detailed discussion of the regelation of pharmaceuticals in Canada *see* Herder, *supra* note 734 at 183; *See also* DuVal, *supra* note 521; Lemmens & Sheldon, *supra* note 720.

414. The Health Canada regulations require that clinical trials receive prior authorization from Health Canada and an REB, that they be conducted in accordance with "good clinical practices," and that any amendments be approved in advance by Health Canada, the REB, and the individual or organization conducting the clinical trial, except in circumstances where changes are merely administrative or are required to eliminate an immediate danger to participants.[737] Clinical trials must be "scientifically sound" and conducted in accordance with the approved protocol by a qualified investigator. Processes for monitoring the safety of participants must be in place, and any safety issues must be reported to REBs and Health Canada. As well, any new information that may affect the safety of a participant or their willingness to continue to participate must be reported to the REB and the participant. Arrangements for medical care must be made to address any harms suffered by a participant during the trial, and any provisions made for treatment and compensation for research-related injuries must be described in the consent form.[738]

415. As part of their guidance documents, Health Canada has adopted and implemented the "good clinical practices" set out in the International Conference on Harmonisation of Technical Requirements for the Registration of Pharmaceuticals for Human Use (ICH) *Guideline for Good Clinical Practice* (ICH-GCP).[739] The ICH-GCP was developed by the ICH, an organization established by European, Japanese, and American regulatory agencies and industry representatives.[740] The ICH-GCP is intended to "harmonize" standards across jurisdictions and sets out guidelines to be followed in clinical trials to protect the rights, safety and well-being of trial participants and to produce credible clinical data for submission to regulatory authorities.[741]

416. The ICH-GCP draws on the Declaration of Helsinki, a set of international rules and principles regarding the ethical conduct of medical research involving human subjects.[742] The Declaration of Helsinki was originally developed by the World Medical Association in 1964 and has since undergone numerous revisions, most recently in October 2013.[743] As the references to the Helsinki Declaration in

737. DuVal, *supra* note 521 at 250; Herder, *supra* note 734 at 193; *Food and Drug Regulations*, C.R.C., c 870.
738. DuVal, *supra* note 521 at 250; Herder, *supra* note 734 at 193; *Food and Drug Regulations*, C.R.C., c 870; International Council for Harmonisation of Technical Requirements for Pharmaceuticals for Human Use, *Integrated Addendum to ICH E6(R1): Guideline for Good Clinical Practice E6(R2)* (Nov. 9, 2016) [ICH-GCP].
739. Health Canada, *Guidance Document: Part C, Division 5 of the Food and Drug Regulations "Drugs for Clinical Trials Involving Human Subjects,"* Catalogue No H14-313/2019E-PDF (Ottawa, Health Canada: Aug. 20, 2019) (Health Canada, *Guidance Document: Part C, Division 5*); Lemmens & Sheldon, *supra* note 720 at 225; DuVal, *supra* note 521 at 233, 250.
740. ICH-GCP, *supra* note 737 at 1; DuVal, *supra* note 521 at 233.
741. DuVal, *supra* note 521 at 233; ICH-GCP, *supra* note 737 at 1.
742. ICH-GCP, *supra* note 737 at 1, Art. 2.1, 4.8.1.
743. World Medical Assembly, "Declaration of Helsinki: Recommendations Guiding Doctors in Clinical Research" (Jun. 18, 1964), online (pdf) www.wma.net/wp-content/uploads/2018/07/DoH-Jun1964.pdf; World Medical Association, "Declaration of Helsinki: Ethical Principles for Medical

the ICH-GCP would suggest, the Declaration has influenced many of the policies adopted internationally to guide the ethical conduct of medical research involving human subjects.[744] The influential nature of the ethical principles originating in the Declaration is evidenced in Health Canada's regulatory policies both through the adoption of the ICH-GCP and through referencing the Declaration directly in certain guidance documents.[745]

417. In addition to these international standards, Health Canada's regulatory policies also draw on the *TCPS 2*.[746] For example, Health Canada recommends that REBs overseeing clinical trials follow the guidelines for REBs set out in the *TCPS 2*, and that researchers follow the guidance on informed consent set out in that policy as well.[747]

3. Common Law and Civil Law Requirements for Research Involving Human Subjects

418. Though there are no federal or provincial laws specifically governing research involving human subjects, the basic common law and Quebec Civil Code requirements must be met relating to standards of care and the requirements for a valid consent. Under the CCQ, liability would arise from a breach of the contractual relationship between the researcher and the human subject. Although liability is primarily the responsibility of the researcher, the institution also bears a duty to the subject.[748] In terms of consent, the *Civil Code* provides that an adult may consent to participate in research, if the risk is not disproportionate to the anticipated benefits and the research is approved and monitored by an REB.[749] The *Code* also provides specific requirements for consent on behalf of minors (*see* discussion below).

Research Involving Human Subjects" (June 1964, as amended, October 2013), online www.wma.net/policies-post/wma-declaration-of-helsinki-ethical-principles-for-medical-research-involving-human-subjects/. *See also* DuVal, *supra* note 521 at 233. *See* in general Ulf Schmidt, Andreas Frewer & Dominique Sprumont, eds., *Ethical Research: The Declaration of Helsinki, and the Past, Present, and Future of Human Experimentation* (USA: Oxford University Press, 2020).

744. D Sprumont, S Girardin & T Lemmens, "The Helsinki Declaration and the Law: An International and Comparative Analysis" in A Frewer & U Schmidt, eds., *History and Theory of Human Experimentation: The Declaration of Helsinki and Modern Medical Ethics* (Stuttgard: Franz Steiner Verlag, 2007) at 223.
745. *See* Lemmens & Sheldon, *supra* note 720 at 226; *See also* for example, Health Canada, *Guidance Document: Part C, Division 5*, *supra* note 738; Health Canada, *Guidance Document: Applications for Medical Device Investigational Testing Authorizations*, Catalogue No H13-9/16-2018E-PDF (Ottawa: Health Canada, Oct. 1, 2018) [Health Canada, *Guidance Document: Applications for Medical Device*] at 6, 21.
746. Lemmens & Sheldon, *supra* note 720 at 225; *See* for example, Health Canada, *Guidance Document: Part C, Division 5*, *supra* note 738; Health Canada, *Guidance Document: Applications for Medical Device*, *supra* note 744.
747. Health Canada, *Guidance Document: Part C, Division 5*, *supra* note 738.
748. CCH Canadian Limited, *Canadian Health Facilities Law Guide* (Toronto: LexisNexis Canada, 2019) at para. 7495 (QL).
749. Article 20 CCQ; *See also* Arts. 22–25 CCQ.

419. Some examples of the leading Canadian cases dealing with liability in a research context are as follows.

a. *Halushka v. University of Saskatchewan*

420. A university student volunteered to test a new anesthetic agent but was not told that the drug had not been tried by the investigators, nor that there was a risk associated with its use. He was told that a catheter would be inserted in his arm, but not that it would be advanced into his heart. During the test, the subject had a complete cardiac arrest, resulting in unconsciousness for four days and, ultimately, brain damage.[750]

421. The case discussed the extent of disclosure required for a valid consent in research involving human subjects. The Saskatchewan Court of Appeal found liability against the research physicians. In experimental procedures, the duty to obtain consent is as great as, if not greater than, that in routine treatment. The subject should be given a complete and candid disclosure of all the probabilities and facts which a reasonable person might be expected to consider before giving his or her consent. The inaccurate information was in essence a non-disclosure, making the consent ineffective. There is a duty of complete disclosure for researchers. Despite the fact that the subject signed a consent form, the omissions and misstatements of the doctors constituted a failure in the duty of disclosure.

b. *Weiss v. Solomon*

422. Doctors were conducting non-therapeutic research on ophthalmic drops. The subject died during the experiment from an adverse reaction to another substance used in the test. The physician failed to reveal all known risks to the research subject, including those that were rare or remote. The Quebec Superior Court found that the researcher had failed in his duty to disclose. The duty to inform in matters relating to purely scientific experimentation is the most exacting possible and includes the revelation of "all known risks including those which are rare or remote, especially if they may entail grave consequences." The subject was told the risks were extremely rare and were relatively minor. He was never told about the risk of death, even though the risk was remote. The hospital was also held accountable in that it did not ensure that appropriate selection criteria were used to select would be human subjects.[751]

c. *Brock (Litigation Guardian of) v. Hsu*

423. The infant plaintiff in this case was diagnosed with acute lymphoblastic leukemia (ALL) and entered into a study by the Pediatric Oncology Group (POG) at the Ottawa Children's Hospital of Eastern Ontario. As part of the study, she

750. *Halushka v. University of Saskatchewan* (1965), 53 DLR (2d) 436 (Sask. CA).
751. *Weiss v. Solomon* (1989), 48 CCLT 280 [1989] 1 RJQ 731 (Que. Sup. Ct.).

received a higher dosage of the drug methotrexate during her chemotherapy treatment than was standard for ALL patients under a prior protocol, which allegedly caused her to suffer irreversible brain damage. The only reported judgment emerging from this case addressed a motion by one of the defendants, the chair of POG who was not a treating physician of the plaintiff but allegedly had final responsibility for the treatment protocol, to dismiss the action against her. The Ontario Superior Court of Justice dismissed the motion, holding that it was reasonably foreseeable that the protocol would be used by the treating physicians, who were all members of POG, and thus that the pleadings arguably supported that the harm to the plaintiff was a reasonably foreseeable consequence of the POG chair's actions.[752]

d. *Stirrett v. Cheema*

424. The plaintiff's deceased spouse was admitted to hospital for an angioplasty. On the same day, before the successful angioplasty, he was recruited for a study which would require him to submit to a follow-up angiogram six months afterward for purely research purposes. The principal investigator failed to inform the participant of changes in funding and number of participants in the study, and these changes were not reflected in the consent form the participant signed. The participant suffered complications from the follow-up angiogram, ultimately leading to his death. A jury found that the principal investigator had breached the standard of care, but that it was not the cause of the participant undergoing the angiogram. However, the trial judge ruled that a fiduciary duty existed and that the principal investigator breached this fiduciary duty to the participant as his research subject in failing to inform him of the new information. The trial judge concluded that the "finding of a fiduciary duty and a breach of that duty obviated the need to consider the issue of causation" and allowed the plaintiff to recover.

425. The ONCA found that the trial judge erred in failing to consider causation and reversed the damages award on the basis that even if it were established that a fiduciary duty was owed to the participant and that the principal investigator had breached this duty, the plaintiff/respondent was not entitled to recover because "there was no causal link" between the breach and the participant's decision to undergo the angiogram that led to his death. As the causation issue was dispositive of the appeal, the Court did not address the issue of whether an ad hoc fiduciary duty was in fact owed to the participant. The Court thus left open the question of whether a fiduciary relationship may be found to exist between a medical researcher and a study participant, noting that their reasons should be read neither as "foreclosing" nor "requiring" such a finding and that the existence or absence of a fiduciary relationship in any given case would have to be decided on the particular circumstances of that case.[753] As the Court of Appeal did not decide the issue, it will

752. *Brock (Litigation Guardian of) v. Hsu* (2006), 82 OR (3d) 786 (Ont. SCJ).
753. *Stirrett v. Cheema*, 2020 ONCA 288.

be interesting to see how this case, both the trial judge and Court of Appeal decisions, may influence determinations in future cases where questions are raised about whether a fiduciary duty is owed by a researcher to a study participant.

e. *Barker v. Barker*

426. This case was launched by twenty-eight former patients who, while involuntarily hospitalized at a maximum-security state-run psychiatric hospital in Ontario between 1966 and 1983, were subjected to various experimental programs. The programs included: giving patients high doses of hallucinogenic drugs (including LSD); handcuffing or strapping patients together for long periods of time; locking groups of naked patients together for weeks in a small, windowless, constantly lit room with no furniture and an exposed toilet, where they were fed through straws in the wall and were monitored by patient observers through closed-circuit television and a one-way mirror; putting patients in solitary confinement in an unfurnished cell with only a heavy sack gown to wear and a raised cement platform to sleep on, and fully depriving them of any outside contact for three or four days before placing them in a group setting where they could either earn "privileges" like clothing or a cushion by meeting stringent requirements, or be punished again by returning them to solitary confinement. The programs were primarily administered by two doctors (the personal defendants), who published widely in medical journals about the programs and the theories that underpinned them.

427. After winding its way through the legal system for nearly two decades, a trial at the Ontario Superior Court of Justice was ultimately scheduled to take place in two parts. A judgment on the first part, dealing with liability, causation, defense and limitation issues was released in June 2020. The second part of the trial, dealing with quantification of damages, has yet to be heard. In adjudicating the first part of the trial, Justice Morgan was obliged to consider whether the programs were "professionally acceptable treatment" or whether they were "non-therapeutic and callous experimentation." In addressing this central question, Justice Morgan turned first to the issue of informed consent, finding that the ethical standards relating to informed consent had not been met as, even where there was a "semblance of consent," the plaintiffs' purported consent was not "fully informed" and was "coerced in the sense that it was tied" to recommendations regarding their release from the institution. On the issue of treatment versus medical research, Justice Morgan concluded that the impugned programs were a hybrid, being both "therapeutic/ treatment approaches" as well as "experimental research projects," that, as such, they were "required to conform to the ethical standards applicable to both categories" (including oversight by an independent REB), and that "[i]n failing to do so, the programs were conducted in a way that violated the applicable ethical principles." In the result, Justice Morgan concluded that the doctors who ran the programs, and the provincial crown, who was responsible for the hospital facility, had breached their fiduciary duties to the plaintiff patients.

428. In addition to pleading a breach of fiduciary duties, the plaintiffs also sought to ground liability in two intentional torts, battery and assault and intentional infliction of emotional distress. With regards to battery, Justice Morgan found that the defendants had "failed to establish a defense of consent to battery" and that each of the programs amounted "to a non-consensual, non-trivial invasion of the Plaintiff's bodily integrity." He further found that the "design, administration, and implementation" of one of the programs, a "strict physical disciplinary regime," "amounted to an assault" against all of the plaintiffs, both those patients who had been in the program and those who, by virtue of being detained in the facility, "were on reasonable grounds in believing that they were in danger" of also being subjected to the program. Finally, while Justice Morgan agreed with the plaintiffs that the conduct at issue was "flagrant and outrageous," and that the impugned acts "produced 'serious and prolonged' mental harm," he nevertheless concluded that the tort of intentional infliction of emotional distress was not made out as the "programs were not plainly calculated to produce the lasting, harmful effects" that were experienced by many of the plaintiffs.[754]

4. Other Sources of Regulation

429. While there are currently no federal or provincial laws that specifically govern how or when research involving human subjects may be conducted, various pieces of legislation may regulate certain aspects of particular research projects. As discussed above, these legislated regulatory frameworks include those established by the federal government for the importation and sale in Canada of drugs and medical devices for investigational testing involving human subjects.[755] Outside of the Health Canada regulatory framework, legislated regulatory frameworks for research involving human subjects may be found in various other federal and provincial statutes.

430. Legislative acts governing specific health-related matters may be applicable to, and therefore govern, research with human subjects. For example, the federal government has made attempts to legislate the uses of new reproductive and genetic technologies as they relate to research involving humans and their genetic material. Specifically, certain subsections of the *Assisted Human Reproduction Act* purported to regulate the conduct of in vitro embryonic research, embryonic stem cell research, and certain clinical trials mostly through outright criminal prohibitions. While many of the *act's* provisions were struck down as unconstitutional by the SCC,[756] the *act* still contains provisions which may regulate embryonic research. For example, the *act* prohibits the creation of an in vitro embryo for any purpose outside of creating a human being or improving or providing instruction in assisted

754. *Barker v. Barker*, 2020 ONSC 3746.

755. *Food and Drug Regulations*, C.R.C., c 870, ss. C.05.002–C.05.017; *Medical Devices Regulations*, SOR/98–282, ss. 79–88.

756. *See Reference re Assisted Human Reproduction Act,* 2010 SCC 61 [2010] SCJ No. 61; *See also* Chapter 3, §3 Reproductive Technologies.

reproduction procedures, and the *Regulations* establish specific provisions regarding the requirements for consent to use an embryo for research purposes.[757]

431. Provisions in provincial health legislation may also be a source of governance for research with human subjects in certain circumstances. For example, in British Columbia, the *Health Care (Consent) and Care Facility (Admission) Act* includes "participation in a medical research program approved by an ethics committee designated by regulation" within its definition of "health care."[758] Thus, valid consent in accordance with the legislation is required.

432. Provincial and federal privacy legislation governing the use of personal information may also play a role in the regulation of research involving human subjects by establishing rules and requirements for researchers seeking to access and use health information for research purposes. For example, under Alberta's *Health Information Act*, a researcher may be permitted to access and use health information in the possession of health-care facilities for research purposes, without obtaining informed consent from the patients, if the proposal and REB review requirements in the act are met. These requirements include, among other things, that the REB assess whether the importance of the research is such that "the public interest in the proposed research outweighs to a substantial degree the public interest in protecting the privacy of the individuals who are the subjects of the health information to be used in the research."[759]

433. The laws of other countries, as well as private pharmaceutical or medical device firms, may also have their own requirements for the conduct of research involving human subjects. Efforts must be made to ensure compliance with all applicable regulations and guidelines (including international) and institutional standards of care (institutional policies for review and conduct of human research).[760] The various ethical standards which may apply to research with human subjects may lead to confusion, particularly as there appears to be no clear guidance as to how to deal with potential conflicts.[761]

757. *Assisted Human Reproduction Act*, SC 2004, c 2, s. 5(1)(b). *See also Consent for Use of Human Reproductive Material and In Vitro Embryos Regulation*, SOR/2007-137.
758. *Health Care (Consent) and Care Facility (Admission) Act,* RSBC 1996, c 181, s. 1.
759. *Health Information Act*, RSA 2000, c H-5, ss. 1(1), 27(1)(d), 49, 50, 51; Consider also *Personal Health Information Protection Act, 2004*, SO 2004 c 3, Sch. A, ss. 3, 44; *Privacy Act*, RSC 1985, c P-21, s. 8.
760. CCH Canadian Limited, *Canadian Health Facilities Law Guide* (Toronto: LexisNexis Canada, 2019) at para. 7305 (QL).
761. Lemmens & Sheldon, *supra* note 720 at 226.

II. The Creation, Authority and Membership of REBs

A. Creation of REBs

434. REBs play a central role in the regulation of research involving human subjects. Each of the federal research agencies and Health Canada, as well as certain federal and provincial Acts, require prior approval from an REB before any research involving human subjects can commence. The federal research agency requirements governing the composition and activities of REBs are set out in the *TCPS 2*, whereas Health Canada's requirements for REB composition and activities are established in the regulations and through the adoption of other policy documents, namely the *TCPS 2* and ICH-GCP.

435. Both the *TCPS 2* and the ICH-GCP delegate the primary responsibility for decisions on research ethics to REBs. The REB is to be established under the authority of the institution where the research is being conducted. REBs have a clear mandate to review all proposals for research involving human subjects, which may include research with living human participants or with human biological materials, as well as human embryos, fetuses, fetal tissue, reproductive materials and stem cells.[762]

436. The *TCPS 2* and the ICH-GCP, as well as certain federal and provincial Acts, set out general principles and minimal expectations regarding membership and the process of REBs, which operate in accordance with the policies of their local institutions.[763] The REB should be a standing body which meets regularly, has a defined membership which turns over periodically, and has a sufficient workload to ensure an experienced Board.

B. Authority of REBs

437. An REB's evaluation of a research protocol is the major step through which the values of the community in the research are addressed.

438. Ongoing research will be subject to continuing reviews by the REBs to ensure that the actual implementation and conduct of the project continue to meet the standards of ethics. At a minimum, researchers are required to submit an annual status report (for multi-year projects) and an end-of-study report (for projects lasting less than a year).[764]

762. TCPS 2, *supra* note 718 at Arts. 6.1–6.3, 2.1; ICH-GCP, *supra* note 737 at Art. 1.27, 1. 31, 2.6, 3.1.
763. TCPS 2, *supra* note 718 at Arts. 6.4, 6.11–6.14; ICH-GCP, *supra* note 737 at Arts. 1.27, 1.31, 3.1–3.4; Consider also, for example, *Food and Drug Regulations*, C.R.C., c 870, s C.05.001; *Personal Health Information Protection Act, 2004*, SO 2004 c 3, Sch. A, s. 44; Ont. Reg. 329/04, s. 15; *Health Research Ethics Authority Act*, SNL 2006, c H-1.2.
764. TCPS 2, *supra* note 718 at Art. 6.14; *See also* ICH-GCP, *supra* note 737 at Arts. 3.1.4, 4.10.

C. Membership of REBs

439. The *TCPS 2* deals with the membership criteria of REBs for research to which the *TCPS 2* applies. They are to contain a minimum of five people, including both men and women, at least one of whom is a community member not affiliated with the institution. Two members must have expertise in research disciplines, fields, and methodologies relevant to the REB. One member must have expertise in ethics. For biomedical research, one member must be knowledgeable in the area of biomedical law. At a minimum, the REB must have members appointed in one capacity only for each; any additional members may fulfill more than one capacity.[765] When reviewing research proposals, REB members are required to disclose real, potential or perceived conflicts of interest. Where such conflicts exist, members may be asked to withdraw from deliberations and decisions.[766]

440. REB membership criteria may also be prescribed by legislation or the regulations emanating from them. For example, the membership criteria for REBs overseeing clinical drug trials are prescribed in the *Food and Drug Regulations*, which require that these REBs be comprised of at least five members, including both men and women, and a majority of whom must be Canadian citizens or permanent residents. At least two members must have primary experience and expertise in a scientific discipline, and specifically a medical discipline for one of them, and they must have "broad experience in the methods and areas of research to be approved." One member must be knowledgeable in ethics and one knowledgeable in Canadian laws relevant to the biomedical research at issue. One member's primary experience and expertise must be in a non-scientific discipline and, one member must be from the community or a representative of an organization with an interest in the areas of research (but who is not affiliated with the individual or organization conducting the clinical trial or with the site where it will be conducted).[767]

441. In addition to the requirements established under the two main sources of governance for research with human subjects (federal research agencies and Health Canada), REB membership criteria may also be prescribed by provincial legislation. For example, in Ontario, the regulations under the *Personal Health Information Protection Act*, require that REBs have at least five members, including one member with no affiliation with the person who established the REB, one member who is knowledgeable in research ethics, two members with expertise in the methods or areas of the research at issue, and one member who is knowledgeable in privacy issues.[768] The regulations also stipulate that the REB can only act in regards to a proposal where there is no conflict of interest between the REBs duties and any member's personal interests.[769]

765. TCPS 2, *supra* note 718 at Art. 6.4.
766. *Ibid.*, at Art. 7.3.
767. Section C.05.001.
768. Ont. Reg. 329/04, s. 15.
769. *Ibid.*

III. Criteria for REB Approval of Research

442. REBs are to adopt a proportionate approach when assessing proposed research for approval. This proportionate approach is based on the general principle that the more invasive the research, the greater care should be taken in its assessment. The higher the level of risk, the higher the level of scrutiny.[770]

443. The policies governing research with human subjects address special populations as research subjects in the interests of fairness and equity. For example, the *TCPS 2* sets out particular considerations where research populations are comprised of women, Indigenous peoples, children and adults who lack decision-making capacity.[771] The ICH-GCP also recognizes that some subjects, such as members of groups with hierarchical structures, people who have incurable diseases, impoverished persons, ethnic minority groups, refugees, minors, and people who lack the capacity to consent, may be more vulnerable to being unduly influenced to participate in research, and call upon REBs to pay particular attention to safeguarding the rights, safety, and well-being of these individuals.[772]

IV. Informed Consent to Participate in Research as a Human Subject

A. *Generally*

444. The cardinal principle of research on human subjects is that, to the extent that it is possible, a subject's involvement should be informed and voluntary. Ideally, subjects should be fully informed and should make their decision on whether to participate in leisure and in complete freedom from any pressure.[773]

445. To be legally effective the consent must be informed and given by a person with the legal capacity to consent. The doctrine of informed consent is governed by provincial law and common law.

446. The obtaining of informed consent is only one step in a continuing process. Continuing consent must be elicited during the progress of the research.

447. Prospective participants are entitled to full disclosure of the information necessary to make an informed decision regarding participation.[774]

770. TCPS 2, *supra* note 718 at Art. 2.9. *See also* Art. 6.11-6.14 for discussion on levels of REB review.
771. *Ibid.*, at Arts. 4.2–4.7, 9.1–9.22.
772. ICH-GCP, *supra* note 737 at Arts. 1.61, 3.1.1.
773. TCPS 2, *supra* note 718 at Art. 3.1; ICH-GCP, *supra* note 737 at Art. 4.8.3.
774. TCPS 2, *supra* note 718 at Art. 3.2; ICH-GCP, *supra* note 737 at Art. 1.28, 4.8.10.

B. Elements of Informed Consent

448. Informed consent by research participants is usually required by the REB.[775] The *TCPS 2* and the ICH-GCP set out the features generally required for informed consent. These features include: a statement about the research purpose, procedures, foreseeable harms and/or benefits, assurance that participation is voluntary and the participant may withdraw, a description of how participants will be identified or confidentiality maintained, and who may have access to the information collected about participants.[776] Additional information may also be required in some circumstances to conform to the values of informed consent. For example, where real, potential, or perceived conflicts of interests may exist (e.g., where there is the possibility of commercialization of the research findings), this information must be disclosed to the participants.[777]

C. Waivers and Alteration of Informed Consent Requirements

1. Non-consensual Research

449. In some cases, an REB may approve research without requiring participant consent, if the REB is satisfied, and documents, that a specified list of requirements are met, namely:

(1) the research involves no more than minimal risk to the participants;
(2) the lack of consent is unlikely to adversely affect the welfare of the participants;
(3) it is impossible or impracticable to conduct the research properly if prior consent is required;
(4) the precise nature and extent of the alteration to the requirements for consent is defined; and
(5) whenever possible and appropriate, after participation, participants will be debriefed, provided with additional pertinent information and given the opportunity to refuse consent and request the withdrawal of their data or biological materials.[778]

2. Deception

450. In view of the critical importance of informed and free consent, consideration of deception seems incongruous. However, some areas of behavioral or psychological research can only be carried out if the research subject is not aware of

775. While informed consent is usually required, the *TCPS* does allow consent that is not fully informed when circumstances enumerated are warranted: *TCPS 2*, *supra* note 718 at Art. 3.7A.
776. TCPS 2, *supra* note 718 at Art. 3.2; ICH-GCP, *supra* note 737 at Art. 4.8.10.
777. TCPS 2, *supra* note 718 at Art. 3.2.
778. *Ibid.*, at Art. 3.7A-3.7B.

the reasons for the research. Deception involves the intentional misleading of prospective subjects or withholding information from them so that subjects believe that the procedures or the objectives of the research are different from what they actually are. Deception may include deliberate presentation of false information, suppression of material information, or selection of revealed truths in a way designed to mislead. Should research situations arise where it is essential to scientific integrity that the subjects remain unaware of the nature of the research, the REB must determine whether the situation warrants an altered consent procedure.[779]

V. Access to REB Records

A. *Generally*

451. The general rule in research is that confidentiality cannot be breached without the research subject's consent. When subjects have given consent to the research, access to information that personally identifies them, and its use in the research, must be guarded.[780] Investigations of the genetic or familial aspects of a disease give rise to a particular problem of confidentiality. The *TCPS 2* includes a section on guidance on Human Genetic Research.[781] It is recognized that this is a sensitive area, and places the onus on researchers to propose ways in which to deal with the outcome of genetic research and the impact it will have on families and others in the community. While many statutes now recognize a "right to warn" third parties of a "threat of serious harm," at present, however, there is no statutory duty to warn family members of genetic conditions.[782]

452. Research records are liable to subpoena. Courts and judicial tribunals always have the final power to require disclosure either in a restricted or public way.

453. The REB must keep its own internal records that may be accessed by authorized representatives of the institution, researchers and funding agencies.[783]

779. *Ibid.,* at Art. 3.7A.
780. *Ibid.*, at Art. 5.1; ICH-GCP, *supra* note 737 at Art. 2.11.
781. TCPS 2, *supra* note 718 at Arts. 13.1–13.7.
782. Gibson, *supra* note 408 at 223; Consider Adrian Thorogood & Bartha Maria Knoppers, "The Ethical and Legal Duties of Physicians in Clinical Genetics and Genomics" in Y Joly & BM Knoppers, eds., *Routledge Handbook of Medical Law and Ethics* (New York: Routledge, 2015) 319 at 323, 324; *See also Liss v. Watters*, 2012 QCCA 257 at para. 111, leave to appeal to SCC refused 2012 CarswellQue 8879 (QL), where the court noted that the usual "imminence of danger" criterion for the professional duty to warn third parties is not easily transposed to genetic risk circumstances.
783. TCPS 2, *supra* note 718 at Art. 6.17; ICH-GCP, *supra* note 737 at Art. 3.4.

B. Applicability of Access to Information Act (Canada) and Privacy Act

454. As a federal agency, CIHR records are subject to the *Access to Information Act*[784] and the *Privacy Act.*[785] Section 20 of the *Access to Information Act* addresses the exemption of confidential information from requests for information. It is not clear whether this section offers protection from the requirements of disclosure of information during the peer review process. REBs which have been delegated ethics review functions under the *TCPS 2*, and which may operate in provincial or university institutions, may potentially come within the scope of provincial Public Records Acts in some cases. Many provinces have Privacy Acts which protect personal information held by government agencies.

455. The Access to Information Act gives Canadian citizens and people present in Canada a limited right of access to information in federal government records. The *Privacy Act* gives the same individuals a limited right of access to personal information about themselves held in government records and sets out rules and fair practices for the management of personal information by federal institutions. All information collected by CIHR is subject to these laws.

456. An individual seeking access to records held by the CIHR under the *Access to Information Act* must make a request in writing or online. Certain records may be withheld from disclosure in accordance with legislative exceptions that apply when disclosure of information could be expected to injure private or public interests. For example, CIHR would not disclose personal information about identifiable individuals or proprietary technical information submitted in confidence by researchers or companies without consulting with the third parties.

457. The *Privacy Act* sets out limits to the right of access similar to those contained in the *Access to Information Act.* For example, a person seeking access to their personal information would not be given access to personal information about another person. An individual seeking access to personal information held about them by CIHR can submit a written or electronic request under the *Privacy Act.* Under the *Privacy Act,* the written opinion of a reviewer about a grant proposal or scholarship is available to the applicant, but the name of the reviewer is not.[786]

C. Rules of Discovery

458. The records of the REB may also be obtained through ordinary discovery in litigation, according to the discovery rules of the jurisdiction.

784. RSC 1985, c A-1.
785. RSC 1985, c P-21.
786. *Privacy Act*, RSC 1985, c P-21, s. 3.

VI. Regulation of Research Performed upon Special Groups of Subjects

A. Children

1. Generally

459. The age of majority, fixed by provincial statute, is either 18 or 19 years of age. Except for the province of Quebec, there is no specific legislation in force on research involving children either at the federal or provincial level.[787]

460. The *TCPS 2* sets out protective guidelines with respect to those who may lack legal decisional capacity, including children, who are research subjects.[788] Specifically, the harms that children may experience in research are to be taken into consideration by researchers when presenting protocols to REBs, and precautions and ameliorating measures should be presented.[789]

2. Categories of Risk or Benefit

461. The *TCPS 2* only allows a representative to consent to research on behalf of a child (or other person lacking legal decisional capacity) where the research does not expose them to more than minimal risks without the potential for direct benefits to him or her.[790]

3. Consent

a. Consent of Parties Other Than the Child

462. The *TCPS 2* provides that consent from an authorized representative is required if a person, including a child, is not capable of giving consent.[791] However, the representative's consent is not necessarily a sufficient condition. If the person lacks legal decisional capacity but understands the nature and consequences of the research, his or her dissent will preclude participation.[792]

463. In Canada, the age of majority is not the same as the age of consent. Nothing in common law prevents a minor from making their own treatment decisions. The "mature minor" rule does not establish an age below which parental consent

787. Bartha Maria Knoppers, "Legal Aspects of Research Involving Children in Canada" in *Canadian Child Health Law* (Toronto: Thompson Educational Publishing, 1991) at 298; Consider also DuVal, *supra* note 521 at 234–235.
788. TCPS 2, *supra* note 718 at Art. 3.9.
789. *Ibid.,* at Arts. 3.9, 4.4.
790. *Ibid.,* at Art. 3.9.
791. *Ibid.,* at Art. 3.9.
792. *Ibid.,* at Art. 3.10.

would be required, and many provinces have enacted legislation which similarly recognize that minors may have the capacity to consent to treatment on their own behalf.[793]

464. In Quebec, the CCQ governs consent as it pertains to integrity of the person. Under the Civil Code, minors[794] who are incapable of giving their consent may alienate their body parts only if: the body parts are capable of regeneration; no serious risk to their health results; the person with parental authority, the mandatary, the tutor or curator consents; and only with the authorization of the court.[795]

465. Under the C.C.Q minors who are incapable of giving consent may participate in an experiment only if they have no objection and only in the absence of any serious risk to their health.[796] The minor must understand the nature and consequences of the research. The person having parental authority, the mandatary, the tutor or the curator must give consent. If an experiment is carried out on only one minor, a benefit to that person's health must be expected. An experiment conducted on a group of minors must involve an expected benefit to persons of that age group with the same illness or handicap. The research project must be approved and monitored by a competent research ethics committee formed by the Minister of Health and Social Services or designated by that Minister.

466. If a body part is removed as part of the care of the minor, this body part may be used for research purposes with the consent of the person qualified to give consent.[797] If a court is called to rule upon an application to remove a body part or conduct an experiment, it must obtain the opinions of experts, of the person having parental authority, of the mandatary, of the tutor or the curator, and of the tutorship council. It may also obtain the opinion of any person who shows a special interest in the person concerned by the application.[798]

b. Consent of the Child

467. Whether a child will be able to consent to becoming a research subject will depend on the development of the individual child and the surrounding circumstances.

468. While a child may be incapable of giving consent to participate in research, if he or she understands the nature and consequences of the research, the researcher has the onus to ascertain the wishes of the child concerning participation. If the subject does not want to participate, they will not be required to.[799]

793. CCH Canadian Limited, *Canadian Health Facilities Law Guide* (Toronto: LexisNexis Canada, 2019) at paras. 2305, 2310 (QL); *See also* Chapter 2, §1, The Minor Patient.
794. The age of majority in Quebec is 18.
795. Article 19 CCQ.
796. The contents of this paragraph are set out in Art. 21 CCQ.
797. Article 22 CCQ.
798. Article 23 CCQ.
799. TCPS 2, *supra* note 718 at Art. 3.10.

469. In the common law provinces, since no legislation prohibits mature minors from consenting to therapeutic or non-therapeutic research, it could be argued that a mature minor could legally consent alone to participate in medical research.[800] The legal capacity of children to consent must be adjusted, of course, to relevant provincial legislation or regulation on the age of consent to medical treatment and, when this gives no guidance, to the maturity of the individual child.

470. The CCQ states that any person 14 years of age or over can consent to care and treatment. The care and treatment given to the minor must be "required by the state of health" of the child, therefore excluding elective surgery with no therapeutic benefit. The physician must inform the person with parental authority where the minor's state of health requires that he or she remains in a health or social services establishment for more than twelve hours, or for extended treatment.[801] Where a minor is under 14 years of age, the consent of the person with parental authority must be obtained; with very limited exceptions (i.e., emergency).[802]

471. In Quebec a minor 14 years of age or over may consent to a body part removed as part of care being used for the purposes of research.[803] When a court is called to rule upon an application for an experiment, it is bound to obtain the opinion of the person concerned unless that is impossible, and to respect the person's refusal.[804]

472. As discussed in Chapter 2, §1, The Minor Patient, a number of other provinces have also enacted legislation proscribing an age of consent for medical treatment.

B. *Fetuses and Embryos*

1. Fetuses *in Utero*

473. Studies directed at the fetus may concern prenatal diagnosis or *in utero* methods of treating the fetus. However, as the mother and fetus are inextricably linked, any research involving the fetus requires the consent of the mother.[805]

800. Bernard M Dickens, "The Legal Challenge of Health Research Involving Children" (1998) 6 Health L J 131 at paras. 37–38 (QL); Bartha Maria Knoppers, "Legal Aspects of Research Involving Children in Canada" in *Canadian Child Health Law* (Toronto: Thompson Educational Publishing, 1991) at 199.
801. Article 14 CCQ.
802. *Ibid.*
803. Articles 17 and 22 CCQ.
804. Article 23 CCQ.
805. TCPS 2, *supra* note 718 at Art. 12.9.

2. Fetuses *ex Utero*

474. A fetus living at birth, even if it is not viable, is treated under the *Criminal Code* as a human being, whether or not it has breathed, has an independent circulation, or the umbilical cord is severed.[806] Fetuses born alive and viable are treated as children with their own independent interests under *TCPS 2* and must be treated under principles applicable to children.[807]

3. Embryos

475. The *TCPS 2* states that, in accordance with the provisions of the *Assisted Human Reproduction Act*, it is not acceptable to create embryos in vitro for research purposes only, except where the embryo is created for the purpose of improving or providing instruction in assisted reproduction procedures.[808] It is also acceptable, with the consent of the gamete or embryo donors, to use embryos that were created for a reproductive purpose that are no longer required for that purpose.[809] Embryo research is an evolving area where Canada has no social consensus. A broad prohibition of all research on embryos, however, is neither justified nor wise. Research on embryos may only take place up to the fourteenth day of its development, excluding any time during which development was suspended.[810] Canada's *Assisted Human Reproduction Act* prohibits genetic alteration of in vitro embryos as well as human beings in a manner capable of being transmitted to descendants.[811]

476. With the advent of new stem cell research and therapies, the CIHR implemented a separate set of ethical guidelines directly related to stem cell research.[812] It has been integrated into *TCPS 2* since 2014.[813]

C. Research Involving Adults Lacking Legal Decisional Capacity

477. Persons with mental and physical disabilities cannot be presumed to lack the capacity to comprehend information and exercise choice. The issues must be determined on the facts of each case. Such adults may not be under clear legal guardianship. Their guardians, whether de jure guardians properly appointed, or de

806. *Criminal Code*, RSC 1985, c C-46, s. 223.
807. TCPS 2, *supra* note 718 at Art. 12.9.
808. *Ibid.*, at Art. 12.7; *Assisted Human Reproduction Act*, SC 2004, c 2, s. 5(1)(b).
809. TCPS 2, *supra* note 718 at Art. 12.8; *Assisted Human Reproduction Act*, SC 2004, c. 2, s. 8; *Consent for Use of Human Reproductive Material and In Vitro Embryos Regulations*, SOR/2007-137, ss. 4, 8, 13.
810. TCPS 2, *supra* note 718 at Art. 12.8; Consider also *Assisted Human Reproduction Act*, SC 2004, c 2, s. 5(1)(d).
811. SC 2004, c 2, s. 5(1)(f).
812. Canadian Institutes of Health Research, *Human Pluripotent Stem Cell Research: Guidelines for CIHR Funded Research* (Ottawa: Canadian Institutes of Health Research, 2002).
813. TCPS 2, *supra* note 718 at Ch. 12, s. F.

facto guardians such as family members, may not have legal power to give effective consent to invasive procedures. Legal protections for people with mental and physical disabilities are strengthened under the *Canadian Charter of Rights and Freedoms*,[814] reducing the likelihood that provincial public hospital, mental health or mental capacity and consent legislation would be construed to allow research not related to therapy. The authorized representative of an adult who lacks legal decisional capacity, like that of a minor, may only consent to research that exposes the participant to no more than minimal risk without the prospect of direct benefit.[815] In addition, as with children, if an adult who otherwise lacks legal decisional capacity understands the nature of the research and its consequences, his or her dissent will be determinative of his or her participation in the research.[816]

478. The conduct of research with adults who lack legal decisional capacity and who are also institutionalized can raise particular ethical issues. The ethical issues raised in these cases are similar to those that arise where research is conducted with patients, prisoners, or members of the military forces. These individuals will or may be conditioned by their surroundings and by the influence of personnel having control of their comforts and environments. They may also be induced by the promise of advantages to which those in free circumstances would not respond.

VII. Research Involving First Nations, Inuit and Métis Peoples

479. The *TCPS 2* provides a specific framework for research involving Indigenous peoples in Canada, including First Nations, Inuit and Métis peoples.[817] This framework is intended to recognize that research involving Indigenous peoples has often been carried out primarily by non-Indigenous researchers, using approaches that did not reflect Indigenous world views and producing research that was often not beneficial to the communities being studied.[818] Indeed, research with Indigenous communities has a "violent" and "exploitative" history in Canada.[819] Indigenous peoples in Canada have been the subject of a great deal of research, with projects being carried out to achieve interests that are unrelated to the priorities of the studied community, that do not involve consultation or collaboration with the community, and that have extracted data which is (mis)used without consent and in ways that have been detrimental to the subject community.[820] The *TCPS 2* framework is "not intended to override or replace ethical guidance offered by Indigenous

---

814. *Canadian Charter of Rights and Freedoms,* Part I of the *Constitution Act, 1982,* being Sch. B to the *Canada Act 1982* (UK), 1982, c 11.
815. TCPS 2, *supra* note 718 at Art. 3.9.
816. *Ibid.,* at Art. 3.10.
817. *Ibid.,* at Ch. 9.
818. *Ibid.,* at Ch. 9, Preamble.
819. Julia K Ridell et al., "Laying the Groundwork: A Practical Guide for Ethical Research with Indigenous Communities" (2017) 8:2 Intl Indigenous Policy J 1 at 10–11.
820. The First Nations Information Governance Centre, *Ownership, Control, Access and Possession (OCAP™): The Path to First Nations Information Governance* (Ottawa: The First Nations Information Governance Centre, May 2014) at 6–10 [OCAP]; Ridell et al., *supra* note 818 at 2–3, 10–11.

peoples themselves," but rather to "ensure, to the extent possible, that research involving Indigenous peoples is premised on respectful relationships."[821]

480. The *TCPS 2* framework promotes respect, collaboration and engagement between researchers and participants and their communities. The framework provides for ongoing engagement and collaboration with Indigenous communities where the research is likely to affect the welfare of those communities, with the level and nature of involvement and participation being jointly decided and being appropriate to the community's characteristics and the nature of the research.[822] The *TCPS 2* framework also encourages reciprocity, providing that, where possible, the research should be relevant to community needs and priorities and should benefit the participating community as well as extending "the boundaries of knowledge."[823] And, it recognizes the importance of researchers, communities, and institutions considering and agreeing upon issues related to access and use of the knowledge or data related to the research.[824]

481. Research with Indigenous communities may also be guided by a community's customs and/or any codes or guidelines for research practices developed or adopted by the community. Many First Nations communities have adopted the *Ownership, Control, Access and Possession (OCAP™): The Path to First Nations Information Governance*, a standard for conducting research with First Nations which sets out a set of principles relating to ownership of, control of, access to, and possession of information and data.[825] In addition to OCAP, various other frameworks have been authored and adopted by Indigenous governing bodies, organizations, and communities.[826] These include, but are by no means limited to, the *USAI: Utility, Self-Voicing, Access, Inter-Relationality Research Framework* developed by the Ontario Federation of Indigenous Friendship Centres, the *Guiding Ethical Principles* developed by the Urban Aboriginal Knowledge Network, and *Negotiating Research Relationships with Inuit Communities: A Guide for Researchers* prepared by the Inuit Tapiriit Kanatami and Nunavut Research Institute.[827]

482. Researchers interested in conducting research with Indigenous communities should engage with the community or communities from the earliest stages of research design and must ensure that they are familiar with and respect the community's norms and values, and any customs and/or codes or guidelines for research

---

821. TCPS 2, *supra* note 718 at Ch. 9, Preamble.
822. *Ibid.,* at Arts. 9.1–9.7, 9.10, 9.15, 9.16, 9.17, 9.18.
823. *Ibid.,* at Art. 9.13.
824. Consider *Ibid.,* at Arts. 9.18, 9.19.
825. OCAP, *supra* note 819; *See also* TCPS 2, *supra* note 718 at Art. 9.8, Application.
826. *See* Ridell et al., *supra* note 818; TCPS 2, *supra* note 718 at Art. 9.8, Application.
827. Ontario Federation of Indigenous Friendship Centres, *USAI Research Framework: Utility Self-Voicing Access Inter-Relationality*, 2nd ed. (Toronto, ON: Ontario Federation of Indigenous Friendship Centres, 2016); Urban Aboriginal Knowledge Network, "UAKN Guiding Ethical Principles" (Dec. 3, 2016), online (pdf): *Urban Aboriginal Knowledge Network* uakn.org/wp-content/uploads/2014/10/Guiding-Ethical-Principles_Final_2015_10_22.pdf; Inuit Tapiriit Kanatami and Nunavut Research Institute, *Negotiating Research Relationships with Inuit Communities: A Guide for Researchers* (Ottawa & Iqualuit: Inuit Tapiriit Kanatami and Nunavut Research Institute, 2007).

practice that are relevant to or have been adopted by the community.[828] Researchers must also ensure that they comply with any institutional, or other, applicable research governance frameworks (e.g., *TCPS 2*). Where adherence to community-based customs or codes are inconsistent with institutional policies, the researcher must address and resolve these issues before the research begins and may also be required to revise and adapt research practices as the research process unfolds.[829]

VIII. Liability of REBs

483. As Canada has no statutory regulation of research on human subjects, there is no clear statement of who might be legally responsible if there is abuse, accident or carelessness in the course of research causing injury to a research subject.[830] REB members act only as individuals and may be liable only as individuals, as the REB is not a legal entity.[831]

484. While the REB does exercise some control over the researcher, it does so only as an agent of the institution. REB members and researchers could be viewed as fellow agents of the institution and not responsible for one another. There appears to be no basis for holding a member of an advisory REB vicariously liable for the negligence of a researcher.[832]

485. Regarding the duty of the institution or REB member to research subjects to properly review protocols, the law has not generally required one person to take positive steps to prevent injury to another, unless there is a special relationship between them. Canadian courts have recently shown a willingness to expand the situations in which a positive duty to act will be imposed.[833] The individual REB members who perform protocol reviews appear to be in the same position as the research institution with respect to research subjects. There is no reason to believe that individual REB members might not also have a duty to properly direct the conduct of a researcher in order to prevent injury to a research subject.[834]

---

828. TCPS 2, *supra* note 718 at Art. 9.8; *See also* Ridell et al., *supra* note 818.
829. TCPS 2, *supra* note 718 at Art. 9.8, Application; Consider also Riddell et al., *supra* note 818 at 8, 10, 11–12.
830. Medical Research Council of Canada, *Report of the Working Group on Liability* (Ottawa: MRC, 1991) at 2. *See also* Jennifer L Gold, "Watching the Watchdogs: Negligence, Liability, and Research Ethics Boards" (2003) 11 Health L J 153 (QL); Amy Zarzeczny & Timothy Caulfield, "Legal Liability and Research Ethics Boards: The Case of Neuroimaging and Incidental Findings" (2012) 35 Intl J L & Psychiatry 137 at 139.
831. Medical Research Council of Canada, *Report of the Working Group on Liability* (Ottawa: MRC, 1991) at 29.
832. *Ibid.*
833. *Ibid.*, at 31. For further discussion of special relationships giving rise to a positive duty to act, *see Childs v. Desormeaux*, 2006 SCC 18.
834. Medical Research Council of Canada, *Report of the Working Group on Liability* (Ottawa: MRC, 1991) at 33. *See also* Zarzeczny & Caulfield, *supra* note 829 at 141, 142.

486. A research institution or REB member which initially owed no duty to subjects may be viewed as undertaking to protect them from the negligence of a researcher once a protocol review is commenced. The very act of conducting protocol reviews could be seen as creating a duty.[835] Once a policy of protocol review is undertaken, however, the "manner and quality" of the review would appear to be an operational aspect and the institution's acts are subject to a duty of care. The distinction lies in the difference between formulating policy and implementing policy by operational decisions.[836]

487. While the standard of care required of a research institution cannot be precisely defined since there do not appear to be any Canadian cases directly on point, the institution might be expected, as a minimum, to hire competent researchers, to have adequate research facilities and to conduct any review of protocols according to Canadian and international codes and guidelines governing such research. It might also be expected to appoint only competent people to act as an REB.

488. The minimum standard of care required of an REB member would be to carry out a proper risk or benefit analysis and a review of the consent form and procedures having regard to all relevant guidelines.[837] In *Weiss v. Solomon,*[838] the court held that the hospital, through its REB, was liable for failing to put the well-being of subjects ahead of the interests of the community and science, as it was required to do by the Declaration of Helsinki. The fault of the researcher engaged the liability of the hospital, even though there was a contract between the research subject and the researcher. The case also makes clear that a research institution in Quebec can be liable for the negligence of its REB in approving a research protocol or consent form that is inadequate. The hospital was further held liable for its failure to have appropriate emergency equipment available. The individual REB members were not parties to the action on this case.[839]

489. The issue in causation is whether the REB approval caused the subject to consent to an experiment that the subject would not have consented to if he or she had been fully informed.[840] An individual REB member might not be held liable to an injured research subject, even though the REB's decision on the protocol was negligent, if the individual member can show that he or she did not take part in the

835. *Ibid.*
836. Medical Research Council of Canada, *Report of the Working Group on Liability* (Ottawa: MRC, 1991) at 35.
837. Medical Research Council of Canada, *Report of the Working Group on Liability* (Ottawa: MRC, 1991) at 36. *See also* Zarzeczny & Caulfield, *supra* note 829 at 137, 141, 142.
838. *Weiss v. Solomon* (1989), 48 CCLT 280 [1989] 1 RJQ 731, RRA 374 (Que. Sup. Ct.).
839. Medical Research Council of Canada, *Report of the Working Group on Liability* (Ottawa: MRC, 1991) at 36, 40.
840. *Ibid.,* at 37; Consider also Zarzeczny & Caulfield, *supra* note 829 at 143.

particular negligent decision but instead relied on the expertise of another REB member, or possibly even if the individual member can show that he or she dissented from the decision.[841]

IX. Transparency and Access to Data

490. In the wake of public exposure of misrepresentation and fraud in medical research, particularly in the context of clinical trials of pharmaceutical products and medical devices, transparency of research and access to research data have become prominent topics in research governance.[842] Transparency and access to data rules are intended to promote research integrity and accountability by allowing public and independent scrutiny of research findings. Various regulatory and policy initiatives have taken place at the international level,[843] which cannot be discussed here in detail. But the developments in Canada are worth mentioning here for two reasons: first because Canada's drug regulatory agency is now in the process of making a very significant amount of regulatory data publicly available, even retroactively; and second, because this move toward greater regulatory data transparency has been set in motion in part as a result of public interest litigation, which highlights the growing role in Canada of health-related litigation.

491. In line with the recognition of the importance of transparency in the Declaration of Helsinki,[844] the federal funding agencies' *TCPS 2* contains various transparency-related obligations and recommendations. A key obligation is to register clinical trials in a trial registry recognized by the World Health Organization or by the International Committee of Medical Journal Editors prior to the enrolment of any human participant (Article 11.10). The *TCPS 2* also imposes a duty on researchers to disseminate in a timely manner the data analysis and research results (Article 4.8). There is further an—albeit prudent—encouragement to make data available for further analysis or verification and references to transparency in the informed consent requirements (Article 3.2(f)).

841. Medical Research Council of Canada, *Report of the Working Group on Liability* (Ottawa: MRC, 1991) at 37; Consider also Zarzeczny & Caulfield, *supra* note 829 at 142.

842. *See* in general Trudo Lemmens, "Pharmaceutical Knowledge Governance: A Human Rights Perspective" (2013) 41:1 JL Med & Ethics 163; Trudo Lemmens & Candice Telfer, "Access to Information and the Right to Health: The Human Rights Case for Clinical Trials Transparency" (2012) 31:1 Am J L & Med 63; Simon Stern & Trudo Lemmens, "Legal Remedies for Medical Ghostwriting: Imposing Fraud Liability on Guest Authors of Ghostwritten Articles" (2011) 8:8 PLoS Medicine 1 at 1–8.

843. Trudo Lemmens & Carlos Herrera Vacaflor, "Research Transparency in the Americas: The Need to Coordinate Regulatory Spheres" (2018) 362 British Medical J k2493-8; *See also* Herder, *supra* note 734 at 199.

844. Trudo Lemmens & Gregory Ringkamp, "The Declaration of Helsinki and Transparency: When International Ethics Standards Face National Implementation Challenges" in Ulf Schmidt, Andreas Frewer & Dominique Sprumont, eds., *Ethical Research: The Declaration of Helsinki, and the Past, Present, and Future of Human Experimentation* (USA: Oxford University Press, 2020) at 284–309.

492. More stringent transparency obligations have been introduced in the regulatory system surrounding clinical trials for pharmaceutical products and medical devices. Federal access to information law was until recently the only cumbersome tool to obtain clinical trials data submitted to Health Canada. Then in 2014, an amendment to the *Food and Drugs Act* created a disclosure option without consent from the sponsor for data related to approved drugs. It also provided a basis for further regulations about trial registration.[845] Originally, Health Canada still appeared reluctant to facilitate data access. It required, for example, the signing of a confidentiality agreement before providing access to data to researchers who wanted it for public health-related research purposes. But in 2018, a federal court ruled in *Doshi v. Canada (Attorney General)*[846] that requiring a public interest focused researcher to sign a confidentiality agreement was unreasonable and contradicted the public health purpose of Vanessa's Law. The judge also pointed to the fact that at the time of the litigation, the government had drafted already regulations that indicated Canada's plans for more substantial data transparency. Importantly, the court also ruled that the requirement to sign a confidentiality agreement constituted an unreasonable restriction of the researcher's freedom of expression, protected under the Canadian Charter, since it interfered with his ability to communicate his findings.[847] The government did not appeal the decision.

493. In February 2019, new regulations[848] introduced a presumption that information about clinical trials, including safety and efficacy data, ceases to be commercial confidential information once a final decision about approval of a drug product or medical device is made.[849] Health Canada also started implementing a proactive release of such clinical information, including information about drugs approved or rejected in the past. A guidance document[850] lays out an implementation schedule for the publication of all the regulatory data and contains details about what type of data can still be declared commercial confidential information. These developments constitute a major shift in regulatory data sharing in Canada and makes the Canadian drug regulatory agency one of the most transparent in the world, at least when it comes to clinical trials data.

---

845. Parliament of Canada 2014, c 24; *See also* Herder, *supra* note 734 at 199–200.

846. *Doshi v. Canada (AG)* [2018] F.C.J. No. 740.

847. *Ibid.* For more details about the case, *see* Matthew Herder, Peter Doshi & Trudo Lemmens, "Precedent Pushing Practice: Canadian Court Orders Release of Unpublished Clinical Trials Data" (Jul. 19, 2018), online (blog): *BMJ Blogs* blogs.bmj.com/bmj/2018/07/19/precedent-pushing-practice-canadian-court-orders-release-of-unpublished-clinical-trial-data/.

848. Government of Canada, *Regulations Amending the Food and Drug Regulations (Public Release of Clinical Information),* Canada Gazette, II, Mar. 20, 2019, Vol. 153, No. 6, 746.

849. Joel Lexchin, Matthew Herder & Peter Doshi, "Canada finally opens up data on new drugs and devices" (2019) 365 BMJ I1825 doi https://doi.org/10.1136/bmj.l1825.

850. Government of Canada, *Public Release of Clinical Information: Guidance Document* (online: Health Canada, Mar. 12, 2019) www.canada.ca/en/health-canada/services/drug-health-product-review-approval/profile-public-release-clinical-information-guidance/document.html.

§7. LAW AT THE END OF LIFE

I. Recent Developments: The Decriminalization of Medical Assistance in Dying

494. The right to make self-regarding health-care decisions has been a mainstay of Canadian health law. In the context of end-of-life care, both the right to refuse life-sustaining treatment[851] and the right to have such treatment withdrawn have been firmly entrenched in the law since the 1980s. Yet, until recently, this did not include any recognition of a right to have active support in ending one's life, either by receiving a lethal prescription, or having one's life terminated by a health-care provider. In 1993, the Supreme Court explicitly confirmed in *Rodriguez v. British Columbia (Attorney General)*[852] by a 5 to 4 majority the constitutionality of an absolute prohibition on euthanasia and assisted suicide. Although it confirmed that the prohibition impacted on the right to life, liberty and security of the person, the limitation was considered reasonable under the Charter's proportionality test.

495. In 2015, a largely reconstituted Supreme Court overturned this precedent in the case of *Carter v. Canada (Attorney General)*, which was factually quite similar to the Rodriguez case.[853] The Court invoked changing societal perceptions, availability of new evidence from jurisdictions that legalized the practice, and a change in the Court's proportionality test to justify a reconsideration of the 1993 precedent.[854] It ruled that an absolute prohibition on what it termed "physician-assisted dying" was an unjustifiable infringement on the right to life, liberty and security of the person. The criminal law prohibition was deemed unjustifiable to the extent that it prevented a competent adult who has a grievous and irremediable medical condition that causes enduring and intolerable suffering from obtaining the help of a physician in ending their life. Canada thus became the second jurisdiction after Colombia to recognize some form of constitutional right to life-ending termination by physicians.[855]

851. *See* e.g., *Malette, supra* note 325, in which the Ontario Court of Appeal recognized a duty to respect a written instructive not to receive a blood-transfusion by a Jehovah's witness.

852. *Rodriguez v. British Columbia (Attorney General)* [1993] 3 SCR 519, 107 DLR (4th) 342 [*Rodriguez*].

853. *Carter, supra* note 168. For a discussion of the decision, *see* Benny Chan & Margaret Somerville, "Converting the 'Right to Life' to the 'Right to Physician-Assisted Suicide and Euthanasia': An analysis of *Carter v. Canada (Attorney General)* Supreme Court of Canada" (2016) 24:2 Med L Rev 143; Stephanie Palmer, "'The Choice Is Cruel': Assisted Suicide and Charter Rights in Canada" (2015) 74:2 Cambridge LJ 191; Rose M Carter & Brandyn Rodgerson, "Medical Assistance in Dying: Journey to Medical Self-Determination" (2018) 55:3 Alta L Rev 777; and various chapters in Derek Ross, ed., *Assisted Death: Legal, Social and Ethical Issues After Carter* (Toronto: LexisNexis, 2018).

854. For a discussion of the revision of precedent in *Carter*, *see* Debra L Parkes, "Precedent Revisited: *Carter v Canada (AG)* and the Contemporary Practice of Precedent" (2016) 10:1 McGill JL & Health S124.

855. Trudo Lemmens, Heesoo Kim & Elizabeth Kurz, "Why Canada's Medical Assistance in Dying Law Should be C(h)arter Compliant and What It May Help to Avoid" (2017) 11:1 McGill JL & Health S61 at 64. This article also discusses the case and the subsequent debate in Canada about how Parliament had to respond.

496. The Supreme Court suspended the declaration of invalidity of the absolute prohibition for a year and invited Parliament to enact a strict regulatory regime with stringent safeguards, that would permit physician-assisted dying with respect to the general parameters it provided. Noteworthy is that shortly before the Supreme Court 2015 decision in *Carter*, Quebec's National Assembly had already adopted in 2014 an "Act respecting end-of-life care" in which it explicitly authorized active life-ending interventions by physicians (euthanasia and assisted suicide).[856] Quebec's provincial legislature thereby permitted within the context of end-of-life care a practice, based on its power with respect to health care, which contravened for a short period of time the federal criminal law.

497. Following the *Carter* decision, heated societal and parliamentary debate ensued about how broad the legislation had to be in terms of who could have access to it.[857] In 2016, Canadian Parliament enacted *An Act to Amend the Criminal Code and to Make Related Amendments to Other Acts (Medical Assistance in Dying)* [MAiD],[858] thereby becoming one of a handful of jurisdictions internationally that allow active life-ending termination by health-care providers. The law, which continues to treat the practice within the context of the criminal law, permits that health-care providers take active steps, at the patient's request, to end the patient's life where specified criteria are met, or prescribe lethal medication for the patient to self-administer. The partial decriminalization of MAiD represents a significant shift in the country's laws and policies surrounding medical interventions at the end of life.

498. However, policies surrounding the availability and expansion of MAiD in Canada continue to evolve. From its inception, some of the limitations on the practice of MAiD, particularly the restriction to the end-of-life context, which is discussed further, have been contested by advocacy organizations and commentators supportive of broad access to MAiD. In 2019, a Quebec superior court ruled in *Truchon v. Canada (AG)*[859] that the end-of-life restriction in the MAiD law violated both the right to life, liberty and security of the person as well as the equality rights of people whose death is not "reasonably foreseeable." The Federal Government declined to appeal the decision[860] and has recently introduced a Bill that would remove the "reasonably foreseeable" natural death requirement and allow individuals who are not nearing the end of their lives to access MAiD.[861] This proposed legislative change, likely to happen by the end of 2020, will likely significantly broaden access to MAiD, particularly outside the end-of-life context.

---

856. *Act Respecting End-of-Life Care*, S-32.0001.
857. For an overview of the debate, including the publication of several reports, *see* Lemmens, Kim & Kurz, *supra* note 853 at S87–119.
858. *An Act to Amend the Criminal Code and to Make Related Amendments to Other Acts (Medical Assistance in Dying)*, S.C. 2016, c 3.
859. *Truchon v. Canada (AG)*, 2019 QCCS 3792.
860. For a commentary, *see* Trudo Lemmens & Laverne Jacobs, "The Latest Medical Assistance in Dying Decision Needs to Be Appealed: Here's Why" (Oct. 9, 2019), online: *The Conversation* theconversation.com/the-latest-medical-assistance-in-dying-decision-needs-to-be-appealed-heres-why-124955.
861. Bill C-7, *An Act to Amend the Criminal Code (Medical Assistance in Dying),* 1st Sess, 43rd Parl, 2020 (first reading Feb. 24, 2020).

II. The Right to Forgo Life-Sustaining Treatment

A. Competent Adults

499. The law in Canada is that a competent adult may refuse life-sustaining medical treatment. This includes the right to insist that treatment, once commenced, be withdrawn or discontinued.[862] Not only is this right supported by the common law, it is protected by the *Canadian Charter of Rights and Freedoms.* Administering treatment without a patient's consent both constitutes battery and violates the patient's right to life, liberty and security of the person.[863] The ONCA and the SCC have held that the right to make choices concerning one's own body and to control one's physical and psychological integrity is encompassed within the right to security of the person.[864] In addition, the Court acknowledged the common law right to demand that medical treatment which would extend life be withheld or withdrawn. Even if a patient chooses to proceed with beneficial medical treatment, he or she retains choice as to the course of action that treatment will take.

500. Health-care practitioners have a difficult role to play in relation to a dying patient: physicians are to allow death to occur with dignity and comfort and need not prolong life by unusual or heroic means. If a patient refuses medical treatment which will lead to his or her death the only legal and ethical concern that the practitioner must address is whether the patient is competent and capable of making that decision. A physician is also obligated to withdraw life-sustaining treatment if a competent patient requests it.[865] Further, the physician is not under any obligation to continue futile treatment. To totally sedate terminal patients suffering intolerable pain, and to provide pain control treatment aimed at alleviating suffering, is accepted practice and legal, even if it may shorten life.[866] All of these activities are legal if they occur with the consent of the patient or in accordance with an advance directive or other legally accepted substitute decision process. Where the patient's wishes are not known or are left unascertained, any physician who individually takes active or unconventional steps to end a patient's suffering faces the risk of legal prosecution, regardless of the futility of further medical intervention.[867]

---

862. *See Ciarlariello v. Schacter* [1993] 2 SCR 119; *Rodriguez, supra* note 851; and *Malette, supra* note 325.
863. *Ibid.*; and *see Fleming, supra* note 167.
864. *Rodriguez, supra* note 851. *See also Carter, supra* note 168.
865. The Special Senate Committee on Euthanasia and Assisted Suicide, *Report of the Special Senate Committee on Euthanasia and Assisted Suicide: Of Life and Death* (Ottawa: Minister of Supply and Services, June 1995).
866. *Ibid. See also Rodriguez, supra* note 851; *Carter, supra* note 168.
867. As was the case in *B.(N.) v. Hotel-Dieu de Quebec* (1992) 69 CCC (3d) 450 (Que. Sup. Ct.), where the Court affirmed that a mentally competent patient cannot be treated without consent. The patient, Nancy B., suffered from almost total paralysis and weakness of the muscles required for breathing, as a result of Guillain-Barre syndrome. Her request to have life-sustaining treatment removed was denied by her physician and the hospital, so she sought recourse through the courts.

B. Formerly Competent Patients: Anticipatory Decision-Making and Advance Directives

1. Advance Directives or Living Wills

501. If a patient while competent makes his or her wishes known regarding treatment then those wishes are to be respected notwithstanding the patient's subsequent incapacity to make health-care decisions.[868] This position has been expressly protected by legislation in virtually all provinces.[869] Advance directives can be divided into two categories. Instruction directives set out what or how health-care decisions are to be made on a person's behalf when he or she is unable to make them. Proxy directives, or power of attorney, name an individual who is to make the health-care decisions for the patient when he or she is incompetent.

502. As examples, the Manitoba and Ontario laws are discussed in more detail in the following paragraphs.

503. The Manitoba legislation is straight forward and emphasizes the patient and his or her right to refuse treatment. It specifically acknowledges that mentally capable individuals have the right to consent to or refuse treatment. This right is to be respected after individuals are no longer able to participate in decisions respecting their medical treatment. A person may, while capable, make a health-care directive which expresses the maker's health-care decisions or appoints a proxy or both. A person is capable if he or she is able to understand the information that is relevant to making a decision and able to appreciate the reasonably foreseeable consequences of a decision or lack of decision. In the absence of evidence to the contrary it is presumed that a person who is 16 years of age or older is capable. The directive must be in writing, signed by the maker and witnessed by someone other than the proxy, if a proxy is appointed. It is effective once the maker ceases to have capacity or is unable to communicate his or her decisions.[870]

504. Ontario's *Health Care Consent Act* establishes a hierarchical list of persons who may act as a substitute decision maker to give or refuse consent to treatment on behalf of an incapable person. The ranking begins with the person's guardian, and thereafter includes an attorney with power of attorney for personal care (if there

---

868. *Fleming, supra* note 167; *Malette, supra* note 325.
869. *See* Manitoba's *Health Care Directives Act,* CCSM c H27; Ontario's *Health Care Consent Act, 1996,* SO 1996, c 2, Sch. A and *Substitute Decisions Act, 1992,* SO 1992, c 30; Quebec's Art. 11 CCQ; Newfoundland and Labrador's *Advance Health Care Directives Act,* SNL 1995, c A-4.1; Alberta's *Personal Directives Act,* RSA 2000, c P-6; British Columbia *Representation Agreement Act,* RSBC 1996, c 405 and *Health Care (Consent) and Care Facility (Admission) Act,* RSBC 1996, c 181; Saskatchewan *Health Care Directives and Substitute Health Care Decision Makers Act, 2015,* SS 2015, c H-0.002; Prince Edward Island's *Consent to Treatment and Health Care Directives Act,* RSPEI 1988, c C-17.2; Nova Scotia's *Personal Directives Act,* SNS 2008, c 8; New Brunswick's *Advance Health Care Directives Act,* RSNB 2016, c 46; Yukon's *Care Consent* Act, SY 2003, c 21, Sch. B; and the Northwest Territories' *Personal Directives Act,* SNWT 2005, c 16.
870. *The Health Care Directives Act,* CCSM c H27.

is explicit authority with regards to medical treatment), an appointed representative, and family members (also ranked hierarchically). Section 5 recognizes that capable persons may express their wishes with respect to treatment in the form of a power of attorney, a form prescribed by regulation, or in any other written or oral form or any other manner. Later wishes expressed while capable take precedence over earlier expressed wishes. Section 21 then requires the substitute decision maker to give or refuse consent in accordance with the wishes expressed by the incapable person while capable and 16 years of age or older. The substitute decision maker is free to act in the incapable person's best interests only if the latter had not expressed any wish while capable with respect to the circumstances in question, or if it is impossible to comply with the expressed wish. Under the *Health Care Consent Act, 1996,* Ontario now has a capacity test that relies less on a specific age, and more on finding that a person "is able to understand the information that is relevant to making a decision about the treatment ..., and able to appreciate the reasonably foreseeable consequences of a decision or lack of decision."[871] However, other sections of the act indicate that an incapable person's earlier expressed wishes are not binding unless they had been expressed after the person had attained 16 years of age while capable.

2. Powers of Attorney for Health Care

505. In Ontario the *Substitute Decisions Act, 1992* provides that a person may give a written power of attorney for personal care, authorizing the attorney to make, on the grantor's behalf, decisions about health and other personal care decisions. A person is capable of giving a power of attorney if he or she has the ability to understand whether the proposed attorney has a genuine concern for the grantor's welfare and appreciates the need for the attorney.[872] The Manitoba *Health Care Directives Act* allows for a review of the appointment by the court if it is believed that the proxy is not acting in the patient's best interests. A proxy must be apparently mentally competent and at least 18 years of age.[873]

3. Court-Appointed Guardians of the Person

506. In the absence of legislation the only person who has legal authority to consent on behalf of a mentally incapable person is a guardian appointed by the court. In Ontario a court may appoint a guardian who shall make decisions on the incapable person's behalf in accordance with certain principles. For example, if the guardian is aware of the wishes or instructions of the person expressed while capable, then the decision should be made in accordance with these wishes. If the guardian is not aware of such wishes then he or she must attempt to ascertain them by consulting with the patient's family members, friends and caregivers. If the

871. *Health Care Consent Act, 1996,* SO 1996, c 2, Sch. A, s. 4.
872. *Substitute Decisions Act,* 1992, SO 1992, c 30, ss. 46–47.
873. *The Health Care Directives Act,* CCSM, c H27, s. 12.

guardian is still unable to determine the wishes of the patient then he or she is to act in the best interests of the patient. The guardian is to choose the least intrusive and restrictive course of action that is available and is appropriate in the particular case.[874]

507. In Alberta, the relevant legislation is the *Adult Guardianship and Trusteeship Act.*[875] Under it, an interested person may apply to the court for an order appointing a guardian to make decisions regarding personal matters—including health-care matters—for an incapable adult. Such an order will be made if the court is satisfied that: the adult does not have the capacity to make decisions about the personal matters that are to be referred to in the order; less intrusive and less restrictive alternative measures than the appointment of a guardian have been considered or have been implemented and would not likely be or have not been effective to meet the needs of the adult; and it is in the adult's best interests to make the order. In urgent cases—in cases of immediate danger of death or serious physical or mental harm—the court may dispense with documents, notice and evidence that are otherwise necessary, and appoint a temporary guardian—either an individual or the Public Guardian.[876]

4. Family Consent Laws

508. It is often presumed that the family may make decisions relating to the incapable person's health care. This is not true at common law, but some provinces have taken this approach in the development of their consent legislation. The statute generally sets out a list of relatives in descending order of proximity to the patient (spouse, adult children, parents, siblings) who may give health-care directions on the patient's behalf. In Ontario, however, the statute's prioritized list gives first precedence to an incapable person's guardian of the person. The person's relatives fall last on the list, ranked in an order that begins with the person's spouse or partner, and ends with "any other relative of the incapable person."[877] In Alberta, where an adult has been assessed as lacking the capacity to make a decision respecting the adult's health-care or temporary admission to a residential facility, a health-care provider may select a nearest relative to act as "specific decision maker." Such a person must: be 18 years of age or older; be available and willing to make the decision; be able to make the decision; have been in contact with the adult in the previous twelve months; have knowledge of the adult's wishes respecting the decision to be made or of the beliefs and values of the adult; and not have a dispute with the adult that might affect the relative's ability to comply with the duties of a specific decision maker.[878]

874. *Substitute Decisions Act, 1992,* SO 1992, c 30, s. 66.
875. SA 2008, c A-4.2.
876. *Ibid.*, ss. 26–27.
877. *Health Care Consent Act, 1996,* SO 1996, c 2, Sch. A, s. 20.
878. *Adult Guardianship and Trusteeship Act,* SA 2008, c A-4.2, ss. 87(2), 89.

C. Patients Who Have Never Been Competent

509. Patients who have always been mentally incompetent to consent to medical care must rely upon other persons to make those decisions for them. Such persons may be court-appointed guardians or, in some provinces, they may be the "nearest relative," as has been discussed in the foregoing. Because there is no way to ascertain the wishes of patients who have never been competent, heavy reliance is placed upon the "best interests" approach. In Ontario, for example, a person who gives or refuses consent on an incapable person's behalf shall do so in accordance with the best interests of the patient. The decision maker shall consider the values and beliefs of the patient, the wishes expressed while incapable, whether the patient's condition will improve with treatment, and whether the benefits of treatment outweigh the risks. Only a person who is at least 16 years of age and is capable with respect to the treatment may give or refuse consent on the incapable person's behalf. However, a person who is less than 16 years of age may give or refuse consent on behalf of his or her child if the person is capable with respect to the treatment.[879]

510. There are no Canadian cases which turn on the right of adult incapable persons to refuse life-sustaining treatment. Both Ontario's and Manitoba's legislation recognize that patients may be incapable at one time and not another, and that patients may be incapable regarding one form of treatment and not another.[880] Although incapable adults may have the right to refuse treatment, therefore, a difficulty arises regarding how they may express that right. As discussed earlier,[881] substitute decision makers and legal guardians make decisions on behalf of children who require life-sustaining treatment and who have not reached a level of maturity allowing them to make their own decisions. Legislation in British Columbia directs a representative to comply with an incapable person's current wishes if it is reasonable to do so, but also requires substantial agreement among the health-care providers involved with the person's care that it is medically appropriate to refuse substitute consent to care necessary to preserve life.[882] In the absence of legislation addressing the issue of substitute decision-making, however, it is suggested that the incompetent patient's rights, including the right to life as guaranteed by the *Canadian Charter of Rights and Freedoms,* would have to be protected and would supersede the concerns regarding personal autonomy and dignity. The SCC has acknowledged, however, that the principle of sanctity of life is no longer seen to

879. *Health Care Consent Act, 1996,* SO 1996, c 2, Sch. A, s. 20(2)(b).
880. *The Health Care Directives Act,* CCSM c H27, s. 6(2) and *Health Care Consent Act, 1996,* SO 1996, c 2, Sch. A, s. 15.
881. *See* Chapter 2. III.
882. *Representation Agreement Act*, RSBC 1996, c 405, s. 16(2)-(3); *Health Care (Consent) and Care Facility (Admission) Act*, RSBC 1996, c 181, ss. 18–19.

require that all human life be preserved at all costs. The Court noted that the principle is not absolute but involves a consideration of the quality of life and is subject to certain limitations and qualifications reflective of personal autonomy and dignity.[883]

III. Requests for Continuation of Futile Treatment

511. In its *Code of Ethics and Professionalism,* the CMA encourages its members to "respect the decisions of the competent patient to accept or reject any recommended assessment, treatment, or plan of care." Physicians are to "respect the values and intentions of a patient deemed incompetent as they were expressed previously through advance care planning discussions when competent," and where specific intentions are unknown and in the absence of a formal mechanism for treatment decisions (e.g., valid substitute decision maker) to "act consistently with the patient's discernable values and goals of care."[884] CMA policy distinguishes "the withholding or withdrawal of inappropriate, futile or unwanted medical treatment or the provision of compassionate palliative care" from both euthanasia and assisted suicide.[885]

512. The position that physicians are not legally obligated to commence or continue futile medical treatment is recognized at Canadian common law, at least where a patient is clinically brain dead and death of the body is inevitable. At least one Canadian jurisdiction's appellate court has stated that "[t]here is no legal obligation on a medical doctor to take heroic measures to maintain the life of a patient in an irreversible vegetative state."[886] Courts have acknowledged that, in some cases, the withdrawal of medical treatment may be in the best interests of the patient.[887] The Special Senate Committee on Euthanasia and Assisted Suicide has also acknowledged that futile treatment could be withheld even against a competent patient's wishes. It defined "futile" treatment as that which, in the opinion of the health-care team, would be completely ineffective. It is recommended that this be interpreted very narrowly.[888] On the other hand, the court has equally refused to insulate physicians from potential legal responsibility for the decision to withhold or withdraw treatment. In *London Health Sciences Centre v. R.K. (Guardian ad litem of),*[889] the court refused to grant caregivers a declaration of immunity from prosecution for withdrawing life support from an elderly patient in a severe persistent vegetative

883. *Rodriguez, supra* note 851. *See also Carter, supra* note 168.

884. Canadian Medical Association, *CMA Code of Ethics and Professionalism,* at ss. 12, 15–16, online (pdf): *Canadian Medical Association* https://policybase.cma.ca/documents/policypdf/PD19-03.pdf

885. Canadian Medical Association, *Euthanasia and Assisted Suicide* (Ottawa: Canadian Medical Association, 1998) at 1. *See also* Canadian Medical Association, *Medical Assistance in Dying* (Ottawa: Canadian Medical Association, 2017) at 1, online: policybase.cma.ca/en/permalink/policy13698.

886. *Child and Family Services of Central Manitoba v. Lavallee* (1997), 154 DLR (4th) 409 (Man. CA).

887. *See* discussion in *Alberta (Child, Youth, and Family Enhancement Act, Director) v. D.L.*, 2012 ABQB 562, affirmed 2012 ABCA 275.

888. *Report of the Special Senate Committee on Euthanasia and Assisted Suicide: Of Life and Death* (Ottawa: Minister of Supply and Services, 1995) at 45 (hereinafter: "Senate Committee Report").

889. (1997), 152 DLR (4th) 724 (Ont. Gen. Div.).

state, whose family members initially had refused their consent. In their reasons, the court cited a disinclination to interfere with either the Attorney General's prosecutorial discretion, or Parliament's purview to declare the physician's legal right to withdraw life support. In Canada, therefore, the withholding or cessation of futile treatment is generally considered a medical decision and responsibility, but without parliamentary intervention, caregivers who act against a competent patient or substitute decision maker's wishes have no guarantee that their medical decision will not carry legal consequences.

513. In recent years, some Canadian courts have demonstrated a willingness to grant, and continue, interim injunctions prohibiting health-care teams from withdrawing arguably futile medical treatment. In *Golubchuk v. Salvation Army Grace General Hospital,* for example, the Manitoba Court of Queen's Bench continued such an order granted to the committee of a patient suffering kidney and heart failure. As the patient's interest in continued life outweighed the doctor's interest in ceasing treatment, an injunction pending full trial was held appropriate.[890] In *I.H.V. Estate (Re),* on the other hand, the Alberta Court of Queen's Bench refused to grant an injunction that would have prescribed a course of continued treatment contrary to the unanimous view of the patient's health-care providers.[891] Motions for injunctive relief in circumstances such as these are to be made by special application to the court, not by statement of claim.[892]

514. In *Rasouli (Litigation Guardian of) v. Sunnybrook Health Sciences Centre,*[893] the SCC held that withdrawal of life support constitutes "treatment" under Ontario's Health Care Consent Act, and that consent has to be obtained from substitute decision-makers even when physicians are of the opinion that providing further life support is not medically indicated. Physicians could challenge the substitute decision maker's refusal to withdraw life support by appealing to the specialized Consent and Capacity Board under Ontario's consent law. The Board then makes a determination on the basis of the "best interests" of the patient, following specific criteria set out in the legislation.

IV. Medical Assistance in Dying (Euthanasia, Physician-Assisted Suicide)

A. *Terminology*

515. Various terms have been used across jurisdictions to describe the phenomenon of a health-care professional ending the life of a patient or assisting the patient in doing so. In Canada, the terminology that has been adopted in the legislation, and

890. 2008 MBQB 49; 290 DLR (4th) 46. *See also Jin (Next Friend of) v. Calgary Health Region,* 2007 ABQB 593.
891. 2008 ABQB 250.
892. *See Sweiss v. Alberta Health Services,* 2009 ABQB 691; *May v. Alberta Health Services,* 2010 ABQB 213.
893. 2013 SCC 53.

also more widely within society, is "Medical Assistance in Dying" (MAiD). Medical Assistance in Dying (MAiD) captures circumstances in which a health-care professional is involved in the process of assisted dying. Specifically, under Canadian legislation, MAiD encompasses situations where, at a patient's request, a health-care professional (physician or nurse practitioner) administers a substance to the person, or prescribes a substance for the person to self-administer, which causes their death.[894] The use of this terminology, and its statutory definition, reflects according to some the fact that in Canada, it is not only a physician who may assist a patient in ending their lives, but rather that health-care teams, including nurses, pharmacists, and other health-care professionals, may also be involved in the process of assisted dying.[895] Originally, the term appears to have been coined in particular by those promoting legalization of the practice to avoid the negative connotations that for some were attached to the terms euthanasia and assisted suicide. In Canada, the term has been criticized particularly by palliative care specialists, who consider that palliative care has been providing medical support in dying for many decades, and that the term "MAiD" misleadingly fails to state clearly that direct life-ending interventions are involved.[896] In this chapter, we nevertheless use the term "Medical Assistance in Dying" or "MAiD" to encompass both physician-assisted suicide and euthanasia since it is the term now widely used in Canada and the term of the law.

516. The MAiD rules provide an exemption to the rules in the criminal code that prohibit causing a person's death or aiding a person to die by suicide. Specifically, under the exemptions for MAiD, medical practitioners, nurse practitioners, persons aiding a medical or nurse practitioner, and pharmacists dispensing a substance prescribed by a medical practitioner or nurse practitioner will not be guilty of an offense for providing a person with MAiD in accordance with the criteria established in section 241.2 of the *Criminal Code*.[897]

517. Outside of the more recent MAiD context, the term "euthanasia" has been used in Canada in previous cases, and still seems to be attached to the practice of involuntary life-ending interventions. In the case of *R. v. Latimer,* the Saskatchewan appellate court explicitly noted that the accused's severely handicapped, quadriplegic 12-year-old daughter "was not in a position to make an informed and voluntary choice to exercise a hypothetical right. Furthermore, this case does not involve medical decisions concerning continuation or termination of life-sustaining treatment."[898] In 2001, the SCC upheld his conviction for second-degree murder and the mandatory minimum sentence of life imprisonment without parole eligibility for ten

894. *Criminal Code,* RSC 1985, c C-46, s. 241.1. *See also Act Respecting End-of-Life Care*, RSQ, c S-32.0001.
895. J Nicol & M Tiedemann, *Legislative Summary: Bill C-14, An Act to Amend the Criminal Code and to Make Related Amendments to Other Acts (Medical Assistance in Dying)*, Publication No. 42-1-C14-E (Ottawa: Library of Parliament, Sep. 27, 2018) at 2.
896. *See* the discussion in Lemmens, Kim & Kurz, *supra* note 853 at S71-72.
897. *Criminal Code,* RSC 1985, c C-46 at ss. 227, 241(2)-(5.1).
898. *R v. Latimer* [1995] 8 W.W.R. 609 [1995] S.J. No. 402.

years, holding that the defense of necessity could not apply (killing his daughter not being a proportionate response to the non-life-threatening suffering caused by her condition).[899]

B. Background: Partial Legalization of MAiD in Canada

518. The landmark 2015 SCC decision in *Carter v. Canada (Attorney General)*[900] and the subsequent enactment of legislation partially permitting MAiD as an exemption of the overall criminal law prohibition represent a significant shift in the legal landscape in Canada. This unprecedented change was preceded by decades of debates surrounding MAiD. Prior to the *Carter* decision, MAiD was addressed in numerous studies, including a Special Senate Committee on Euthanasia and Assisted Suicide in 1995, and in a Royal Society of Canada (RSC) report on end-of-life decision-making, including MAiD, in 2011.[901] It was also addressed through private members' bills that proposed amendments to the *Criminal Code* to permit physician-assisted suicide, with "Right to die with dignity" amendments being debated in the federal House of Commons in 2005, 2008, 2009 and 2014 (though none were successful).[902] In addition, prior to *Carter,* MAiD was also addressed in various court cases, most notably in the case of *Rodriguez v. British Columbia (Attorney General)*, an unsuccessful challenge to the *Criminal Code's* prohibition on assisted suicide.

519. Attempted suicide was decriminalized in 1972. However, assisting an individual in dying remained a criminal offense under the Criminal Code.[903] Section 241 of the *Criminal Code* makes it a criminal offense to counsel a person to commit suicide or to aid or abet a person to commit suicide. "Aid or abet" includes providing information or the means to a person who commits suicide.

520. The prohibition in the Criminal Code was unsuccessfully challenged in the 1993 case, *Rodriguez v. British Columbia (Attorney General).*[904] The challenge was brought under the *Canadian Charter of Rights and Freedoms*, on the basis that the assisted suicide prohibition infringed on an individual's right to liberty and security of the person and discriminated against persons with physical disabilities. Sue Rodriguez was suffering from amyotrophic lateral sclerosis (also known as "Lou Gehrig's Disease"). She asked that the *Criminal Code* be declared invalid and that a

899. *R v. Latimer*, 2001 SCC 1.
900. *Carter, supra* note 168.
901. J Nicol & M Tiedemann, *Legislative Summary: Bill C-14, An Act to Amend the Criminal Code and to Make Related Amendments to Other Acts (Medical Assistance in Dying)*, Publication No. 42-1-C14-E (Ottawa: Library of Parliament, Sep. 27, 2018) at 2; *Senate Committee Report, supra* note 886; Royal Society of Canada, U Schuklenk et al., *End-of-Life Decision Making* (Ottawa: Royal Society of Canada, November 2011).
902. J Nicol & M Tiedemann, *Background Paper: Euthanasia and Assisted Suicide in Canada by Julia Nicol & Marlisa Tiedemann*, Publication No. 2015-139-E (Ottawa: Library of Parliament, Dec. 15, 2015) at 15.
903. *Criminal Code*, RSC 1985, c C-46.
904. *Rodriguez, supra* note 851.

qualified physician be allowed to set up the technological means by which she could, by her own hand, and at the time of her choosing, end her life. The SCC held that although the prohibition against suicide offended Ms. Rodriguez's right to liberty and security of the person, this infringement was not contrary to the principles of fundamental justice. The majority of the Court held that the purpose of section 241 is to protect the weak and the vulnerable. This is grounded in the state's interest in protecting life and is reflective of the state's policy that human life should not be depreciated by allowing life to be taken. Although the section was upheld by the Court, it is important to note that it was by a slim majority; five judges upheld the prohibition and four rejected it. The dissenting judges based their decisions on the view that the legislative scheme which makes suicide lawful, as it is in Canada, but assisted suicide unlawful, denies some people the choice of ending their lives solely because they are physically unable to do so. This prevents them from exercising the autonomy over their bodies that is available to other people. The denial of this ability is arbitrary and amounts to an unjustifiable infringement of their rights.[905]

C. *The Current Legal Status*

1. Permissible Acts: MAiD Eligibility

521. In 2015, over two decades after *Rodriguez*, the SCC released a unanimous decision in *Carter v. Canada (Attorney General)* declaring the prohibitions in the *Criminal Code* that prevent assistance in dying unconstitutional insofar as they prohibit competent adults meeting specified criteria from accessing MAiD.[906] Specifically, the SCC ruled that the then prohibitions on a person consenting to the infliction of death (section 14) and to aiding a person to die by suicide (section 241(b)) under the Criminal Code, "unjustifiably infringe[d] s[ection] 7 of the Charter and are of no force or effect to the extent that they prohibit physician-assisted death for a competent adult person who (1) clearly consents to the termination of life and (2) has a grievous and irremediable medical condition (including an illness, disease or disability) that causes enduring suffering that is intolerable to the individual in the circumstances of his or her condition."[907]

522. The Supreme Court agreed with the trial court that an absolute prohibition infringed on people's right to make important self-regarding decisions, and impacted on their autonomy and dignity. It also infringed on their right to security because it forced people to endure intolerable suffering. The court confirmed that the concept of right to life included a notion of sanctity of life, which the state has to protect, but it ruled that the right to life could not mean a duty to live. The court agreed with the trial court's analysis of the proportionality of the absolute prohibition under sections 7 and 1 of the Charter of Rights and Freedoms. Recognizing that the prohibition aimed at the protection of vulnerable people who might otherwise

905. *Ibid. See also* the *Senate Committee Report, supra* note 886 at 51–89.
906. *Carter, supra* note 168.
907. *Ibid.*

commit suicide in a moment of weakness, the trial judge had analyzed in detail comparative evidence. She had concluded that this evidence demonstrated that an absolute prohibition was not required to protect vulnerable people, and that Parliament could enact a strict regulatory regime to ensure proper protection. For that reason she found the restriction overbroad. Noteworthy is that the Supreme Court did not discuss whether the prohibition was discriminatory (as the trial judge had ruled), but only analyzed the issues on the basis of section 7. The Supreme Court also explicitly refused to confirm, as the plaintiff claimed, that the "right to life include[s] a right to die with dignity" or the "right to determine whether to take one's own life."[908] While agreeing that an absolute prohibition violated, in certain respects, the right to life, liberty and security of the person, the SCC thus confirmed that the state continues to have an obligation to uphold the right to life, and it emphasized the need for a strict regulatory regime.

523. In order to give Parliament time to be able to effectively respond with legislative changes to the *Carter* decision, the SCC suspended its decision by a period of one year; the suspension was subsequently extended for an additional four months. In suspending the declaration of invalidity, the Court noted that Parliament needed an "opportunity to craft an appropriate remedy" and that it would be for physicians' colleges, Parliament, and the provincial legislatures to construct legislative and regulatory regimes which recognized the *Charter* rights of patients while also considering physicians' freedom of conscience and religion.[909]

524. In 2014, just prior to the Supreme Court *Carter* decision, the Quebec legislature passed the *Act respecting end-of-life care.*[910] The Quebec Act established the rights of "end-of-life patients" and set out a framework for end-of-life care, including palliative care for end-of-life patients and MAiD. In the act, "medical assistance in dying" is defined as "care consisting in the administration by a physician of medications or substances to an end-of-life patient, at the patient's request, in order to relieve their suffering by hastening death."[911] To be eligible for MAiD under the *Act respecting end-of-life care*, a patient must meet the following criteria:

(1) be an insured person within the meaning of the Health Insurance Act;
(2) be of full age and capable of giving consent to care;
(3) be at the end of life;
(4) suffer from a serious and incurable illness;
(5) be in an advanced state of irreversible decline in capability; and
(6) experience constant and unbearable physical or psychological suffering which cannot be relieved in a manner the patient deems tolerable.

---

908. *See* the discussion of these claims in *Carter, supra* note 168 at paras. 59–62. *See also* Karine Millaire, "Le concept d'autonomie dans l'arrêt *Carter* c. *Canada* : Au-delà du libre-choix" (2017) 63:2 RD McGill 283 at 302.
909. *Ibid.*
910. *Act Respecting End of Life Care*, RSQ, c S-32.0001.
911. *Ibid.*

525. In 2016, approximately eighteen months after *Carter*, the Parliament of Canada passed Bill C-14, *An Act to Amend the Criminal Code and to Make Related Amendments to Other Acts (Medical Assistance in Dying).*[912] The Bill amended the *Criminal Code* to provide exemptions from various offenses for health-care professionals providing or assisting in the provision of MAiD and to establish requirements for MAiD.

526. Pursuant to the amendments, medical practitioners, nurse practitioners, and any persons aiding them are exempted from liability for culpable homicide (i.e., causing the death of a person at their request) if they are providing the person with MAiD in accordance with section 241.2 of the *Criminal Code.*[913] Further, medical practitioners, nurse practitioners, and any persons aiding them are exempted from liability for aiding a person to die by suicide, if they are providing them with MAiD in compliance with the *Criminal Code*. As well, under the amendments, pharmacists are also exempt from criminal liability for assisting a person to die by suicide where they dispense a substance that was prescribed to a patient by a medical practitioner or nurse practitioner in providing MAiD in accordance with the *Criminal Code.*[914]

527. In the *Criminal Code*, "Medical Assistance in Dying" is defined as:

- the administering by a medical practitioner or nurse practitioner of a substance to a person, at their request, that causes their death (also known as voluntary euthanasia) or
- the prescribing or providing by a medical practitioner or nurse practitioner of a substance to a person, at their request, so that they may self-administer the substance and in doing so cause their own death (also known as medically- or physician-assisted suicide).[915]

528. In order for a person to be eligible for MAiD (and for a health-care provider to avoid liability for assisting in their death), the person must meet all of the following criteria:

(a) they are eligible—or, but for any applicable minimum period of residence or waiting period, would be eligible—for health services funded by a government in Canada;
(b) they are at least 18 years of age and capable of making decisions with respect to their health;
(c) they have a grievous and irremediable medical condition;

912. Bill C-14, *An Act to Amend the Criminal Code and to Make Related Amendments to Other Acts* (Medical Assistance in Dying), 1st Sess, 42nd Parl, 2016 (assented to Jun. 17, 2016), SC 2016, c 3.
913. *Criminal Code*, RSC 1985, c C-46, s. 227.
914. *Ibid.*, s. 241.
915. *Ibid.*, s. 241.1.

(d) they have made a voluntary request for medical assistance in dying that, in particular, was not made as a result of external pressure; and
(e) they give informed consent to receive medical assistance in dying after having been informed of the means that are available to relieve their suffering, including palliative care.[916]

For purposes of the eligibility requirements, a "grievous and irremediable medical condition" means that:

(a) the person has a serious and incurable illness, disease or disability;
(b) they are in an advanced state of irreversible decline in capability;
(c) the illness, disease or disability or the state of decline causes them enduring physical or psychological suffering that is intolerable to them and that cannot be relieved under conditions that they consider acceptable; and
(d) their natural death has become reasonably foreseeable.[917]

529. In addition to describing conditions of eligibility, the legislation also establishes procedural safeguards including requiring medical practitioners and nurse practitioners to satisfy themselves that the eligibility criteria have been met, that the request for MAiD was made in writing, signed, and dated, that the person is aware that they may withdraw the request, that another medical practitioner or nurse practitioner has provided a written opinion confirming the criteria are met, and that a period of at least ten days has elapsed between the making of the request and its implementation (a shorter period may be found to be appropriate if the person's death or loss of capacity is imminent).[918] It also establishes criteria for determining whether a medical practitioner or nurse practitioner is independent, for filing of information, and for the making of regulations and guidelines by the Minister of Health.[919] As well, the legislation created new offenses for health-care professionals who fail to comply with the requirements set out regarding MAiD.[920]

---

916. *Ibid.*, s. 241.2(1).
917. *Ibid.*, s. 241.2(2). The term 'reasonably foreseeable death' has been the topic of much discussion and debate, both during the discussion of the Bill in Parliament and afterwards. Some argue that the restriction is not in line with the criteria set out in the *Carter* decision and unduly restricts access to MAiD (see the discussion and references in Thomas McMorrow, "MAID in Canada? Debating the Constitutionality of Canada's New Medical Assistance in Dying Law" (2018) 44:1 Queen's LJ 69, in particular at pp. 81-86). Others have defended it as a restriction but acknowledged that it left room for interpretation (see e.g. Lemmens, Kim & Kurz, *supra* note 855 at pp. 111-118). Others, including some who opposed the introduction of the term during the parliamentary discussion, have put forward a very broad interpretation of the definition that has opened up the practice outside the end-of-life context (see in particular Jocelyn Downie & Jennifer A Chandler, *Interpreting Canada's Medical Assistance in Dying Legislation: IRPP Report* (Ottawa: Institute for Research on Public Policy, 2018), online: https://irpp.org/wp-content/uploads/2018/03/interpreting-Canadas-Medical-Assistance-in-Dying-Legislation.pdf)
918. *Ibid.*, s. 241.2(3).
919. *Ibid.*, ss. 241.2(6), 241.31.
920. *Ibid.*, ss. 241.3, 241.31(4).

2. Exclusions from MAiD Eligibility

530. The following three aspects were intentionally omitted from the legalization of MAiD: (1) requests by mature minors; (2) advance requests; and (3) requests where a mental disorder is the sole underlying medical condition.[921] The legislation explicitly stated that further review and assessment of these issues should be undertaken to determine their inclusion in the legislation.[922] To assess the legislation generally and more specifically to determine whether the three omissions should be included within the legislation, in December 2016, the then Ministers of Health and Justice requested the Council of Canadian Academies (CCA) to undertake an independent review of the evidence in relation to these more controversial areas.[923] The CCA is an independent, not-for-profit organization founded and supported by the RSC, the Canadian Academy of Engineering, and the Canadian Academy of Health Sciences.[924] Reviews are undertaken by a multidisciplinary panel of experts.[925] The government's mandate to the CCA Expert Panel on Medical Assistance in Dying was to study and report on the evidence. The Committee was explicitly instructed not to make any recommendations but to inform Parliament about the evidence from current Canadian and international practice directly or indirectly related to these areas.

531. The CCA released the following three reports in December 2018, setting out their findings of the evidence on the three aspects in the Medical Assistance in Dying legislation: (1) *The State of Knowledge on Medical Assistance in Dying for Mature Minors*; (2) *The State of Knowledge on Advance Requests for Medical Assistance in Dying*; and (3) *The State of Knowledge on Medical Assistance in Dying Where a Mental Disorder is the Sole Underlying Medical Condition.*[926]

a. MAiD for Mature Minors

532. The CCA was asked to study the evidence in relation to MAiD for mature minors; the concept of "mature minor" to be defined by his/her capacity for decision-making and not by chronological age.[927] The two primary arguments against making mature minors eligible for MAiD are: (a) they are typically considered to be vulnerable, and hence should receive more protection as compared to

921. Council of Canadian Academies, "Medical Assistance in Dying: The Expert Panel on Medical Assistance in Dying" (Dec. 12, 2018), online: scienceadvice.ca/reports/medical-assistance-in-dying/ [CCA, Expert Panel]; Bill C-14, *An Act to Amend the Criminal Code and to Make Related Amendments to Other Acts* (Medical Assistance in Dying), 1st Sess, 42nd Parl, 2016 (assented to Jun. 17, 2016), SC 2016, c 3.
922. CCA, Expert Panel, *supra* note 918.
923. *Ibid.*
924. Council of Canadian Academies, "State of Knowledge on Medical Assistance in Dying for Mature Minors, Advance Requests, and Where a Mental Disorder Is the Sole Underlying Medical Condition: Summary of Reports" (December 2018), at iii-iv, online (pdf): scienceadvice.ca/wp-content/uploads/2018/12/MAID-Summary-of-Reports.pdf [CCA, State Of Knowledge].
925. CCA, State of Knowledge, *supra* note 921 at iii-iv.
926. CCA, Expert Panel, *supra* note 918.
927. CCA, State of Knowledge, *supra* note 921 at 5–15.

adults; and (b) the difficulty in determining the capacity of a minor to give informed consent.[928] The report indicated that a key question is how to balance the need to protect mature minors from harm, while at the same time not unfairly and unethically restricting them from exercising their rights.[929] The CCA concluded that "[t]he capacity of a minor to consent to a healthcare intervention must be determined on a case-by-case basis by considering their experiences, maturity, circumstances, and the gravity of the decision at hand … rather than denying healthcare choices to groups frequently labelled as vulnerable, society must provide the accommodations to ensure that everyone is protected not only from exploitation, but also from being ignored and excluded."[930]

b. Advance Requests

533. An advance request is a request that patients would make long before MAiD is needed and before they lose their ability to provide consent. Current Canadian legislation requires that patients provide consent at a time when they fulfill the eligibility criteria for access to MAiD, and doctors and nurses must obtain a confirmation of consent immediately prior to providing, MAiD.[931] Hence, a request for MAiD becomes void if the patient has lost his/her ability to provide consent.[932] The primary argument in favor of advance requests is that it would alleviate suffering at the end of life for people who would wish to avail of MAiD but no longer have the mental capacity to give their consent in those last stages. In opposition, the concern is that reliance on advance requests may result in MAiD being applied to individuals who would no longer wish to end their lives at that stage but would be unable to communicate their wishes. The CCA opined that while certain safeguards can be put in place to accompany advance requests in certain situations, there were significant knowledge gaps and further research was needed on end-of-life practices.[933] There appeared to be disagreement among the experts as to whether existing evidence from other jurisdictions supports the claim that advance requests for MAiD can be safely introduced.

c. Mental Disorder Is the Sole Underlying Medical Condition

534. MAiD is only available to competent adults who suffer from a "grievous and irremediable medical condition" who are in an advanced state of irreversible decline in capabilities and whose natural death is "reasonably foreseeable." While people suffering from mental illness can qualify for MAiD if they suffer from a condition that fulfills these criteria, it seems clear that mental illness alone will generally not fulfill these criteria.[934] The report discusses the various arguments invoked

928. *Ibid.*
929. *Ibid.*
930. CCA, State of Knowledge, *supra* note 921 at 14–15.
931. *Ibid.*, at 16–25.
932. *Ibid.*
933. CCA, State of Knowledge, *supra* note 921 at 25.
934. *See* Lemmens, Kim & Kurz, *supra* note 853 at pp. S112–119.

in the context of this debate, and the evidence from the very few jurisdictions (Belgium and the Netherlands) that allow MAiD for the sole reason of mental illness. The report of this subcommittee reflects how providing MAiD for the sole reason of mental illness is clearly one of the most contentious issues, and how experts of this subcommittee strongly disagreed about the interpretation of the evidence, let alone about the desirability of legalizing MAiD in this context.[935]

535. Following the publication of the CCA reports, some members of the subcommittee on "MAID Where a Mental Disorder is the Sole Underlying Medical Condition" came together as a new expert committee (outside of the CCA mandate) and published a report in which they recommended that MAiD should be legally available for people who request MAiD with mental illness as the sole underlying condition.[936] In response, other members of the same CCA subcommittee, joined by members of other subcommittees and some people with lived experience, published a report in which they countered the findings and recommendations of this group.[937] They argued that the report of the so-called Halifax Group was not accurately reflecting the evidence produced in the CCA report. They recommended that the law should recognize that mental illness cannot be considered "irremediable" in the same way as other medical conditions. They also recommended that any expansion of MAiD should include an obligation to explore all other reasonable treatment options prior to providing access to MAiD outside the end of life context.

D. The Ongoing Development of MAiD Laws in Canada

1. Conscientious Objections to MAiD

536. Medical professionals have the right to restrict the health-care services they provide on the basis of freedom of conscience or religion. However, the physician's right to refuse to participate in services to which they have conscientious and religious objections must be balanced against the rights of patients to access care. Where these competing rights lead to irreconcilable conflicts, a determination must be made as to whose rights will prevail. This issue was recently addressed by the ONCA in *Christian Medical and Dental Society of Canada v. College of Physicians and Surgeons of Ontario*, with the Court holding that where a patient's access to

935. CCA, State of Knowledge, *supra* note 921 at 38.

936. The Halifax Group, *MAiD Legislation at a Crossroads: Persons with Mental Disorders as Their Sole Underlying Medical Condition, IRPP Report* (Montreal: Institute for Research on Public Policy, 2020).

937. Expert Advisory Group on Medical Assistance in Dying, *Canada at a Crossroads: Recommendations on Medical Assistance in Dying and Persons with a Mental Disorder: An Evidence-Based Critique of the Halifax Group IRPP Report* (Toronto: EAG, 2020). For a brief discussion of the context of these two reports, *see* Michael Cook, "Competing Canadian Reports on Mental Illness and Euthanasia" (Feb. 16, 2020), online (newsletter): *BioEdge* www.bioedge.org/bioethics/competing-reports-on-canadians-with-mental-illness-and-euthanasia/13330.

medical services such as MAiD conflicts with a physician's freedom to refuse to participate in health-care services, the patient's interests should prevail.[938]

537. Christian Medical and Dental Society of Canada v. College of Physicians and Surgeons of Ontario involved constitutional challenges to two policies enacted by the College of Physicians and Surgeons of Ontario which required physicians to provide an "effective referral" to patients where they objected to providing MAiD or prescribing pharmaceuticals for the purpose of self-administration, on the basis of their conscience or religion. The policies did not require that the physicians provide the services (except in emergency situations), but rather required them to provide "a referral made in good faith, to a non-objecting, available, and accessible physician, other health-care professional, or agency." The appellants, individual physicians and organizations representing physicians in Ontario, argued that the "effective referral" requirements in the policies infringed their constitutional rights by obliging them "to be complicit in procedures that offend their religious beliefs" and by discriminating against physicians "based on their religions." Finding against the appellants, the ONCA observed that "the fiduciary nature of the physician-patient relationship requires physicians to act at all times in their patients' best interests, and to avoid conflicts between their own interests and their patients' interests" and that "[o]rdinarily, where a conflict arises between a physician's interest and a patient's interest, the interest of the patient prevails." The Court concluded that the College's policies, which did not oblige objecting physicians to personally provide patients with services or to make formal referrals, represented a compromise and struck a "reasonable balance between patients' interests and physicians' *Charter*-protected religious freedom."[939]

538. Under their current policy, the College of Physicians and Surgeons of Ontario does not require physicians who have a conscientious or religious objection to MAiD to provide this service to patients. However, where a physician declines to provide MAiD on the basis of a conscientious objection, they are required to decline in a manner which respects patient dignity and does not impede access to MAiD, to be clear that the objection is personal and not for clinical reasons, to avoid expressing moral judgments about the patient, to provide the patient with information about *all* options for care that are available or appropriate, to not "abandon the patient" and to provide them with an "effective referral" (i.e., take "positive action to ensure the patient is connected to a non-objecting, available, and accessible physician, other health-care professional, or agency").[940] Other provincial and territorial colleges also have standards of practice where physicians refuse to provide services on conscientious or religious grounds, generally requiring the physician to communicate clearly with the patient, not withhold information, avoid expressing moral judgments, and offer a means to connect with another, non-objecting, health-care

938. *Christian Medical and Dental Society of Canada v. College of Physicians and Surgeons of Ontario*, 2019 ONCA 393 [*Christian Medical and Dental Society of Canada*].

939. *Ibid.* at paras. 2, 3, 187.

940. "Medical Assistance in Dying" (last modified December 2018), online: *College of Physicians and Surgeons of Ontario* www.cpso.on.ca/Physicians/Policies-Guidance/Policies/Medical-Assistance-in-Dying#endnote16.

provider.[941] Some of these standards are arguably easier to reconcile with conscientious or religious objection, since they do not require a specific referral, but rather an obligation to provide information, for example, a phone number of an agency that provides further information about how to have access to the service.

2. MAiD for Persons Not at the End of Life and for Persons Who Have Lost Capacity

539. In the recent decision of *Truchon v. Attorney General of Canada*, the Quebec Superior Court of Justice concluded that the provisions in both the Federal and Quebec legislation restricting MAiD to people nearing the end of life violated the *Charter*.[942] The applicants in *Truchon* were two individuals who argued that they were experiencing enduring, intolerable and irremediable suffering from physical conditions but were ineligible for MAiD as they were not yet at the end of life and their deaths were arguably not "reasonably foreseeable." In concluding that the provisions were unconstitutional, the Court found that the reasonably foreseeable natural death requirement exposes individuals, like the applicants, to a "heightened risk of death" as "due to the prolongation of their life and the accompanying suffering, some patients will be inclined to end things prematurely, and often in a degrading

941. *See* for example, "Standard of Practice: Conscientious Objection" (reissued June 2016), online: *College of Physicians and Surgeons of Alberta* www.cpsa.ca/standardspractice/conscientious-objection/; "Practice Standard: Medical Assistance in Dying" (last modified Jun. 20, 2019), online (pdf): *College of Physicians and Surgeons of British Columbia* www.cpsbc.ca/files/pdf/PSG-Medical-Assistance-in-Dying.pdf; "Moral Factors and Medical Care" (amended June 2017), online: *College of Physicians and Surgeons of New Brunswick* cpsnb.org/en/medical-act-regulations-and-guidelines/guidelines/445-moral-factors-and-medical-care; "Standard of Practice: Medical Assistance in Dying" (updated Mar. 29, 2016), online (pdf): *The College of Physicians and Surgeons of Newfoundland and Labrador* www.cpsnl.ca/web/files/2017-Mar-11%20-%20MAID.pdf; "Professional Standard Regarding Medical Assistance in Dying" (Oct. 13, 2017), online: *College of Physicians and Surgeons of Nova Scotia* cpsns.ns.ca/wp-content/uploads/2016/06/Medical-Assistance-in-Dying-Standard.pdf; "Policy on Conscientious Objection to Provision of Service" (Nov. 4, 2019), online (pdf): *College of Physicians and Surgeons of Prince Edward Island* cpspei.ca/wp-content/uploads/2019/12/Conscientious-Objection-to-Provision-of-Service-Nov-2019.pdf; "Policy—Conscientious Objection," online: *College of Physicians and Surgeons of Saskatchewan* www.cps.sk.ca/imis/CPSS/For_Physicians/Patient_Care/Conscientious_Objection/CPSS/Legislation__ByLaws__Policies_and_Guidelines/Legislation_Content/Policies_and_Guidelines_Content/Conscientious_Objection.aspx?PhysiciansCCO=2&hkey=7d265724-0d8c-4e24-a663-5cb2c456e04a; *Code de Déontologie Des Médecins*, c M-9, r 17, online www.cmq.org/publications-pdf/p-6-2015-01-07-fr-code-de-deontologie-des-medecins.pdf?t=1582844264480; "Medical Practice: Moral or Religious Beliefs Affecting Medical Care," online (pdf): *Yukon Medical Counsel* yukonmedicalcouncil.ca/pdfs/Moral_or_Religious_Beliefs_Affecting_Medical_Care.pdf; *See also* "Standards of Practice of Medicine" (revised up to Dec. 13, 2019), online (pdf): *College of Physicians and Surgeons of Manitoba* www.cpsm.mb.ca/assets/Standards%20of%20Practice/Standards%20of%20Practice%20of%20Medicine.pdf; Government of Northwest Territories, *Medical Assistance in Dying Interim Guidelines for the Northwest Territories* (Northwest Territories: Department of Health and Social Services, Nov. 1, 2018), online (pdf) www.hss.gov.nt.ca/sites/hss/files/maid_interim_guidelines_-_in_force_november_1_2018_-_english.pdf.

942. *Truchon*, *supra* note 857.

or violent manner, before being in mortal agony, or having completely lost their dignity or being in the final stage of life." The Court further found that, by enacting the reasonably foreseeable natural death requirement, the state "directly interferes with their physical integrity, causes them physical and psychological pain and deprives them of the opportunity to make a fundamental decision that respects their personal dignity and integrity." And, the Court found that in excluding people who were not at the end of life from being eligible for MAiD, the Government was depriving people, like the applicants, of exercising choices essential to their dignity as human beings based on their personal characteristics and held that individuals in the position of the applicant "must be allowed to exercise full autonomy not only at the end of life, but also at any moment during their life, even if this means death, where the other eligibility conditions for medical assistance in dying are met."[943] The court also found that the prohibition discriminated between those who are suffering intolerably from a condition that makes their death reasonably foreseeable and who can thus obtain access to MAiD, and those who suffer intolerably from a medical condition that is not associated with a reasonably foreseeable death.

540. To permit the Federal and Quebec legislatures time to enact new legislation, the Court suspended the declaration of constitutional invalidity for six months, while also granting a constitutional exemption to the applicants so they could access MAiD during the suspension period if they met the eligibility requirements. The decision came out shortly before federal elections, and likely as a result of the perceived popularity of expanding access to MAiD, particularly in the province of Quebec, the incumbent government declared in election debates that it would not appeal the decision. The failure to appeal the decision was criticized, because of the importance of the issues at stake, the fact that this was a first instance decision by one trial judge, based in part on the concept of discrimination that had never been endorsed by the Supreme Court in the end-of-life context, and the fact that the existing law already raised concerns.[944] The government requested two extensions, first because of the time lost during the elections, subsequently because of the suspension of parliament as a result of COVID-19. This was in turn criticized by those arguing that the government was prolonging suffering as well as an ongoing violation of people's constitutional rights.[945]

---

943. *Ibid.*, at paras. 521, 522, 534, 681, 682.

944. *See* Trudo Lemmens & Laverne Jacobs, "The Latest Medical Assistance in Dying Decision Needs to Be Appealed: Here's Why" (Oct. 9, 2019), online: *The Conversation* theconversation.com/the-latest-medical-assistance-in-dying-decision-needs-to-be-appealed-heres-why-124955; *see also* a letter by various advocacy organizations, "Advocates Call for Disability-Rights Based Appeal of the Quebec Superior Court's Decision in Truchon & Gladu" (Oct. 4, 2019), online: *Canadian Association for Community Living* cacl.ca/2019/10/04/advocates-call-for-disability-rights-based-appeal-of-the-quebec-superior-courts-decision-in-truchon-gladu/; *see also* John Sikkema, "Opinion: Federal Leaders Still Don't Seem to Understand the Attorney General's Role," *The National Post* (Oct. 10, 2019), online: nationalpost.com/news/politics/election-2019/opinion-federal-leaders-still-dont-seem-to-understand-the-attorney-generals-role.

945. Jocely Downie & Jon Goud, "Four Years (and Counting) of Unconstitutional Barriers to Maid" (Jun. 26, 2020), online (blog): *Impact Ethics* impactethics.ca/2020/06/26/four-years-and-counting-of-unconstitutional-barriers-to-maid/.

541. In response to the *Truchon* decision, in late February 2020, the Federal Government introduced a Bill that would permit individuals who are not nearing the end of their lives to be eligible for MAiD. Bill C-7, *An Act to amend the Criminal Code (Medical Assistance in Dying)* would amend the *Criminal Code* to repeal the requirement that a person's natural death be reasonably foreseeable in order for them to be eligible for MAiD. If passed, the Bill would also amend the *Criminal Code* to create two sets of safeguards, with one set being applicable in cases where a person seeking MAiD is nearing their natural death and the other being applicable where the person is not nearing the end of life.[946]

542. For people whose natural death is reasonably foreseeable, the proposed amendments would ease the current procedural safeguards by permitting a person who has been found eligible for MAiD and who has lost the capacity to consent, to receive MAiD on the basis of a prior arrangement in writing with the medical practitioner or nurse practitioner. The safeguards are also eased to allow MAiD to be provided in cases where people have lost the capacity to consent to MAiD after self-administering a substance that was provided to them to cause their own death under the MAiD provisions. For advance consent to be binding in these cases, before losing the capacity to consent the person must enter into an arrangement in writing with the medical practitioner or nurse practitioner which provides that they will be present when the person self-administers the substance and that if after administering the substance the person loses the capacity to consent and does not die within a specified period, the health-care professional will then administer a second substance for purposes of causing their death. If passed, the Bill would also remove the requirement for a ten-day waiting period in cases where natural death is reasonably foreseeable.[947]

543. The proposed amendments would also establish specific, separate safeguards for MAiD in cases where the person's natural death is not reasonably foreseeable. A number of these procedural safeguards are similar to those applicable in cases where natural death is reasonably foreseeable, including that medical practitioners and nurse practitioners must confirm that the person meets the eligibility criteria for MAiD (which criteria would no longer include reasonably foreseeable natural death), and ensure that the request is made in writing, signed and dated, and that the person is aware they may withdraw the request.[948]

544. But the Bill also establishes additional safeguards for people whose death is not "reasonably foreseeable." These safeguards include ensuring that the person is informed of the "means available to relieve their suffering" including, as applicable, counseling services, mental health and disability support services, community services and palliative care and that they have been offered consultations with

946. Bill C-7, *An Act to Amend the Criminal Code (Medical Assistance in Dying)*, 1st Sess, 43rd Parl, 2020 (first reading Feb. 24, 2020).
947. *Ibid.*
948. Bill C-7, *An Act to Amend the Criminal Code (Medical Assistance in Dying)*, 1st Sess, 43rd Parl, 2020 (first reading Feb. 24, 2020).

professionals who provide those services. The safeguards also require that a written opinion confirming that the person meets the eligibility criteria is obtained from another medical practitioner or nurse practitioner and that either that health-care professional or the health-care professional providing MAiD has expertise in the person's condition. And, they require that both the health-care professional providing MAiD and the health-care professional providing a written opinion have discussed with the person the "reasonable and available means to relieve" their suffering and agree with the person that the person has "given serious consideration to those means." In addition, the proposed procedural safeguards would require that a period of ninety days elapse between the date of the initial eligibility assessment and MAiD being carried out, although this period may be shortened where the loss of the person's capacity to provide consent is imminent.[949]

545. While the removal of the reasonably foreseeable natural death requirement is in keeping with the *Truchon* decision and is supported by a number of experts, the issue remains hotly contested in Canada. Experts and advocacy groups in favor of removing this restriction argue that the reasonably foreseeable natural death requirement prohibits access to MAiD by people who may be experiencing "enduring and intolerable suffering," but who are not nearing death, thus condemning them to either suffer indefinitely or find a way to kill themselves without assistance. On the other side of the debate, are experts and advocacy groups who argue that the reasonably foreseeable natural death requirement is a key safeguard in balancing autonomous choice on the one hand, with protecting people against their own potential vulnerability, as well as safeguarding the perception of equal value of the life of those who are ill, elderly or disabled, on the other hand. They note that removing the requirement of reasonably foreseeable natural death may mean the premature death of someone who otherwise had years or decades to live, and forecloses the possibility that the illness may have been overcome or adequately addressed or that the person may have changed their minds. Disability rights groups have emphasized that it deprives society, and those supporting people with chronic illness and disabilities, of an opportunity to help them to find renewed purpose and satisfaction in life. It also moves MAiD further away from the other traditionally accepted end of life decisions and medical interventions, such as withdrawing or withholding life-saving or life-sustaining treatment, and makes it even harder to distinguish it from suicide, the prevention of which continues to be an important objective in our society.[950] Experts also caution that the removal of the reasonably foreseeable natural death requirement may open the door to providing premature life-ending interventions to people suffering from mental disorders.[951] Disability rights advocates suggest that singling out people with chronic illness and disabilities for privileged

949. *Ibid.*
950. Trudo Lemmens, "Charter Scrutiny of Canada's Medical Assistance in Dying Law and the Shifting Landscape of Belgian and Dutch Euthanasia Practice" (2018) 85 SCLR (2nd Series) 459 [Lemmens, "Charter Scrutiny"]; *See also* Expert Advisory Group on Medical Assistance in Dying, *Canada at a Crossroads: Recommendations on Medical Assistance in Dying and Persons with a Mental Disorder: An Evidence-Based Critique of the Halifax Group IRPP Report* (Toronto: EAG, 2020).
951. Lemmens, "Charter Scrutiny," *supra* note 947.

access to life-terminating actions within the context of health care is discriminatory because it deprives people of the protection against premature death offered to all others. If adopted, the new law could thus evoke another Charter challenge based on an alleged violation of people with disabilities' right to life and the right to be free from discrimination. Worth noting is that the United Nations Special Rapporteur on the Rights of Persons with Disabilities already stipulated in a 2019 report that access to MAiD, if it is permitted, "should be restricted to those who are at the end of life."[952] In an earlier report of a country visit, she also expressed concern about Canada's MAiD practice under the existing legislation and urged for better safeguards.[953]

3. MAiD for the Sole Reason of Mental Disorder

546. If passed, Bill C-7 will explicitly exclude persons whose sole underlying medical condition is a mental disorder from being eligible for MAiD. However, while excluding mental illness from being considered an "illness, disease or disability" for purposes of MAiD eligibility, the proposed legislation nevertheless signals the possibility that further amendments may be made in the future which would permit MAiD in cases of mental disorder. Specifically, the Preamble to Bill C-7 indicates that "further consultation and deliberation are required to determine whether it is appropriate and, if so, how to provide" MAiD where mental disorder is the sole underlying medical condition. It also notes that the issues surrounding advance requests for MAiD and requests where mental disorder is the sole underlying issue may be considered as part of a review of MAiD and palliative care in Canada being undertaken by Parliament in the near future.[954]

547. Whether to permit MAiD for people where the sole underlying medical condition is a mental disorder remains extremely controversial in Canada. Some experts note that, despite the provision of "adequate or even excellent mental health services and social supports," people with mental disorders may nevertheless experience "great suffering as part of their mental disorder," and argue that this suffering may be as "intolerable and deserving of relief as suffering from physical disorders." They further suggest that excluding people with mental disorders from MAiD on the basis of their mental disorder, is discriminatory and "reinforces the false and stigmatizing view that all persons with mental disorders need to be protected from

952. United Nations, General Assembly, Report of the Special Rapporteur on the Rights of Persons with Disabilities, Human Rights Council, 43rd session A/HRC/43/41 (2019) at para. 70; online: https://undocs.org/en/A/HRC/43/41

953. United Nations Special Rapporteur on the Rights of People with Disabilities, "End of Mission Statement by the United Nations Special Rapporteur on the rights of persons with disabilities, Ms. Catalina Devandas-Aguilar, on her visit to Canada" (12 April 2019) online: https://www.ohchr.org/en/NewsEvents/Pages/DisplayNews.aspx?NewsID=24481&LangID=E; Canada ratified The Convention on The Rights of Persons with Disabilities (A/RES/61/106) in 2010 and acceded to the Optional Protocol in 2018, online: https://www.un.org/development/desa/disabilities/convention-on-the-rights-of-persons-with-disabilities.html

954. Bill C-7, *An Act to Amend the Criminal Code (Medical Assistance in Dying),* 1st Sess, 43rd Parl, 2020 (first reading Feb. 24, 2020).

themselves." They say that, in some cases, health-care professionals can be satisfied that the person's mental disorder is incurable, the person's suffering is enduring and intolerable, and their condition cannot be remedied under conditions acceptable to the person and argue that, with improvements to mental health services and supports and with specific eligibility criteria and procedural safeguards in place, access to MAiD can be allowed for certain people where mental disorder is the sole underlying condition while still protecting against overinclusion.[955]

548. Making the converse argument, other experts submit that unlike other medical conditions, which have known, predictable courses, the course of an individual's mental disorder cannot be known with any certainty and, as such, these disorders "can never be predicted to be irremediable." These experts argue that providing MAiD in cases of mental disorder, "under the false pretense that irremediability can be predicted," is dangerous and discriminates against people with mental disorders. They caution that, should MAiD be permitted for mental disorders, marginalized populations may be provided with MAiD for "all sorts of life suffering," even where recovery or improvement was possible, and MAiD may become "a proxy for lack of access to adequate treatment" and other needed supports.[956]

955. The Halifax Group, *MAiD Legislation at a Crossroads: Persons with Mental Disorders as Their Sole Underlying Medical Condition, IRPP Report* (Montreal: Institute for Research on Public Policy, 2020).

956. Expert Advisory Group on Medical Assistance in Dying, *Canada at a Crossroads: Recommendations on Medical Assistance in Dying and Persons with a Mental Disorder: An Evidence-Based Critique of the Halifax Group IRPP Report* (Toronto: EAG, 2020).

Part III. The Physician and the Health-Care System

Chapter 1. Relations with Health-Care Institutions

§1. HOSPITALS

I. History

549. Basic hospital services have been publicly funded since 1957, when the federal government passed legislation[957,958] which obliged it to reimburse provinces for half the costs of any hospital insurance programs established by them. In the succeeding two decades, hospital construction far outpaced general population growth, and hospitals have since been entrenched as the fundamental site for public health care. However, the trend was subsequently reversed, as the number of acute treatment hospital beds per 1,000 population has generally decreased nationwide.

II. Ownership, Funding and Administration

550. Canadian hospitals may be owned and managed by churches, municipalities, provincial or federal government, or private for-profit corporations, but the great majority are non-profit private institutions. Although not all hospitals were necessarily incorporated, virtually all had a board of directors. While many hospitals continue to have boards which govern the day-to-day operations of the facility, with the establishment of regional health authorities by the provinces, responsibility for the overarching management of hospitals has largely been centralized to regional bodies.

551. Government-owned hospitals in Canada are rare and tend to be specialized. Most provincial hospitals are psychiatric facilities, while federally owned hospitals consist mainly of small institutions for the military or First Nations Peoples.

957. M Rachlis & C Kushner, *Strong Medicine: How to Save Canada's Health-care System* (Toronto: HarperCollins, 1994); RB Deber, *Treating Health Care: How the Canadian System Works and Could Work Better* (Toronto: University of Toronto Press, 2018); GP Marchildon, *Health Systems in Transition: Canada*, 2nd ed. (Toronto: University of Toronto Press, 2013); Halsbury's Laws of Canada (online), *Medicine and Health*, "Hospitals" (V) (2017 Reissue, Molodofsky).
958. *Hospital Insurance and Diagnostic Services Act,* SC 1957, c 28.

552. Despite the variety of hospital ownership and organization in Canada, all hospitals serve the same general function, are subject to the statutory control of the provinces in which they are situated, and share a reliance on public funding. Provincial/territorial governments use a variety of approaches to finance hospitals and there is no one model that can accurately portray the financing of hospitals in Canada. Furthermore, provinces/territories do not use a single method to distribute funds to their hospitals. Most rely on a primary funding approach to allocate the majority of funds and a number of secondary methods to apportion lesser amounts. Methods of hospital funding used in Canada, both primary and secondary, include: line-by-line, ministerial discretion, population-based, global budget, policy-based, facility-based, project-based and service-based.[959]

III. Licensing and Evaluation

553. All hospitals, whether publicly or privately owned, must be licensed by the provincial government in whose jurisdiction they are situated. Provincial hospital statutes establish criteria and procedures for becoming a licensed hospital entitled to operate within the province, and an updated list of such hospitals may be included as part of the act. The province may also grant restrictive licenses; for example, authorizing a private hospital to engage only in specific procedures for particular purposes. The establishment and operation of mental health facilities are also provincially regulated. While the provinces hold virtually unlimited legislative jurisdiction over hospitals, they vary considerably as to: admission policies, operating standards, range of services, quality review, medical staff appointment, financial practices, record keeping, and the making of hospital bylaws.

554. The continuing evaluation of hospitals is carried out by a number of accrediting bodies. Chief among these is Accreditation Canada, formerly the Canadian Council on Health Services Accreditation, which reviews the institutional performance of hospitals and long-term care and mental health facilities. Accreditation Canada publishes various accreditation manuals, administers surveys measuring various facility and staff input and outputs, and performs mandatory prospective medical and nursing audits. Numerous other agencies are involved in hospital accreditation, such as the provincial governments, hospital associations, professional organizations, auditors and researchers. These bodies evaluate particular departments, such as physiotherapy or pharmacy, or certain aspects of hospital performance.

959. For discussion of these methods, *see* Canada, Standing Senate Committee on Social Affairs, Science and Technology, *The Health of Canadians: The Federal Role* (Ottawa: The Senate, 2002), Ch. 2, "Hospital Restructuring and Funding in Canada," online www.parl.gc.ca/37/2/parlbus/commbus/senate/com-e/soci-e/rep-e/repoct02vol6-e.htm/.

§2. RELATIONS BETWEEN PHYSICIANS AND HOSPITALS

I. Staff Privileges

555. Medical staff privileges are initiated through the submission of applications to the hospital or regional authority board. The board may, and often must, according to provincial hospital legislation, consult with the hospital's Medical Advisory Committee. Canadian case law has established that there is no common law or statutory right to medical privileges in a public hospital, even if the applicant is a licensed member of the medical profession with good standing.[960] As long as a hospital board's decision is unbiased, reasonable, and made honestly and in good faith, the Board is under no obligation to allow an applicant physician entry onto the medical staff.[961] However, the lack of an initial *right* to hold privileges does not necessarily prevent a physician from making a civil claim against a hospital for any breach of the relationship that would have arisen between hospital and physician once privileges had been granted.[962]

556. Some provincial hospital statutes direct hospitals to make explicit bylaws regulating the professional conduct of medical staff, procedures for medical staff appointments and the appeal of hospital board decisions. Other provinces reserve to themselves the right to make regulations for the appointment of hospital staff members, and the handling of physician complaints and appeals. A number of court decisions have stated that the hospital appeal board, whether established by provincial regulation or hospital bylaw, generally assumes a judicial function whenever it reviews the procedural requirements for any refusal or removal of hospital privileges. The board is therefore held to a duty to properly exercise judicial discretion according to the rules of natural justice and procedural fairness.[963] Where a province legislatively provides an administrative internal appeal process for decisions to refuse or revoke hospital privileges, the courts will not generally grant judicial remedies until the internal appeal process has been exhausted.[964]

---

960. *Henderson v. Johnston* [1959] SCR 655.
961. *See Young v. Central Health*, 2018 NLCA 24, for discussion of the reasonableness standard. *See also Saskatoon Regional Health Authority v. Johnson*, 2014 SKQB 266.
962. *See Shephard v. Colchester Regional Hospital Commission* (1991), 103 NSR (2d) 361 (NSTD); *Hassall v. British Columbia Children's Hospital* (1997), 45 BCLR (3d) 297 (BCTD); *Macdonald v. Mineral Springs Hospital*, 2008 ABCA 273.
963. *Sreedhar v. Outlook Union Hospital* [1973] 2 WWR 120 (Sask. CA), in which a hospital appeal board was held to have violated a requirement of natural justice when its refusal to grant an adjournment denied a physician the right to be heard; but *see Hicks v. Langley Memorial Hospital* (1992), 16 Admin. L.R. (2d) 33 (BCSC), in which a medical appeal court confirmed the revocation of a physician's hospital privileges, and the court restricted itself to reviewing on the grounds of an overriding jurisdictional error or a patently unreasonable finding of law or fact. *See also Saskatoon Regional Health Authority v. Johnson*, 2014 SKQB 266, where the court applied a "reasonableness" standard.
964. *Haber v. Wellesley* Hospital (1986), 56 OR (2d) 553 (Div. Ct.), affirmed (1988), 63 OR (2d) 756 (CA), in which the existence of a legislated internal review process, establishing natural justice and fair treatment, was considered a threshold issue to the granting of judicial review. *See also Beiko v. Hotel Dieu Hospital St Catharines*, 2007 ONCA 860; and *Khan v. Scarborough Hospital* (2009), 183 ACWS (3d) 572 (Ont. Div. Ct.).

Selected Bibliography

Books

Basen, G, M Eichler & A Lippman, eds., *Misconceptions: The Social Construction of Choice and the New Reproductive and Genetic Technologies* (Hull, Quebec: Voyageur Pub, 1993).

Bourgeault, IL, C Benoit & R Davis-Floyd, eds., *Reconceiving Midwifery* (Montréal: McGill-Queen's University Press, 2004).

Boyer, Y, *Moving Aboriginal Health Forward: Discarding Canada's Legal Barriers* (Saskatoon: Purich Publishing Limited, 2014).

Busse, J, ed., *The 2017 Canadian Guideline for Opioids for Chronic Non-cancer Pain* (Ontario: National Pain Center, 2017).

CCH Canadian Limited, *Canadian Health Facilities Law Guide* (Toronto: LexisNexis Canada, 2019).

Chandler, JA & CM Flood, *Law and Mind: Mental Health Law and Policy in Canada* (Toronto: LexisNexis Canada Inc, 2016).

Collins, KA & RW Bynard, *Forensic Pathology of Infancy and Childhood* (New York: Springer, 2014).

Deber, RB, *Treating Health Care: How the Canadian System Works and Could Work Better* (Toronto: University of Toronto Press, 2018).

Douglas, V, *Introduction to Aboriginal Health and Health Care in Canada: Bridging Health* (New York: Springer Publishing, 2003).

Downie, J, T Caulfield & C Flood, eds. *Canadian Health Law and Policy*, 4th ed. (Markham: LexisNexis, 2011).

Emson, HE, *The Doctor and the Law: A Practical Guide for the Canadian Physician,* 2nd ed. (Toronto: Butterworths, 1989).

Erdman, JN, V Gruben & E Nelson, eds., *Canadian Health Law and Policy,* 5th ed. (Toronto: LexisNexis, 2017).

Flood, CM, K Roach & L Sossin, eds., *Access to Care, Access to Justice: The Legal Debate over Private Health Insurance in Canada* (Toronto: University of Toronto Press, 2005).

Frewer, A & U Schmidt, eds., *History and Theory of Human Experimentation: The Declaration of Helsinki and Modern Medical Ethics* (Stuttgard: Franz Steiner Verlag, 2007).

Gray, JE, MA Shone & PF Liddle, *Canadian Mental Health Law and Policy*, 2nd ed. (Toronto: LexisNexis, 2008).

Inions, NJ, LE Tran & LE Rozovsky, *Canadian Health Information: A Practical Legal and Risk Management Guide,* 4th ed. (Toronto: LexisNexis, 2018).

Irvine, JC, PH Osborne & MJ Shariff, *Canadian Medical Law: An Introduction for Physicians, Nurses and Other Health Care Professionals*, 4th ed. (Toronto: Carswell, 2013).

Joly, Y & B Knoppers, eds., *Routledge Handbook of Medical Law and Ethics* (New York: Routledge, 2015).

Jones, DP & AS de Villars, *Principles of Administrative Law*, 6th ed. (Scarborough: Carswell, 2014).

Kennedy, I & A Grubb, *Medical Law: Text with Materials*, 2nd ed. (London: Buttersworth, 1994).

Knoppers, BM, *Canadian Child Health Law* (Toronto: Thompson Educational Publishing, 1991).

Kulig, JC & AM Williams, eds., *Health in Rural Canada* (Vancouver: UBC Press, 2012).

Lemmens, T et al., eds., *Regulating Creation: The Law, Ethics, and Policy of Assisted Human Reproduction* (Toronto: University of Toronto Press, 2017).

Linden, AM et al., *Canadian Tort Law*, 11th ed. (LexisNexis Canada, 2018).

Marchildon, GP, *Health Systems in Transition: Canada*, 2nd ed. (Toronto: University of Toronto Press, 2013).

McLaren, A, *Our Own Master Race: Eugenics in Canada 1885–1945* (Toronto: McClelland and Stewart, 1990).

Meagher, AJ, PJ Marr & RA Meagher, *Doctors and Hospitals: Legal Duties* (Toronto: Butterworths, 1991).

Norton, L, C Goodleaf & National Indian & Inuit Community Health Representatives Organization, *Coping with HIV/AIDS in Aboriginal Communities: A 1998 Resource Manual* (NICCHRO, 1998).

Rachlis, M & C Kushner, *Strong Medicine* (Toronto: Harper-Collins, 1994).

Robertson, GB, *Mental Disability and the Law in Canada,* 2nd ed. (Toronto: Carswell, 1994).

Robertson, G & Justice E Picard, *Legal Liability of Doctors and Hospitals in Canada*, 5th ed. (Toronto: Thomson Reuters Canada Limited, 2017).

Ross, Derek, ed., *Assisted Death: Legal, Social and Ethical Issues After Carter* (Toronto: LexisNexis, 2018).

Rozovsky, LE & FA Rozovsky, *The Canadian Law of Patient Records* (Toronto: Butterworths, 1984).

Rozovsky, L, *Canadian Law of Consent to Treatment,* 3rd ed. (Toronto: LexisNexis Butterworths, 2003).

Sappideen, C & P Vines, eds., *Fleming's The Law of Torts,* 10th ed. (Sydney: The Law Book Company Ltd., 2011).

Schmidt, U, A Frewer & D Sprumont, eds., *Ethical Research: The Declaration of Helsinki, and the Past, Present, and Future of Human Experimentation* (USA: Oxford University Press, 2020).

Sharpe, G, *The Law & Medicine in Canada,* 2nd ed. (Toronto: Butterworths, 1987).

Steel, FM & SM Rodgers-Magnet, eds., *Issues in Tort Law* (Toronto: Carswell, 1983).

Ubelaker, DH, ed., *The Global Practice of Forensic Science* (West Sussex, UK: Wiley-Blackwell, 2015).

Waddams, SM, *The Law of Contracts*, 2nd ed. (Toronto: Canada Law Book, 1984).

Waldram, JB et al., *Aboriginal Health in Canada: Historical, Cultural, and Epidemiological Perspectives*, 2nd ed. (Toronto: University of Toronto Press, 2006).

Articles

Adelson, Naomi, "The Embodiment of Inequity: Health Disparities in Aboriginal Canada" (2005) 96 Can J of Public Health S45-S61.

Andrews, Lori B, "Torts and the Double Helix: Malpractice Liability for Failure to Warn of Genetic Risk" (1992) 29:1 Houston L Rev 149.

Antoniou, Tony et al., "'Like Being Put on an Ice Floe and Shoved Away': A Qualitative Study of the Impacts of Opioid-Related Policy Changes on People Who Take Opioids" (2019) 66 Intl J Drug Policy 15.

Barer, Morris & Gregory Stoddart, "Barer Stoddart Report Toward Integrated Medical Resource Policies for Canada" (1991) Centre for Health Economics and Policy Analysis Working Paper No. 91-7.

Caulfield, Timothy A, "Case Comment: ter Neuzen v. Korn and the Standard of Care: A Call for Caution" (1996) 34:4 Alta L Rev 986.

Caulfield, Timothy A, "Health Care Reform: Can Tort Law Meet the Challenge?" (1994) 32:4 Alta L Rev 685.

Carter, Rose M & Brandyn Rodgerson, "Medical Assistance in Dying: Journey to Medical Self-Determination" (2018) 55:3 Alta L Rev 777.

Chan, Benny & Margaret Somerville, "Converting the 'Right to Life' to the 'Right to Physician-Assisted Suicide and Euthanasia': An analysis of *Carter v Canada (Attorney General)* Supreme Court of Canada" (2016) 24:2 Med L Rev 143.

Council of Canadian Academies, "State of Knowledge on Medical Assistance in Dying for Mature Minors, Advance Requests, and Where a Mental Disorder Is the Sole Underlying Medical Condition: Summary of Reports" (December 2018), online (pdf): scienceadvice.ca/wp-content/uploads/2018/12/MAID-Summary-of-Reports.pdf.

Crouch, Robert et al., "Complementary/Alternative Health Care and HIV/AIDS: Legal, Ethical & Policy Issues in Regulation" (2001), online (pdf): *Canadian HIV/AIDS Legal Network* at 23 http://www.aidslaw.ca/site/wp-content/uploads/2013/04/Complimentary+Alternative+Healthcare+-+ENG.pdf.

Dickens, Bernard M & Rebecca J Cook, "Patients' Refusal of Recommended Treatment" (2015) 131 International J Gynecology & Obstetrics 105.

Dickens, Bernard M & Rebecca J Cook, "Types of Consent in Reproductive Health Care" (2015) 128 International J Gynecology & Obstetrics 181.

Dickens, Bernard M, "Legal Approaches to Genetic Diagnosis and Counselling" (1980) 1:25 Health L in Can.

Dickens, Bernard M, "Conflicts of Interest in Canadian Health Care Law" (1995) 21 Am J L & Med 259.

Dickens, Bernard M, "The Legal Challenge of Health Research Involving Children" (1998) 6 Health L J 131.

Dickens, Bernard M & Rebecca J Cook, "Dimensions of Informed Consent to Treatment" (2004) 85 International J Gynecology & Obstetrics 309.

Selected Bibliography

Downar, James et al., "Deceased Organ and Tissue Donation after Medical Assistance in Dying and Other Conscious and Competent Donors: Guidance for Policy" (2019) 191:22 CMAJ E604.

Downie, Jocelyn & Jennifer A Chandler, *Interpreting Canada's Medical Assistance in Dying Legislation: IRPP Report* (Ottawa: Institute for Research on Public Policy, 2018), online: https://irpp.org/wp-content/uploads/2018/03/interpreting-Canadas-Medical-Assistance-in-Dying-Legislation.pdf.

DuVal, Gordon, "Creutzfeldt-Jakob Disease: The Problem of Recipient Notification" (1997) 25:1 JL Med & Ethics 34.

Expert Advisory Group on Medical Assistance in Dying, *Canada at a Crossroads: Recommendations on Medical Assistance in Dying and Persons with a Mental Disorder: An Evidence-Based Critique of the Halifax Group IRPP Report* (Toronto: EAG, 2020).

The First Nations Information Governance Centre, *Ownership, Control, Access and Possession (OCAP™): The Path to First Nations Information Governance* (Ottawa: The First Nations Information Governance Centre, May 2014).

Flood, Colleen M & Bryan Thomas, "A Successful Charter Challenge to Medicare? Policy Options for Canadian Provincial Governments" (2018) 13:3-4 Health Economics, Policy, and Law 433.

Flood, Colleen M, Bryan Thomas & Leigh Harrison Wilson, "Cosmetic Surgery Regulation and Regulation Enforcement in Ontario" (2010) 36 Queen's Law Journal 31.

Fox, Dov, I Glenn Cohen & Eli Y Adashi, "Editorial: Fertility Fraud, Legal Firsts, and Medical Ethics" (2019) 134:5 Obstetrics & Gynecology 918.

Gold, Jennifer L, "Watching the Watchdogs: Negligence, Liability, and Research Ethics Boards" (2003) 11 Health L J 153 (QL).

Gomes, Tara et al., "Comparing the Contribution of Prescribed Opioids to Opioid-Related Hospitalizations Across Canada: A Multi-Jurisdictional Cross-Sectional Study" (2018) 191 Drug & Alcohol Dependence 86.

The Halifax Group, *MAiD Legislation at a Crossroads: Persons with Mental Disorders as Their Sole Underlying Medical Condition, IRPP Report* (Montreal: Institute for Research on Public Policy, 2020).

Healy, Patrick, "Statutory Prohibitions and the Regulation of New Reproductive Technologies under Federal Law in Canada" (1990) 40 McGill LJ 905.

Hyshka, Elaine et al., "Principles, Practice, and Policy Vacuums: Policy Actor Views on Provincial/Territorial Harm Reduction Policy in Canada" (2019) 71 Intl J Drug Policy 142.

Ikonomidis, S & F Lowy, "Access to *in vitro* Fertilization in Canada" (1994) 16 J SOGC 50.

Inuit Tapiriit Kanatami and Nunavut Research Institute, *Negotiating Research Relationships with Inuit Communities: A Guide for Researchers* (Ottawa & Iqualuit: Inuit Tapiriit Kanatami and Nunavut Research Institute, 2007).

Irvine, John C, "Case Comment: Law Estate v. Simice," CCLT 21 (2d) (1994).

Karamouzian, Mohammad et al., "Correlates of Seeking Emergency Medical Help in the Event of an Overdose in British Columbia, Canada: Findings from the Take Home Naloxone Program" (2019) 71 Intl J Drug Policy 157.

Khan, Saman, "Aboriginal Mental Health: The Statistical Reality" (2008) 5:1 Visions J 6.

Knoppers, Bartha Maria, "Modern Birth Technology and Human Rights" (1985) 33:1 Am J Comp Law 1.

Knoppers, Bartha Maria, "Physician Liability and Prenatal Diagnosis," CCLT 18 (1981).

Lavallee, Lynn & Jennifer Poole, "Beyond Recovery: Colonization, Health and Healing for Indigenous People in Canada" (2010) 8:2 International J of Mental Health & Addiction 271.

Law Commission of Ontario, *Legal Capacity, Decision-Making and Guardianship: Final Report* (Toronto: Law Commission of Ontario, March 2017).

Lemmens, Trudo, "Charter Scrutiny of Canada's Medical Assistance in Dying Law and the Shifting Landscape of Belgian and Dutch Euthanasia Practice" (2018) 85 SCLR (2nd. Series) 459.

Lemmens, Trudo, "Pharmaceutical Knowledge Governance: A Human Rights Perspective" (2013) 41:1 JL Med & Ethics 163.

Lemmens, Trudo & Candice Telfer, "Access to Information and the Right to Health: The Human Rights Case for Clinical Trials Transparency" (2012) 31:1 Am J L & Med 63.

Lemmens, Trudo & Carlos Herrera Vacaflor, "Research Transparency in the Americas: The Need to Coordinate Regulatory Spheres" (2018) 362 British Medical Journal k2493.

Lemmens, Trudo, Heesoo Kim & Elizabeth Kurz, "Why Canada's Medical Assistance in Dying Law Should Be C(h)arter Compliant and What It May Help to Avoid" (2017) 11:1 McGill JL & Health S61.

Lemmens, Trudo & Kanksha Mahadevia Ghimire, "Regulation of Health Professions in Ontario: Self-Regulation with Statutory-Based Public Accountability" (2019) 19:3 Revista de Direito Sanitário / Journal of Health Law 124.

Letendre, Angeline Dee, "Aboriginal Traditional Medicine: Where Does It Fit?" (2002) 1:2 Crossing Boundaries: An Interdisciplinary J 79.

Lexchin, Joel, Matthew Herder & Peter Doshi, "Canada finally opens up data on new drugs and devices" (2019) 365 BMJ I1825 doi: https://doi.org/10.1136/bmj.l 1825.

Madeira, Jody Lynee, "Uncommon Misconceptions: Holding Physicians Accountable for Insemination Fraud" (2019) 37:1 Law & Ineq 45.

Martins, Diana et al., "Impact of Delisting High-Strength Opioid Formulations from a Public Drug Benefit Formulary on Opioid Utilization in Ontario, Canada" (2019) 28 Pharmacoepidemiology & Drug Safety 726.

McConnell, Moira L, "Abortion: Provincial Legislation—Control over Health Care: *R. v. Morgentaler*" (1994) 73 Can Bar Rev 417.

McNamara, Linette, "Case Comment: Waldman v. British Columbia (Medical Services Commission)" (1997) 6:2 Health L Rev 24.

McMorrow, Thomas, "MAID in Canada? Debating the Constitutionality of Canada's New Medical Assistance in Dying Law" (2018) 44:1 Queen's LJ 69.

Millaire, Karine, "Le concept d'autonomie dans l'arrêt *Carter* c. *Canada* : Au-delà du libre-choix" (2017) 63:2 RD McGill 283.

Mulder, Johannes, "Facilitating the Wishes of Patients Who Choose Both MAiD and Organ Donation" (2019) 191:22 CMAJ E595.

Mundel, Erika & Gwen E Chapman, "A Decolonizing Approach to Health Promotion in Canada: the Case of the Urban Aboriginal Community Kitchen Garden Project" (2010) 25:2 Health Promotion International 166.

Nelson, Erin & Gerald Robertson, "Liability for Wrongful Birth and Wrongful Life" (2001) 2 ISUMA: Can J of Policy Research 102.

Obomsawin, Raymond, "Traditional Medicine for Canada's First Peoples" (March 2007), online (pdf): *Faculty of Land and Food Systems, Indigenous Research Partnerships* https://lfs-Indigenous.sites.olt.ubc.ca/files/2014/07/RayObomsawin.traditional.medicine-1.pdf.

Ontario Federation of Indigenous Friendship Centres, *USAI Research Framework: Utility Self-Voicing Access Inter-Relationality*, 2nd ed. (Toronto, ON: Ontario Federation of Indigenous Friendship Centres, 2016).

Palmer, Stephanie, "'The Choice is Cruel': Assisted Suicide and Charter Rights in Canada" (2015) 74:2 Cambridge LJ 191.

Parkes, Debra L, "Precedent Revisited: *Carter v Canada (AG)* and the Contemporary Practice of Precedent" (2016) 10:1 McGill JL & Health S124.

Pioro, Mark et al., "Wrongful Birth Litigation and Prenatal Screening" (2008) 179:10 CMAJ 1027.

Renke, Wayne, "The Confidentiality of Health Information in the Criminal Law" (1998) 6:3 Health L Rev 3.

Ridell, Julia K et al., "Laying the Groundwork: A Practical Guide for Ethical Research with Indigenous Communities" (2017) 8:2 Intl Indigenous Policy J 1.

Robertson, Gerald B, "Civil Liability Arising from Wrongful Birth Following an Unsuccessful Sterilization Operation" (1978) 4 Am J L & Med 131.

Robertson, G, "Informed Consent Ten Years Later: The Impact of Reibl v Hughes" (1991) 70:3 Can Bar Rev 423.

Robertson, GB, "Informed Consent 20 Years Later" (2003) Health LJ (Spec Ed).

Robertson, GB, "Ontario's New Informed Consent Law: Codification or Radical Change?" (1994) 2 Health LJ 88.

Robertson, GB et al., "Legal Norms Relevant to the Practice of Human Genetics: A Background Paper" (1995) 3 Health LJ 187.

Sawyer, Douglas M & Timothy M Caulfield, "Creutzfeldt-Jakob Disease and Blood Transfusion: Policy Issues" (1997) 6 Health L Rev 12.

Sherwood, Juanita & Tahnia Edwards, "Decolonisation: A Critical Step for Improving Aboriginal Health" (2006) 22 Contemporary Nurse: A J for the Australian Nursing Profession 178.

Somerville, Margaret, Law Reform Commission of Canada, *Consent to Medical Care, Protection of Life Series, A Study Paper* (Ottawa: Department of Justice Canada, 1980).

Somerville, Margaret A, "Structuring the Issues in Informed Consent" (1981) 26:4 McGill LJ 740.

Stern, Simon & Trudo Lemmens, "Legal Remedies for Medical Ghostwriting: Imposing Fraud Liability on Guest Authors of Ghostwritten Articles" (2011) 8:8 PLoS Medicine 1.

Tadrous, Mina et al., "Evaluation of the Fentanyl Patch-for-Patch Program in Ontario, Canada" (2019) 66 Intl J Drug Policy 82.

Toews, Maeghan & Timothy Caulfield, "Physician Liability and Non-Invasive Prenatal Testing" (2014) 36:10 J Obstetrics & Gynaecology Can 907.

United Nations, General Assembly, Report of the Special Rapporteur on the Rights of Persons with Disabilities, Human Rights Council, 43rd session A/HRC/43/41 (2019), online: https://undocs.org/en/A/HRC/43/41.

United Nations Special Rapporteur on the Rights of People with Disabilities, "End of Mission Statement by the United Nations Special Rapporteur on the rights of persons with disabilities, Ms. Catalina Devandas-Aguilar, on her visit to Canada" (12 April 2019) online: https://www.ohchr.org/en/NewsEvents/Pages/DisplayNews.aspx?NewsID=24481&LangID=E.

Vachon, J, V Gallant & W Siu, "Tuberculosis in Canada" (2016) 44:3/4 Can Commun Dis Rep 75.

Wilson, Kumanan & Paul C Hebert, "The Challenge of an Increasingly Expensive Blood System" (2003) 168:9 CMAJ 1149.

Zarzeczny, Amy & Timothy Caulfield, "Legal Liability and Research Ethics Boards: The Case of Neuroimaging and Incidental Findings" (2012) 35 Intl J L & Psychiatry 137.

Zawati, Ma'n H & Adrian Thorogood, "The Physician Who Knew Too Much: A Comment on *Watters v White*" (2014) 21 Health LJ 1.

Government Documents

Canada, *A Prescription for Canada: Achieving Pharmacare for All, Final Report of the Advisory Council on the Implementation of National Pharmacare, June 2019* (Ottawa: Health Canada, June 2019).

Canada, Commission of Inquiry on the Blood System in Canada, *Final Report* (Ottawa: Minister of Public Works and Government Services Canada, 1997).

Canada, Royal Commission on Aboriginal Peoples, *Volume 3: Gathering Strength*, in *Report of the Royal Commission on Aboriginal Peoples* (online: Government of Canada, 1996) www.bac-lac.gc.ca/eng/discover/aboriginal-heritage/royal-commission-aboriginal-peoples/Pages/final-report.aspx.

Canada, Royal Commission on New Reproductive Technologies, *Proceed with Care: Final Report of the Royal Commission on New Reproductive Technologies* (Ottawa: Minister of Government Services Canada, 1993).

Canada, Standing Senate Committee on Social Affairs, Science and Technology, *The Health of Canadians—The Federal Role* (Ottawa: The Senate, 2002), online: www.parl.gc.ca/37/2/parlbus/commbus/senate/com-e/soci-e/rep-e/repoct02vol6-e.htm/.

Canadian Institute for Health Information, *Pan-Canadian Trends in the Prescribing of Opioids and Benzodiazepines, 2012 to 2017*, ISBN 978-1-77109-719-2 (Ottawa: Canadian Institute for Health Information, 2018).

Canadian Institutes of Health Research, *Human Pluripotent Stem Cell Research: Guidelines for CIHR Funded Research* (Ottawa: Canadian Institutes of Health Research, 2002).

Canadian Institutes of Health Research, Natural Sciences and Engineering Research Council of Canada, and Social Sciences and Humanities Research Council of

Canada, *Tri-Council Policy Statement: Ethical Conduct for Research Involving Humans* (Ottawa: Secretariat on Responsible Conduct of Research, 2018).

Health Canada, *Government of Canada: Actions on Opioids, 2016 and 2017*, Catalogue No H14-236/2017E-PDF (Ottawa: Health Canada, November 2017).

Health Canada, *Guidance Document: Applications for Medical Device Investigational Testing Authorizations*, Catalogue No H13-9/16-2018E-PDF (Ottawa: Health Canada, October 1, 2018).

Health Canada, *Guidance Document for Clinical Trial Sponsors: Clinical Trial Applications* (Ottawa: Ministry of Health, adopted June 25, 2003, revised date, March 17, 2016).

Health Canada, *Guidance Document: Part C, Division 5 of the Food and Drug Regulations "Drugs for Clinical Trials Involving Human Subjects,"* Catalogue No H14-313/2019E-PDF (Ottawa: Health Canada, August 20, 2019).

Health Canada, *Joint Statement of Action to Address the Opioid Crisis: A Collective Response, Annual Report, 2016-2017* (Ottawa: Canadian Centre on Substance Use and Addiction, 2017).

Medical Research Council of Canada, *Report of the Working Group on Liability* (Ottawa: MRC, 1991).

Nicol, Julia & Marlisa Tiedemann, *Background Paper: Euthanasia and Assisted Suicide in Canada by Julia Nicol & Marlisa Tiedemann*, Publication No. 2015-139-E (Ottawa: Library of Parliament, December 15, 2015).

Ontario, *Inquiry into Pediatric Forensic Pathology in Ontario*—Report (Toronto: Ministry of the Attorney General, 2008).

Ontario, *Public Inquiry into the Safety and Security of Residents in the Long-Term Care Homes System* (Toronto: the Honourable Eileen E. Gillese, Commissioner, July 31, 2019).

Royal Commission of Inquiry into the Confidentiality of Health Records in Ontario, *Report of the Commission of Inquiry into the Confidentiality of Health Information* (Toronto: Queen's Printer, 1980) (Commissioner: The Hon. Mr. Justice Horace Krever).

Royal Society of Canada, Udo Schuklenk et al., *End-of-Life Decision Making* (Ottawa: Royal Society of Canada, November 2011).

Special Advisory Committee on the Epidemic of Opioid Overdoses, *National Report: Apparent Opioid-Related Deaths in Canada* (Ottawa: Public Health Agency of Canada, April 2019), online: *Government of Canada* infobase.phac-aspc.gc.ca/datalab/national-surveillance-opioid-mortality.html.

The Special Senate Committee on Euthanasia and Assisted Suicide, *Report of the Special Senate Committee on Euthanasia and Assisted Suicide: Of Life and Death* (Ottawa: Minister of Supply and Services, June 1995).

Standing Senate Committee on National Finance on Canada's Aging Population, *Getting Ready: For a New Generation of Active Seniors* (June 2017) (Chair: Percy Mockler).

Truth and Reconciliation Commission of Canada, *Truth and Reconciliation Commission of Canada: Calls to Action*, online (pdf): www.trc.ca/websites/trcinstitution/File/2015/Findings/Calls_to_Action_English2.pdf.

Truth and Reconciliation Commission of Canada, "TRC Findings" (Winnipeg: Truth and Reconciliation Commission of Canada, 2015) www.trc.ca/websites/trcinstitution/index.php?p=890.

Selected Bibliography

Index

The numbers here refer to paragraph numbers.

Index

Index

www.ingramcontent.com/pod-product-compliance
Lightning Source LLC
Chambersburg PA
CBHW071441230926
51846CB00001B/300
* 9 7 8 9 4 0 3 5 3 0 1 5 4 *